DINING WITH THE SAINTS

DINING
WITH THE
SAINTS

THE SINNER'S GUIDE TO A
RIGHTEOUS FEAST

FATHER LEO PATALINGHUG AND MICHAEL P. FOLEY

REGNERY
HISTORY
Washington, D.C.

Regnery History™ is a trademark of Salem Communications Holding Corporation Regnery® is a registered trademark and its colophon is a trademark of Salem Communications Holding Corporation

Cataloging-in-Publication data on file with the Library of Congress

ISBN: 978-1-68451-247-8
eISBN: 978-1-68451-396-3

Published in the United States by
Regnery History, an Imprint of
Regnery Publishing
A Division of Salem Media Group
Washington, D.C.
www.Regnery.com

Manufactured in the United States of America

10 9 8 7 6 5 4 3 2 1

Images of Saint Damien de Veuster and Saint Thérèse of Lisieux courtesy of Geoffrey Butz and Katherine Makowsky, respectively

Book interior design by Jason Sunde

Books are available in quantity for promotional or premium use.
For information on discounts and terms, please visit our website: www.Regnery.com.

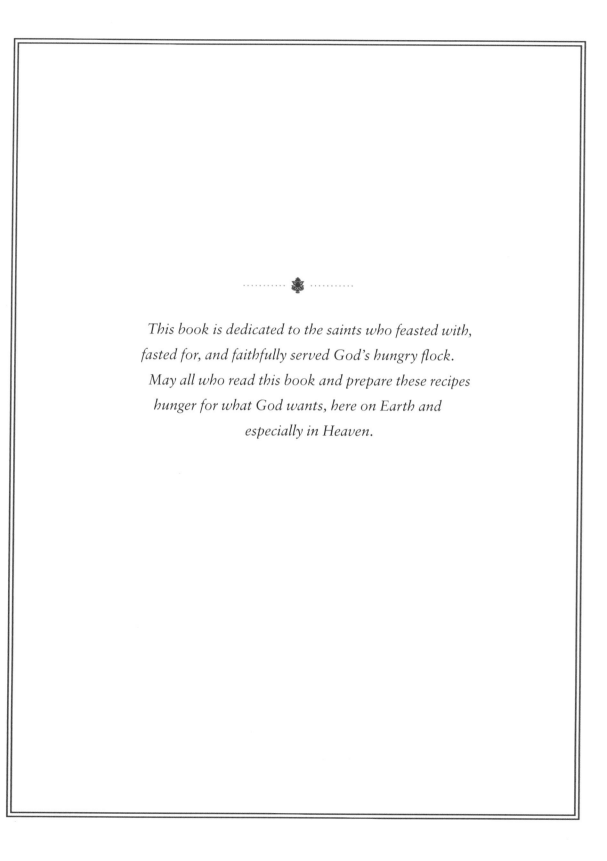

This book is dedicated to the saints who feasted with,
fasted for, and faithfully served God's hungry flock.
May all who read this book and prepare these recipes
hunger for what God wants, here on Earth and
especially in Heaven.

Contents

.... ❧ ....

INTRODUCTION

.... ⚜ ....

AND EVERY THING THAT MOVETH AND LIVETH SHALL
BE MEAT FOR YOU: EVEN AS THE GREEN HERBS HAVE
I DELIVERED THEM ALL TO YOU.
—Genesis 9:3

IT IS BETTER TO BE INVITED TO HERBS WITH LOVE,
THAN TO A FATTED CALF WITH HATRED.
—Proverbs 15:17

THE WHENCE AND WHY OF THIS BOOK

Some matches are made in Heaven, some on earth, and some in both places. When the powers that be at Regnery Publishing suggested that we, Fr. Leo Patalinghug and Dr. Mike Foley, team up to write *Dining with the Saints: The Sinner's Guide to a Righteous Feast*, they created a worldly partnership with a celestial aim. Father Leo is an award-winning chef, author, a popular radio and TV host, and founder of Plating Grace, a fun, family-focused, dynamic ministry seeking to bring about a future of stronger families, closer relationships, and a deeper understanding of Jesus as Food for our minds, bodies, and souls. Mike is the author of three bestselling liturgical cocktail books (*Drinking with the Saints*, *Drinking with Saint Nick*, and *Drinking with Your Patron Saints*) and an authority on the feast days of the Church. For the sake of food, festivity, and family, we are pleased to present to you this book, the product of our labors in the Lord's kitchen, library, and chapel.

And perhaps just in time. In the United States, family dinners—and with them, family conversation—have dropped alarmingly in the last couple of decades, the results being increased substance abuse, unwanted pregnancies, depression, obesity, lower academic performance, smaller vocabularies, and reduced literary skills among children and poorer mental and physical health and higher divorce rates among adults.[1] We fear that the loss of the family dinner will also have a bad effect on the very source and summit of our worship. If the Eucharist is, as we Catholics believe, both a sacrifice and a banquet, what will happen to our understanding of the Blessed Sacrament when we no longer understand the simple activity of a shared meal? What will happen to our appreciation of a solemn sacrifice when we lose even the simple etiquette of the table? Perhaps to Father Patrick Peyton's wise aphorism "The family that prays together stays together" we should add, "The family that dines together shines together."

THE UNIQUENESS OF THIS BOOK

Dining with the Saints gives you the resources you need for a healthy and uplifting family meal, a memorable couple's night, or a merry dinner party. It stands humbly in a long line of fine religious-themed cookbooks, beginning with Florence Berger's 1949 classic *Cooking for Christ*. But our book differs from its predecessors in three respects.

First, like the householder in the Gospel, *Dining with the Saints* brings out of the storeroom treasures both new and old (see Matthew 13:52). Some Catholic cookbooks favor only traditional recipes; others have only novel suggestions; ours aspires to the perfect blend of both. We delight in introducing you to the vast and wonderful array of old folk dishes from around the world, but we also realize that not all of these are feasible today. For instance, there is a tradition of having sheep's head on Saint Andrew's Day. Since eating something that looks like a slightly mummified head staring at you with eyeless sockets would be about as attractive to the average American family as finding half a worm in an apple, we provide a more edible alternative. In fact, *all* of the recipes in this book are specially designed by Father Leo himself to be delicious, easy to make, and a good fit for the liturgical occasion.

Second, whenever possible, *Dining with the Saints* presents what a saint actually ate or a piece of advice he or she gave about eating and drinking, and we connect that information to our recipes. Saint Thomas Aquinas's miracles having to do with food all involve fish, and so we recommend a delicious pasta with cod for his feast. Geneva bishop Saint Francis de Sales worried about spicy food upsetting one's spiritual equilibrium, and so to honor him there is a mild Swiss potato rosti. Granted, not all the saints were merry souls when it came to feasting. Saint Isidore of Alexandria (d. 403) frequently burst into tears at table, saying, "I who am a rational creature, and made to enjoy God, eat the food of brutes, instead of feeding on the bread of angels."[2] You may be surprised to learn that Saint Isidore was not invited to a lot of dinner parties.

Third, *Dining with the Saints* has a special "Food for Thought" feature that will help you profit spiritually from the occasion. A meal in honor of Saint Benedict is also a reminder that the Benedictine motto "Pray and Work" is not just for monks but for everyone; and dinner on the feast of Saint Anthony of Padua is an opportunity to find your faith in times of despair and your courage in times of fear—not just your lost car keys.

PRACTICAL ADVICE

First, do not be scrupulous about preparing meals on the appointed day. Instead, think of these entries as a "moveable feast" and transfer them to whenever it is most convenient. And be creative with the calendar. Like *Drinking with the Saints* and its sequels, this volume follows the old 1962 Roman calendar (which has more feast days); the traditional dates appear in boldface, followed by dates in italics for the Novus Ordo calendar if they differ from the traditional dates. Consult the appendix for cross-referencing, and be opportunistic with both calendars, landing on what works for you and your family. Finally, feel free to mix and match. Sometimes the entry for the day is only a dessert or a dipping sauce. Pair this with other entries to come up with a complete banquet (and for adult beverages, turn to *Drinking with the Saints*). The important thing is to carve out special time for the refreshment of body and soul and for the enjoyment of each other's company.

Second, just as it does not take much to turn the carnal fueling of the body known as eating into the exercise of civility known as dining (all you need are table manners and polite conversation), so too it does not take much to turn an exercise of civility into an almost sacred moment of fellowship and good cheer. We recommend starting off by saying a prayer before and after you sup. We include below the traditional Grace before Meals. You can, of course, improvise a prayer of your own, but don't go on for too long or the food will get cold, and don't forget to *bless* the food. Lay persons have the power to bless two things, their families and their comestibles; a blessing extends the peace and goodness of the Incarnate Word to other incarnate things, such as the things that are about to go into our mouths.

While most Catholics know the standard Grace before Meals, few know the Grace after Meals (see below). The first prayer blesses the food, the second gives thanks for it. We find the arrangement mildly amusing: while Protestants usually offer a thanksgiving before the meal, Catholics don't thank God for the food on their table until they've finished it! (Cynical, perhaps?) But the prayer reminds us to be thankful not only for the food we have just enjoyed but for *all* of God's benefits. It's a good attitude to have.

Moreover, in the Grace after Meals we pray for the dead: we remember those who are absent from the table and whom we yearn to see again at the Wedding Feast of the Lamb. The pagan Roman chef Apicius claimed that the dining room was a microcosm of the universe: the ceiling represented the gods; the table, the earth; and the floor, the underworld or realm of the dead. If Apicius could think like that, we Christians can certainly imagine our humble repasts as an echo of the communion of saints and a foreshadowing of the eternal banquet over which death has no dominion. And finally, saying grace before and after the meal bookends the time and provides recognizable markers. Children, for example, learn not to leave the table until the second grace is said. Saint Margaret of Scotland used this technique to civilize the crude Scots in her realm: she would not allow her guests to drink Scotch until after they had prayed the Grace after Meals. As a result, in some parts of Scotland the postprandial round of wine or liquor was known as the Grace Cup.

Third, we include an interesting comment made by Saint Josemaría Escrivá: "The day you leave the table without having done some small mortification you have eaten like a pagan." That may sound like a bit of a downer, but Escrivá's point is that if we approach feasting as an end unto itself, we will eventually become enslaved to our appetites. In C. S. Lewis's *Screwtape Letters*, the demon Screwtape advises his nephew Wormwood to encourage humans to have "an ever increasing craving for an ever diminishing pleasure." Even a tiny act of mortification, such as taking one less bite of food or using one less shake of salt, militates against this devilish trap. That's actually good news: all it takes is a little pinch (with God's grace) to keep the vices away. And it makes it easier to live up to Saint Paul's great and inspiring rule: "Whether you eat or drink, or whatsoever else you do, do all to the glory of God" (1 Corinthians 10:31).

Fourth, use this book liberally! Take advantage of the recipes and other ideas, and when it is time to sit at table, read aloud not only the "Food for Thought" but the biography of the saint or the explanation of the feast. One of the greatest compliments that Mike received after *Drinking with the Saints* came out was when the father of a family asked his children at dinnertime what their favorite book was and the five-year-old replied, "*Drinking with the Saints*." The young lad wasn't mixing himself a martini every night; what he enjoyed were the saints' stories, which his parents read aloud to him and which he had never heard before. *Dining with the Saints* has equally entertaining stories, with the added advantage that you don't have to explain to Junior the difference between whisky and brandy.

And so here's to eating and drinking to the glory of God, to the memory of His friends the saints, and to the culinary treasures of the Church. We pray that you and yours find as much joy using this book as we did writing it.

GRACE BEFORE MEALS

Bless us, O Lord, and these Thy gifts,
which we are about to receive from Thy bounty,
through Christ our Lord.
Amen.

GRACE AFTER MEALS

We give Thee thanks, Almighty God, for all Thy benefits,
who livest and reignest forever and ever.
Amen.

May the souls of the faithful departed, through the mercy of God, rest in peace.
Amen.

PART I

. . . . ❧ . . . .

The Feasts of the Saints
(The Sanctoral Cycle)

CHAPTER 1

January Saints

For January 1 through 6, see chapter 15, the Twelve Days of Christmas, and chapter 16, Epiphany and the Time Thereafter.

JANUARY

JANUARY 8
OUR LADY OF PROMPT SUCCOR

As every son and daughter of New Orleans knows right well, the patroness of their city, of the Archdiocese of New Orleans, and of the state of Louisiana is Our Lady of Prompt Succor ("quick help," if you need a more modern idiom). It was devotion to Our Lady under this title that obtained victory for the United States during the Battle of New Orleans on January 8, 1815. The night before the battle, the Ursuline nuns who had introduced this devotion to the city prayed that if God saved New Orleans from the British they would have a Mass of Thanksgiving celebrated every year. Their prayers were answered. The battle lasted roughly thirty minutes and claimed over two thousand British casualties but only a few dozen Americans. General Andrew Jackson, though a Protestant, personally thanked the Ursuline nuns for their intercession. And a Mass of Thanksgiving continues to be said every year on January 8 in the Ursuline convent.

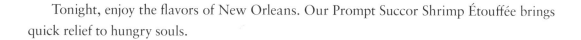

Tonight, enjoy the flavors of New Orleans. Our Prompt Succor Shrimp Étouffée brings quick relief to hungry souls.

Prompt Succor Shrimp Étouffée
Serves: 4–6   **Cooking time: 90 minutes**

2 lbs. shrimp, peeled and deveined (save the shells)

½ cup of bacon grease or lard

¼ cup flour

½ large onion, chopped (1 cup)

1 green bell pepper, chopped

2 jalapeno peppers, diced

1 large stalk celery, chopped (½ cup)

4 cloves garlic, minced

1 pint seafood stock

¼ cup clam juice

1 tsp. paprika

½ tsp. garlic powder

½ tsp. onion powder

½ tsp. dried oregano

1 tsp. cayenne pepper

2 tsps. salt

1 tsp. black pepper

1 tsp. dried thyme

½ tsp. celery salt

3 scallions, chopped

1 Tbsp. (or more) of your favorite hot sauce

1 cup white rice

1 Tbsp. vegetable oil

1. Add the rice, water, and vegetable oil to a small saucepan, bring to a simmer, cover with a tight-fitting lid, and cook for 20 minutes.
2. In a large stock pot, combine the seafood stock, clam juice, and shrimp shells and boil for 5 minutes. Strain out and discard the shells, reserving the stock.
3. In a Dutch oven, heat the bacon grease or lard over medium heat until it is fully melted and beginning to smoke. Add the flour and whisk together until it turns copper brown. Continue to stir for about 10 minutes.
4. Add the celery, green pepper, jalapeno, and onion and mix together until onions become translucent, approximately 4 minutes.
5. Add the stock 1 cup at a time so that you can judge how thick you want the sauce for the étouffée to be. Add more for a looser sauce or less for a thicker sauce.
6. Add the shrimp, paprika, garlic powder, onion powder, dried oregano, cayenne pepper, salt, black pepper, thyme, and celery salt, along with your favorite hot sauce. Reduce the heat, stir to mix together, and simmer for 10 minutes.
7. When the shrimp are fully cooked (opaque with a slight pinkish hue), turn off the heat, add the fresh green onions, and pour a couple of ladles of the étouffée over rice. Garnish with scallions and more hot sauce.

JANUARY 17
SAINT ANTHONY THE ABBOT

Saint Anthony is the founder of monasticism. At the age of twenty, he walked into church just as the Gospel was being proclaimed: "If thou wilt be perfect, go sell what thou hast" (Matthew 19:21). Interpreting the verse to refer to himself then and there, he relinquished his possessions and took up the ascetic life. Initially he stayed near his village, residing in a tomb outside of town, where he was assaulted by the devil in the form of terrifying beasts. Later, he withdrew into the Egyptian desert, where for twenty years he did not set sight on another human being. Eventually, however, a group of disciples gathered around him, and so he agreed to become their spiritual director. He instructed this community of monks for five years and then withdrew again, spending the last forty-five years of his life as a hermit and dying at the age of 105.

Saint Anthony could be a party pooper. At meals he often burst into tears and had to leave the table without eating because, reflecting on the blessed spirits in Heaven, he contrasted their constant praise of God with our low earthly needs. Thus he exhorted his brethren to pay little heed to the care of the body. How funny that Anthony's symbol in Christian iconography should be a pig, that gluttonous creature which loves to wallow in the mud and mire. One theory for this association is that a medieval order bearing his name, the Order of Hospitallers of Saint Anthony, was allowed the special privilege of letting their swine run free in the streets (an obsolete term for the runt of a sow's litter is an Anthony pig). Another theory is that Anthony was often tempted in the desert by the devil in the form of a pig. Regardless of the cause, Anthony is typically pictured in Christian art with a pig beside him, and pork became the traditional fare for his feast day.

You can honor this tradition with one of our pork recipes, such as Kalua Pork (see May 10) or Stamppot (June 6). Or you can imitate Anthony's own eremitical austerity. We imagine that a solitary life in the desert requires energy-packed food with lots of flavor. This Egyptian rice takes a meatless meal to a new level of boldness.

Egyptian Rice (Koshari Rice), Chickpeas, and Lentils with Crispy Onions
Serves: 4   **Cooking time: 1 hour**

THE CRISPY ONIONS

1 onion, thinly sliced

2 tsps. salt

½ cup all-purpose flour

½ cup vegetable oil

1. Season the onion slices with the salt and dredge them in flour until coated; shake off and discard excess flour.
2. On medium-high, heat oil in a cast-iron skillet or heavy frying pan, add the onion slices, and stir until they begin to brown.
3. Scoop out the onion slices and spread them on a plate lined with paper towels to soak up grease.
4. Set aside.

THE VINEGAR-BASED TOMATO SAUCE

2 Tbsps. vegetable oil

1 small onion, minced

4 garlic cloves, minced

1 tsp. ground coriander

½–1 tsp. red pepper flakes

28–30 oz. tomato sauce

½–1 tsp. salt

½–1 tsp. black pepper

2 Tbsps. distilled white vinegar

1. In a saucepan, heat oil over medium heat.
2. Add onion, garlic, coriander, and red pepper flakes and cook until onions become translucent.
3. Add tomato sauce, salt, and black pepper, stir, cover the saucepan, and cook until the sauce thickens, about 4–5 minutes.
4. Turn off the heat, stir in distilled vinegar, and set aside.

THE RICE

1 cup brown lentils

1½ cups medium-grain rice

1 tsp. salt, divided

½ tsp. black pepper

½ tsp. coriander

15 oz. can chickpeas

2 tsps. vegetable oil

7 cups water

2–3 Tbsps. fresh parsley, minced

1. Rinse the rice, soak in water for 20 minutes, and drain.
2. Rinse and drain the lentils and the chickpeas.

JANUARY

3. Combine lentils, 4 cups water, and ½ tsp. salt in a saucepan and partially cook for 15 minutes. Lentils should be tender but not mushy.

4. To a separate saucepan add 3 cups of water, the drained rice, vegetable oil, and ½ tsp. each salt, pepper, and coriander. Cover and cook over medium heat for 15–20 minutes, or until rice is soft.

5. Add the chickpeas to the rice and stir. Add the lentils to the rice and warm for 5–10 minutes.

6. To assemble the dish, use a fork to fluff the rice and lentils. Add a scoop of rice and lentils to each plate. Ladle some tomato sauce over the rice, add some crispy onions on top, and sprinkle with fresh parsley.

FOOD FOR THOUGHT

Eating slowly allows discernment, and discernment is one of the defining characteristics of a monk. Tonight let us slow down and discern what we are putting into our bodies, our minds, and our hearts.

JANUARY 20
SAINT SEBASTIAN

At your next dinner party, you can ask your guests the following question: Which saint was martyred twice? The answer is the reason for today's festivity. Saint Sebastian (d. 288) was a soldier in the Roman army who exhorted imprisoned Christians to stand firm in their faith despite torture and death and who was responsible for a number of conversions. He was appointed by both Emperors Diocletian and Maximian to be captain of the Praetorian Guard, neither of them knowing that he was a Christian. When Diocletian discovered the truth, he ordered Sebastian to be bound to a tree and killed with arrows. The saint was shot so many times that his biographers say that he looked like a hedgehog. Yet when a saintly widow came to bury his body, she discovered that he was alive and nursed him back to health. (Some biographers suspect that his fellow archer-soldiers did not want to kill him and thus avoided hitting any vital organs.) After he recovered, Sebastian confronted Diocletian and boldly upbraided him. When the stunned emperor recovered from his shock, he again ordered Sebastian to be executed, this time by being beaten to death with clubs. A tough saint through and through, Saint Sebastian is the patron of athletes, soldiers, and archers.

Roman dishes are usually simple, using basic ingredients but cooked in very precise ways. Saint Sebastian would have enjoyed this simple meal, sweetened with honey but with a peppery sprinkle.

Ancient Roman Sweet Omelet (Ova Spongia Dulcia)
Serves: 1–2   **Cooking time: 10 minutes**

4–6 eggs

1 cup whole milk

2 Tbsps. olive oil

½ cup honey at room temperature

½ tsp. salt

½ tsp. black pepper

1. Beat together eggs and milk.
2. Heat olive oil in a nonstick pan over medium heat.
3. When oil is hot, ladle 3–4 oz. of egg mixture into the pan and allow to cook without mixing or flipping.
4. When the omelet is done (no longer loose or runny), slide it onto a plate.
5. Repeat the process, placing each omelet on top of the last.
6. Drizzle honey over omelets and sprinkle with salt and pepper.

FOOD FOR THOUGHT

Like so many in the early Church, Sebastian's martyrdom was torturous and gruesome, yet he maintained a sweet docility and humility. When we feel like we're being pierced with arrows and insults, offer forgiveness and kind words. Sweetness helps with life's bitterness.

JANUARY

JANUARY 21
SAINT AGNES, VIRGIN AND MARTYR

Agnes (291–304) was only thirteen when she dedicated her maidenhood to Christ, much to the outrage of her many suitors. When she refused to change her mind, Agnes was handed over to the authorities. According to one story, they first tried to despoil her purity by putting her in a brothel, but any man who made advances on her was blinded and paralyzed. They then tried to burn her at the stake, but the wood would not ignite. Finally, she was decapitated on the Via Nomentana outside of Rome. Agnes went to her execution, Saint Ambrose tells us, "more cheerfully than others go to their wedding."

The name Agnes is derived from *agnus*, the Latin word for lamb, and it also evokes the Greek word *agnos*, meaning "pure." Her feast day is best known for the charming custom in which two lambs, raised by the Trappist monastery of Tre Fontane outside of Rome, are taken to the Sisters of the Holy Family of Nazareth in Rome, where they are decorated with roses and a mantle. They then go to the basilica Sant'Agnese fuori le mura, where they are blessed on the altar by the abbot. From there they are taken to the Vatican, where the pope himself receives and blesses them. Later, on Tuesday of Holy Week, the lambs are shorn and their wool is used by the nuns of the Benedictine convent of Saint Cecilia in Trastevere, Rome, to make palliums for newly installed metropolitan archbishops and patriarchs.

Agnes used to be a matchmaking saint. On the eve of her feast, maidens in some parts of England would take flour, salt, and water and make "dumb cakes"—so called because without saying a word the young woman would take the dumb cake, walk backyards with it to her room, eat it on her bed, and pray fervently to Saint Agnes. That night, Saint Agnes would show her the face of her future husband!

A less superstitious option is Leg of Lamb Primavera with Herbal Gremolata, a delicious dish that calls to mind Agnes's name, youth, and innocence.

JANUARY

Leg of Lamb Primavera with Herbal Gremolata
Serves: 4–6   Cooking time: 1 hour 30 minutes

THE HERBAL GREMOLATA

2 cloves garlic, minced

1 lemon, zested and juiced

¼ cup fresh parsley, finely chopped

½ cup panko bread crumbs

2 Tbsps. olive oil

1 tsp. cayenne pepper

¼ tsp. salt

¼ tsp. black pepper

1. Heat oil in a sauté pan, add bread crumbs, and cook until golden brown.
2. Remove pan from the heat, add the rest of the ingredients, and mix well.

THE LAMB

4–6 lb. leg of lamb, with the bone in

2–3 Tbsps. olive oil

4–5 cloves garlic, finely minced

4 sprigs fresh rosemary, finely minced

½ cup coarse-ground mustard

1 cup pistachios, chopped

1 cup golden raisins

2 tsps. salt, divided

2 tsps. black pepper, divided

16 oz. frozen spinach, thawed and drained

cooking twine or string

1. Butterfly the leg of lamb: Use a sharp knife to cut along the leg longwise. Then slide the knife along the bone on both sides of the leg to "open" it up, expose bone, and widen the surface area of the meat. Let it sit at room temperature for 30–40 minutes.
2. Preheat oven to 450°F.
3. In a small sauté pan, combine oil, garlic, rosemary, raisins, and spinach. Cook for 2–3 minutes, stirring to mix all ingredients. Set aside to cool.
4. Grease an oven-safe baking dish or sheet pan and lay out the leg of lamb, spreading out the meat to expose the bone.
5. Season with 1 tsp. salt and 1 tsp. pepper and evenly spread out the mustard.
6. Spoon the garlic, rosemary, raisins, and spinach mixture on the lamb and spread evenly.
7. Roll the lamb meat to close in the mixture and secure the leg of lamb by tying it with twine every two inches until the entire lamb leg is secure.
8. Sprinkle the remaining salt and pepper on the outside of the lamb leg.
9. Place lamb in oven and cook for 15 minutes.

JANUARY

10. Reduce the temperature to 350° and cook for another 40–50 minutes, or until the internal temperature reaches 135°.
11. Remove lamb from oven, allow it to rest for 10 minutes, remove the cooking string, and cut the meat into ¼-inch squares.
12. Top each piece of lamb with the herbal gremolata.

FOOD FOR THOUGHT

Purity of heart, a common characteristic of saints, becomes a source of strength in the face of an immoral and depraved world. Even though Agnes was a young girl, her courage, zest for purity, and opposition to the immorality of her generation gave her a holy boldness. Let us try to be that way as well.

JANUARY 27 *(SEPTEMBER 13)*
SAINT JOHN CHRYSOSTOM

John Chrysostom (347–407) was Patriarch of Constantinople, one of the greatest of the Greek Church Fathers, and a Doctor of the Church. In the Eastern churches, he is considered one of the Three Holy Hierarchs, the other two being Saint Basil the Great and Saint Gregory of Nazianzus. Chrysostom had been leading an ascetical life in Syria when he was made Patriarch of Constantinople, the great imperial city of the Eastern Roman Empire. The unimposing but dignified saint did not like the corruption that he saw in both the Church and the state, and he used his considerable skills as a homilist to say so. From the pulpit Saint John chastised the rich for not sharing their wealth and condemned the excesses of imperial court life; in his spare time, he deposed bishops who had bribed their way into office. The empress Eudoxia was particularly offended by Chrysostom's fiery sermons, but he could not have cared less: he was so unbending in the face of threats and criticisms that he was once called "the man without knees." But Eudoxia finally got her way. Teaming up with Theophilus, the Patriarch of Alexandria who was trying to prevent Constantinople's rise in ecclesiastical status, she forced Chrysostom into exile. After his loyal fans threatened to burn down the emperor's palace, he was quickly called back. Soon after, Chrysostom preached against a dedication ceremony of a new statue of Eudoxia for being too pagan; he even compared the empress to Herodias, the wicked wife of King Herod who had demanded the head of Saint John the Baptist on a platter. Chrysostom was exiled a second time, a mob burned down the basilica during the ensuing unrest, and the saint died as he was traveling to a new place of refuge.

Some of the controversies surrounding this saint involved food. Before being ordained a deacon, Chrysostom spent two years in the Syrian desert as a hermit and observed so strict a diet that he suffered from stomach and kidney problems for the rest of his life. When he moved to Constantinople, he refused to host lavish dinner parties and kept a modest table at all times, a practice that endeared him to the common folk but displeased wealthy citizens and the sycophantish bishops who were hanging around the imperial court. In his interpretation of Acts 2:46—"they took their portion of food with gladness and singleness of heart"—Chrysostom argued that the food in question was not dainty because "they that fare daintily are under punishment and pain." Rather, the cause of their gladness was simplicity, "for no gladness can exist where there is no simplicity."[1] Nevertheless, among the many false accusations brought against the saint was the charge that he secretly gorged himself on fine wines and rich foods.

You won't be accused of gorging on rich foods if you go with tonight's recommendation, but you will enjoy it. "Chrysostom" in Greek means "golden tongue," a moniker that Saint John earned because his sermons were so mesmerizing that the crowd had to be careful they would not get pickpocketed! Our Beef Tongue Pita with Tzatziki Cream celebrates the saint's nickname and his modest table, since tongue, though delicious, was the staple of poor folk.

What's that—you are squeamish about this recipe? Bite your tongue! And then bite into this one. Trust us, you won't regret it.

Beef Tongue Pita with Tzatziki Cream
Serves: 4–6   **Cooking time: 2 hours**

THE TONGUE

1 beef tongue

1 onion, roughly chopped

2 cloves garlic

2 stalks celery, roughly chopped

4 qts. beef broth

2 bay leaves

1 Tbsp. salt

2 tsps. black pepper

2 Tbsps. tomato paste

1. Clean the beef tongue by scrubbing it with salt and cold water and rinse it completely.
2. Put tongue, onion, celery, whole garlic cloves, bay leaves, tomato paste, salt, and pepper in a 6-quart Dutch oven and bring to a boil.
3. Turn down heat to reduce to a simmer, and cook 1–1½ hours, periodically using a slotted spoon to remove and discard the thickened foam that rises to the surface of the liquid.
4. Cook until the tongue is fork-tender (that is, a fork can easily pierce the tongue to the center and be easily removed).
5. Remove the tongue from the Dutch oven and set it aside.
6. Continue to cook the broth to reduce it to half.
7. When the tongue is sufficiently cooled, approximately 10 minutes, use a knife to cut through the exterior of the tongue lengthwise, giving you two long pieces of tongue. This cutting will allow you to peel off the two layers of skin (one dark and one lighter colored) and discard them.
8. Cut the tongue meat into thin slices and return it to the broth in the Dutch oven. Cook for another 3–5 minutes over a low heat, just enough to warm the tongue thoroughly.

THE TZATZIKI CREAM

1 cup sour cream

zest of 1 lemon

juice of ½ lemon

1 cup cucumber, minced or shredded

1 clove garlic, minced

1 tsp. salt

1 tsp. black pepper

1. Combine all ingredients and stir together.

THE PITA SANDWICHES

Cooled tongue and broth

Tzatziki cream

4–6 pieces of pita bread, cut in half

2 Tbsps. fresh dill, minced

1. Stuff the pita bread halves with slices of tongue.
2. Drizzle some of the thickened broth into the pita.
3. Top with tzatziki cream and garnish with fresh dill.

FOOD FOR THOUGHT

Our tongues can be great weapons against heresy if we preach the Gospel and speak the truth. But they can also reveal our hypocrisy if we say one thing and act contrarily. Our goal should be to bless God with both our words and our actions.

JANUARY 29 *(JANUARY 24)*
SAINT FRANCIS DE SALES

Francis (1567–1622) was born into the noble Savoyard or Sales family and received a top-notch education in law. His family's great plans for him were dashed when he broke off an arranged marriage to become a priest. Francis tried to be a dutiful son, secretly studying theology while also practicing fencing and riding to please his rather worldly father. One day while riding, Francis fell three times from his horse, and each time his sword and scabbard somersaulted through the air and landed in the shape of a cross. The writing on the wall was clear. After much disagreement with his father, he was finally ordained a priest.

Francis de Sales was a tireless educator: he learned sign language just to teach one deaf man about God (he is now a patron saint of the deaf and of adult education). But he is perhaps best remembered for his skills as a writer. His *Introduction to the Devout Life* is a spiritual and literary classic that was eagerly read by Catholic and Protestant alike. As Pope Pius XI put it, Francis argued "forcefully, but with moderation and charity." Consequently, the pope declared him patron of all those who "make known Christian wisdom by writing in newspapers or in other journals meant for the general

15

public." Oh, and when he was not writing or teaching, he was converting seventy thousand Calvinists to Catholicism as the bishop of Geneva and helping Saint Jane de Chantal found the Order of the Visitation.

Regarding diet, the saint advised not to be too picky, but to be content with what is set before you (see Luke 10:8). He did, however, say that you should avoid food that "may prejudice the health or incommode the spirit, such as hot or highly seasoned meats." We never thought of spicy food as "incommoding" or disturbing the spirit, but we suppose that if your usual diet is Swiss cuisine, a few drops of Tabasco sauce could make you go into a tailspin. On the other hand, Francis de Sales made allowance for occasions "in which nature requires recreation and assistance in order to be able to support some labor for the glory of God."[2] PowerBars?

Switzerland's national dish is fondue. A mixture of mountain-style cheeses and white wine, it is perfect for a cold winter's night, which is what one is likely to have in late January. The dish was originally devised as a farmer's breakfast, when vegetables were rare.

Better yet, try this Swiss Potato Rosti. The simple ingredients evoke Saint Francis's simple language and everyday examples, while the cooking process, which requires technique and patience and heat, reminds us of how to grow in holiness, Salesian-style: with common sense, good habits, and the love of the Holy Spirit.

Swiss Potato Rosti
Serves: 4 (as a side dish)   Cooking time: 30 minutes

2 lbs. potatoes, russet or Yukon Gold

1 tsp. salt

½ tsp. pepper

4 Tbsps. clarified butter (ghee), divided

1 Tbsp. chives or parsley

1. Mince the chives or parsley.
2. Peel the potatoes, shred them in a food processor or grate them, place them in a bowl lined with a cloth towel, and strain out the excess liquid.
3. Season with salt and pepper.
4. Add 1 Tbsp. of the clarified butter, mix thoroughly, and fluff the potatoes with a fork.
5. Pour the remainder of the clarified butter in a cast-iron skillet, heat on a burner on medium-low, and layer in the potatoes gently (do not pack tightly), about ½ inch high.
6. Cook 8–10 minutes, or until the potatoes begin to turn golden brown. If after 8 minutes the potatoes do not crisp up and turn brown, turn the heat up to medium. (Do not press the potatoes with a spatula or spoon, but allow them to cook slowly.)
7. Put a large plate on top of the skillet and carefully flip the potato cake onto the plate. Gently slide it back into the pan in order to cook the other side, another 8–10 minutes.
8. Remove the potato cake and cut it into quarters.
9. Sprinkle with fresh parsley or chives for garnish and serve immediately.

FOOD FOR THOUGHT

Saint Francis was a model of moderation and an excellent teacher on that subject. "Deer cannot run well under two circumstances," he writes, "when they are either too fat or too lean."[3] A continual moderation is therefore preferable to "violent abstinence practiced by fits and followed by intemperance."[4] Let us add to our New Year's resolutions a more consistent (and healthy) moderation.

CHAPTER 2

February Saints

FEBRUARY 1 *(OCTOBER 17)*
SAINT IGNATIUS OF ANTIOCH

Saint Ignatius (d. ca. 98–117) succeeded Saint Peter the Apostle and Saint Evodius to become the third bishop of Antioch. Ignatius is one of the five "Apostolic Fathers," so called because they personally received the Gospel from one or more of the original twelve apostles: in Ignatius's case, it was Saint John the Evangelist. His letters are valuable witnesses to the early Church's belief in the power of the sacraments, the holiness and unity of the Church, the importance of sound doctrine, and the hierarchy of clergy and laity; they are also where we first see the phrase "Catholic Church."

After being condemned for his faith, Saint Ignatius was led from Antioch to Rome to be fed to wild beasts in the Colosseum. Along the way he wrote to various Christian communities. His letter to the Romans is particularly interesting, for in it he begs the Christians there not to interfere with his execution but to let him be martyred. "Allow me to become food for the wild beasts," he tells them. "I am the wheat of God, and let me be ground by the teeth of the wild beasts, that I may be found the pure bread of Christ." He continues, "Entreat Christ for me, that by these instruments [the beasts] I may be found a sacrifice" to God.[1]

According to tradition, the saint got his wish. Tonight we honor Ignatius with Bulgur Wheat and Lamb, the wheat pointing to him as the "wheat of God" and the lamb pointing to the sacrifice of the cross, the altar, and the martyrs such as he.

....

Bulgur Wheat and Lamb

Serves: 4   **Cooking time: 30 minutes**

1 cup medium-coarse bulgur wheat

2 cups chicken, beef, or vegetable broth

1 tsp. salt, divided

1 tsp. black pepper

1 lb. ground lamb

2 cloves garlic, minced

1 Tbsp. olive oil

1 tsp. cumin

1 tsp. coriander

1 shallot, minced

½ cup fresh parsley, roughly chopped

1 lemon, zested and juiced

4 Tbsps. yogurt or sour cream for garnish and topping

1. In a medium saucepan cook the bulgur grain, broth, and a pinch of salt on medium heat. Simmer for 10 minutes, covered. Turn off the heat and let sit for another 10 minutes without removing the lid.
2. In a sauté pan, heat the oil over medium heat. Add garlic, shallot, cumin, coriander, pepper, and the remainder of the salt and cook until the shallots become translucent, about 1 minute.
3. Add the ground lamb and cook until it browns, about 4–5 minutes.
4. Mix the bulgur wheat into the cooked lamb.
5. Add the parsley leaves and zest and juice of the lemon and stir together.
6. Serve immediately with a dollop of yogurt or sour cream.

FOOD FOR THOUGHT

We should never fear to become more like the Eucharist—to make our lives a sacrifice, holy and pleasing to God, that is being offered for the sake of others, in gratitude for our creation and redemption and as a witness to Christ.

FEBRUARY 1
SAINT BRIGID OF KILDARE

Brigid (451–525), one of the three patron saints of Ireland along with Patrick and Columba, is invoked for numerous causes. She is the patroness of milkmaids, cattle, and chicken farmers because of her own experience as a slave on a farm; she is a patron saint of babies because she was so well-loved by the Blessed Mother that she was permitted to mystically nurse the infant Jesus; she is the patron saint of nuns because of her role in founding religious life in Ireland; and she is a patron saint of brewers because she miraculously provided beer on several occasions. Perhaps that is why ale is served on Saint Brigid's Day, along with an Irish bread baked specially in her honor called barmbrack that is made with currants and caraway seeds.

Tonight, pour yourself an ale as you prepare the lamb for Saint Ignatius of Antioch (see above).

FEBRUARY 3
SAINT BLAISE

FEBRUARY

Blaise (d. 316) was the bishop of Sebaste in historic Armenia (now a part of Turkey). Saint Blaise is one of the Fourteen Holy Helpers and is invoked against diseases of the throat because he once saved a boy choking on a fishbone by praying for him at the request of his desperate mother. Saint Blaise received the crown of martyrdom when he was tortured with steel combs and beheaded for the faith.

In the old *Roman Ritual* there is a blessing on the feast of Saint Blaise for bread, wine, water, and fruit (see "Food for Thought"), so those are obvious choices for today. The Basque people have garlic, salt, apples, and chocolate blessed on this day and give them to their livestock and children to protect their throats. They also enjoy a spicy sausage called *loukinkas* and fresh raw oysters; the custom is to eat a *loukinkas* and then chase it with a cooling oyster. We, on the other hand, recommend Blaise's Boneless Baked Armenian Fish. The spices honor Blaise's Armenian heritage, and they have just enough heat to keep the faith blazing in your heart (sorry: couldn't resist), while the boneless fish is to keep you from putting Saint Blaise to the test. The recipe is versatile: you can use snapper, sea bass, or salmon.

Blaise's Boneless Baked Armenian Fish
Serves: 4   **Cooking time: 30 minutes**

4 filets of snapper, sea bass, or salmon (4–6 oz. each)

1 onion, thinly sliced

4 Roma tomatoes, cubed

2 cloves garlic, minced

1 red bell pepper, thinly sliced

1 green bell pepper, thinly sliced

2 tsps. dried oregano

2 tsps. cumin

up to 2 tsps. cayenne pepper (optional)

2 tsps. ground sumac (or you can substitute lemon pepper)

2 tsps. paprika (sweet or hot, according to your preference)

1 tsp. salt

1 tsp. black pepper

2 Tbsps. olive oil

1 Tbsp. vegetable oil

3 cups water

2 cups long-grain rice

1. Add the rice, water, and vegetable oil to a small saucepan, bring to a boil, turn down to simmer, cover with a tight-fitting lid, and cook for 20 minutes.
2. Preheat oven to 400°F.
3. Gently pat the filets on all sides with salt, pepper, oregano, cumin, paprika, and sumac (or lemon pepper) so that the spices adhere to the fish.
4. In an oven-safe pan or large cast-iron skillet, heat the olive oil over medium heat and cook the fish for 2 minutes per side.
5. Remove the fish from the pan and set aside.
6. To the same pan, add the onions, tomatoes, bell peppers, and salt and pepper to taste and sauté for 2 minutes.
7. Spread the vegetable mix evenly in the pan and gently place the fish on top of the vegetables.
8. Cover the pan with an oven-safe lid or aluminum foil and place in the oven for 10–12 minutes.
9. Carefully remove the aluminum foil or lid and serve the fish and vegetables over the rice.

FOOD FOR THOUGHT

The Blessing of Bread, Wine, Water, Fruit for the Relief of Throat Ailments on the Feast of Saint Blaise:

> Let us pray.
>
> O God, Savior of the world, who consecrated this day by the martyrdom of blessed Blaise, granting him among other gifts the power of healing all who are afflicted with ailments of the throat; we humbly appeal to Thy boundless mercy, begging that these fruits, bread, wine, and water brought by Thy devoted people be blessed and sanctified by Thy goodness. May those who eat and drink these gifts be fully healed of all ailments of the throat and of all maladies of body and soul, through the prayers and merits of Saint Blaise, bishop and martyr.
>
> Amen.

"All maladies of body and soul." As dangerous as pesky fish bones are, the things that choke our spiritual lives are even worse.

FEBRUARY 5
SAINT AGATHA

Agatha (d. ca. 251) is one of the saints who has the honor of being mentioned in the Canon of the Mass (also known as Eucharistic Prayer I). A beautiful native of Catania, Sicily, she consecrated her life to God and refused to apostatize, even when a lustful governor had her breasts cut off (hence her depiction in Christian art holding a tray with two breasts on them). Happily, she was miraculously cured that night by a mysterious visitor to her cell who identified himself as an apostle of Christ. Today Agatha is the patron saint of breast cancer patients, wet nurses, torture victims, bellfounders (because of what a bell resembles), and even bakers, as some folks in the Middle Ages thought that her tray was holding loaves of bread!

Agatha eventually died from other wounds inflicted by her tormentors and quickly became a powerful intercessor in Heaven, curing Saint Lucy's mother of an ailment and saving her hometown from a volcano: the year after she died, Agatha stopped the nearby Mount Etna from erupting. To this day Catania celebrates a three-day festival in her honor involving grand candlelit processions, fireworks, games, and an unforgettable treat: Minne di Sant'Agata, a breast-shaped pastry topped with a candied cherry that looks like a nipple.

Now before you channel your inner Puritan and start reaching for the smelling salts or clutching your pearls, you should know that the Minne di Sant'Agata were invented—or at least popularized—by Sicilian nuns. Indeed, it is believed that one of the other names for this pastry, Minne di Virgini, is not in reference to Agatha the Virgin but to the nuns of the Monastero di Vergini in Palermo.

What can we learn from this memorable custom of mamillary munchies? That, fortunately, the American tendency to sexualize the breast is not universal. In Italy and other areas of the world, breasts are innocent symbols of femininity, fertility, and motherhood. That is why there is an artistic tradition that portrays the Blessed Virgin Mary breastfeeding her Divine Son: the *Madonna Lactans*, or "Nursing Madonna."

We'll stop now, and to spare you further embarrassment we won't even talk about the town of Amarante in Portugal and its unbelievably phallic cakes incxplicably baked for the Festival of Saint Gonçalo, a chaste medieval Dominican priest.

The Breasts of Saint Agatha (Minne di Sant'Agata)
Yields: 8 cakes   Cooking time: 1½ hours

THE CREAM FILLING

2 cups sugar

1 lb. ricotta cheese, strained

2 tsps. vanilla extract

1 Tbsp. chocolate chips

1. Combine all ingredients, stirring together until they are thoroughly mixed.

THE SPONGE CAKES

1¼ cups all-purpose flour

2 tsps. vanilla extract

1½ cups granulated sugar

1 lemon, zested and juiced

5 large eggs

8 maraschino cherries, halved

½ tsp. cream of tartar

¼ cup confectioner's sugar

nonstick spray

1. Preheat oven to 375°F.
2. Prepare two 9-inch square baking pans with nonstick spray.
3. Separate egg yolks from whites.
4. In a mixing bowl, combine the egg whites and cream of tartar. Mix with a hand or stand mixer until you see stiff peaks.
5. In another clean mixing bowl, combine the egg yolks and sugar and use a hand or stand mixer on medium-high speed to beat until thickened and lemon-cream color.
6. Lower the mixer speed and add the flour a little at a time, making sure to scrape down the sides until all the flour is fully incorporated.
7. Add the vanilla extract, lemon zest, and lemon juice and mix.
8. Gently fold the egg whites into the batter.
9. Carefully pour the batter into the cake pans and bake in the middle of the oven for 40–50 minutes, or until the center is cooked and a toothpick inserted comes out clean.
10. Turn the cake out on a wire rack to cool.
11. When the cake is completely cooled, cut out 8 separate cakes using a cookie cutter or an upside-down glass, dipped in water and pressed into the cake.
12. Use an ice cream scoop to place a small dome of the ricotta cheese cream on top of each cake round.
13. Use a wet spoon to form the cream into a dome to cover the cake base.
14. Top off each cake with half a maraschino cherry.
15. Sift confectioner's sugar over each cake and serve.

FEBRUARY

FOOD FOR THOUGHT

We live in a schizophrenic age, where we idolatrize the body, degrade the body, fetishize the body, and are oddly squeamish about the body all at the same time. Today's feast is a salutary reminder that the body and all its members are good and created by a loving God, that the body should be accorded respect and dignity, but also that the body is, when you think about it, kind of funny, and it is okay to giggle at it now and then. Saint Agatha, thanks for the mammaries.

FEBRUARY 10

SAINT SCHOLASTICA

Scholastica (480–542) was the sister of Saint Benedict, the founder of Western monasticism (see March 21). After her brother founded his order on Monte Cassino, she founded a community of nuns about five miles away. Benedict and Scholastica used to meet at a house not far from the monastery gate once a year to discuss spiritual matters. At their last meeting Scholastica, perhaps having a premonition of her death, begged Benedict to stay the night and talk. Benedict refused to spend a night outside the cloister and declined. Scholastica then prayed to God, and immediately a violent storm broke out that prevented his departure, the rain pouring down from heaven like the tears running down her face. When Benedict chastised her, she merely replied, "I asked a favor of you, and you said no. I asked a favor of God, and He said yes." Brother and sister then spent the entire night speaking of heavenly things. Gregory the Great praises Scholastica's prayer, for although Saint Benedict was thinking in terms of justice, she was motivated by charity, and since "God is charity" (1 John 4:8), "she rightly did more who loved more." Three days later Benedict had a vision of a white dove ascending to Heaven, and he knew that his sister had passed to her eternal reward.

Since it is not dove season (and in homage to Scholastica's homeland), how about Italian Quail Cacciatore? You can also decorate the table with mimosas, the flower associated with Saint Scholastica.

Italian Quail Cacciatore
Serves: 4   **Cooking time: 1 hour**

4 quail (1 per person), cleaned and cut in half, with the legs and thighs separate from the breast and wings

2 Tbsps. kosher salt

1 Tbsp. black pepper

¼ cup olive oil, divided

1 onion, thinly sliced

2 bay leaves

fresh sprig of rosemary

1 cup cherry tomatoes

½ cup green olives, pitted and sliced

2–3 Tbsps. capers

½ cup dry white wine

1. Prepare an oven-safe baking dish by spreading out a light coating of olive oil in it, place it in the oven, and preheat the oven (and the dish) to 300°F.
2. Season the quail pieces with the salt and pepper.
3. To a large sauté pan over medium heat, add 1 Tbsp. olive oil. Sear 1 piece of the quail, skin side down first, cook for 2 minutes per side, remove from the pan, and set aside. Repeat with the other pieces.
4. To the same pan, add the onion, bay leaves, cherry tomatoes, olives, capers, and dry white wine, stir together, and cook for 1–2 minutes.
5. Carefully remove the hot baking dish from the oven. Pour the ingredients from the pan into the baking dish. Top off the mixture with the partially cooked quail, skin side up. Add the rosemary sprig and bay leaves into the liquid, keeping the rosemary whole for easy removal.
6. Carefully wrap the baking dish with aluminum foil or cover it with a tight-fitting lid, return it to the oven, and bake for 8–10 minutes.
7. Remove from the oven and let rest for 5–8 minutes.
8. Remove the rosemary and bay leaves and serve the quail with crusty bread, rice, pasta, or potatoes.

FOOD FOR THOUGHT
At your next family reunion, cherish the memories together, fortify your time together with prayer, and consider how you can help each other get to Heaven, as these sibling saints did.

FEBRUARY

FEBRUARY 14
SAINT VALENTINE

Valentine was a priest in Rome who was martyred on this day in AD 270. There are several theories regarding his patronage of young lovers. According to one, he administered Holy Communion and last rites to Christian prisoners before becoming imprisoned himself. As a prisoner, he wrote a letter to the jailer's daughter, signing it "Your Valentine." Another version has it that the saintly priest played matchmaker for the jailer's daughter. But the most likely reason is historical happenstance. Valentine's martyrdom falls on the day before the Roman Lupercalia, when young people would choose courtship partners for a year or even propose marriage. It was only natural that once the old gods were dethroned, the Christian faith should baptize some of these harmless customs.

Love involves giving your entire self to the other, holding everything in common, and respecting each other's differences. This Paella for Two puts different ingredients together and is served from one dish: it almost represents what love would look like if it were a recipe! Paella, by the way, hails from the Spanish region of Valencia, the name of which is derived from the same Latin root as the name Valentine (*valens*, being strong).

Paella for Two
Serves: 2   **Cooking time: 1 hour**

1½ cups Spanish or short-grain rice

1 Tbsp. olive oil

1 clove garlic, minced

1 shallot, minced

1 red bell pepper, thinly sliced

8–10 cherry tomatoes, halved

½ cup frozen peas

1–2 Tbsps. fresh parsley, finely minced

1 tsp. saffron

1 tsp. paprika, sweet or spicy

1 tsp. salt

1 tsp. pepper

1–2 bay leaves

4 large shrimp, deveined, but shells and head kept on if possible

4–6 mussels, cleaned and scrubbed

1–2 whole calamari, cleaned and cut into ½-inch pieces

1–2 chicken thighs, skinned, deboned and cut into ½-inch strips

1 cup dry white wine

4 cups seafood or chicken broth

2 Tbsps. butter

½ lemon, cut in wedges

1. Preheat oven to 400°F.
2. To a paella or other large oven-safe pan, add oil and heat over medium heat.
3. Add the chicken and sauté until 1 side of each piece is slightly browned but not fully cooked (1–2 minutes). Remove from pan and set aside.
4. To the same pan, add the shallots, garlic, bell pepper, cherry tomatoes, and frozen peas. Sauté for 1–2 minutes, until shallots turn translucent. Remove from pan and set aside.
5. To the same pan, add the rice and cook for about 12 minutes, until the rice turns slightly translucent around the edges.
6. Add the white wine to deglaze the pan and stir, cooking for about 1–2 minutes, until the wine almost completely evaporates.
7. Add the butter and stir until it is fully melted.
8. Add 1 cup of the broth and stir.
9. Add the sautéed vegetables and chicken thighs and the salt, pepper, paprika, and saffron and stir together.
10. Add 2 more cups of the broth and stir.
11. Add the bay leaves.
12. Now "design" the paella by evenly spreading the calamari pieces and shrimp in some sort of decorative pattern. Insert the mussels into the rice.
13. Pour in the remaining cup of the broth so that the ingredients are submerged. If you need more liquid, just add more water, ½ cup at a time.
14. Carefully wrap the pan with aluminum foil and put into the oven for 10–15 minutes. Check occasionally to make sure there is enough broth so that the rice cooks evenly, as the rice closest to the bottom of the pan begins to caramelize.
15. After 10–15 minutes, check to see if the rice is cooked and tender. The shrimp should turn a bright orange-pink color, and all the mussels will be opened.
16. Remove the pan from the oven, carefully pull off the aluminum foil, and discard the bay leaves.
17. Sprinkle the minced parsley over the dish and decorate with the lemon wedges.

FOOD FOR THOUGHT

Love is not a feeling of goodness or excitement; it is a decision to do the best for the one you love. Similarly, cooking for and serving the people you love does not always feel good (it can be frustrating and exhausting). What is important is choosing to love (and showing your love by cooking) through thick and thin—and not just on one day of the year!

FEBRUARY 18
SAINT SIMEON

FEBRUARY

Simeon (d. 116) is believed to be the son of Cleophas, which makes him the nephew of the Blessed Virgin Mary and of Saint Joseph and a first cousin of Jesus Christ (one of the "brethren" of the Lord mentioned in the New Testament). He was most likely present at the first Pentecost, when the disciples received the Holy Spirit, and he later succeeded his brother Saint James the Lesser as bishop of Jerusalem after the latter was martyred around AD 66. Simeon guided the local Church under difficult circumstances: he was warned in a dream of the impending destruction of Jerusalem by the Romans and relocated his flock to an ancient city called Pella, on the other side of the river Jordan. He also had to deal with the early heresies of the Nazareans and Ebionites, who denied the divinity of Jesus Christ and practiced a strange mix of Judaism and Christianity. It was probably these heretics who snitched on Saint Simeon to the Roman authorities, accusing him of the double crime of being a Christian and a descendent of the House of David residing in Palestine—a capital offense after the Sack of Jerusalem. Simeon was probably crucified in the year AD 110, at the astonishing age of 120. He endured his sufferings with such equanimity that even his persecutors were filled with admiration.

This Lemon-Infused Olive Oil is perfect as a dipping sauce or for drizzling onto bread or savory meats, and it also makes a great sauce for pasta. Both the lemon and the olive oil carry our thoughts to the sunny cities of Jerusalem and Pella. The kosher salt is a nod to Simeon's Jewish heritage, while the red pepper flakes evoke the fiery tongues of the Holy Spirit that Saint Simeon received at Pentecost.

Lemon-Infused Olive Oil
Serves: 4–6   **Cooking time: 10 minutes**

½ cup heavy green and slightly cloudy first-press olive oil ("extra virgin")

1 Tbsp. kosher salt

1 lemon, zested and juiced

½ tsp. red pepper flakes

1 clove garlic, finely minced

1 Tbsp. fresh parsley, finely chopped

1. Pour olive oil into a small saucepan, add all other ingredients, stir to combine, and bring to a low boil.
2. Use this flavored oil as a dipping sauce for bread, or add ½ pound of cooked pasta, stir, and serve.

FEBRUARY

FOOD FOR THOUGHT

We can only imagine what it was like to be part of Jesus's extended family, to call the Queen of the Angels "Auntie" and her most chaste spouse "Uncle" and to address the King of the universe and the Savior of mankind as "Cuz." Then again, as the adopted children of God, we the baptized are part of an even greater intimacy: we get to call Mary not "Aunt" but "Mother," and Jesus is not our cousin but our brother and friend as well as our Lord. Tonight, let us thank God for the privilege of being members of a new and expanding Holy Family.

CHAPTER 3

March Saints

MARCH 3
SAINT KATHARINE DREXEL

Catherine Mary Drexel (1858–1955) was born with a silver spoon in her mouth to a wealthy and elite Philadelphia family. She developed a passionate interest in the plight of black and Native Americans through reading and through touring the United States. During an audience with Pope Leo XIII she told him about the miserable conditions of these minorities and was surprised to hear the pope suggest that *she* should become a missionary. Catherine heeded the suggestion, took the name Mother Katharine (different spelling), and founded the Sisters of the Blessed Sacrament for the purpose of educating and helping Native and African Americans—all a good hundred years before the public cared one whit about the topic. When she renounced her fortune to become a religious, the Philadelphia headlines read: "Miss Drexel Enters a Catholic Convent—Gives Up Seven Million."

Mother Katharine and her sisters encountered resistance virtually everywhere they went. One of their schools was burnt to the ground; another had every window smashed in. In Beaumont, Texas, the KKK threatened to flog, tar, and feather Catholics if the chapel was not closed in one week. A few days later, a violent storm destroyed the Klan's local headquarters (God is good, all the time). Today the Sisters of the Blessed Sacrament continue to work with African Americans and Native Americans in twenty-one states and in Haiti.

In 1915, Katharine Drexel founded Xavier University in New Orleans, the first and only Catholic institution of higher education for black people in the United States. Twenty-one years earlier, she helped to open the first mission school for Indians, in Santa Fe, New Mexico. Native American Frybread pays tribute to Saint Katharine's service. According to a Navajo tradition, the bread was created using U.S. government–issued flour, sugar, salt, and lard when the tribe was forced to relocate from Arizona to New Mexico in 1864. Popular with tribes across the country even though it is, ironically, a non-native Native American food, it is an apt symbol for the very injustice that Mother Katharine was trying to redress and the resilience of the American Indians, whom she so admired.

Native American Frybread
Serves: 4 **Cooking time: 30 minutes**

2½ cups all-purpose flour, divided

2 tsps. baking powder

½ tsp. salt

½ cup milk

½ cup water

2–3 cups vegetable oil

1 Tbsp. confectioner's sugar

½ tsp. cinnamon

1. Sift 2 cups of the flour, the baking powder, and the salt together into a large bowl.
2. Add the milk and water and mix together with a fork.
3. Separate the dough into 4 equal pieces.
4. Use the remaining flour to dust the workstation and your rolling pin.
5. Roll the 4 pieces of dough into circles about 1 inch thick.
6. In a shallow frying pan, heat the oil until the temperature reaches 150°F.
7. When oil is hot, carefully add one piece of the circular dough to the hot grease.
8. Cook about 1–2 minutes on each side, or until golden.
9. When the frybread is cooked, use a spatula or tongs to remove the bread from the oil. Shake off excess grease and place the frybread on the paper towels.
10. Repeat with the other 3 dough circles, avoiding stacking the breads on top of each other.
11. Combine confectioner's sugar and cinnamon and sift over the bread and serve it as a hearty dessert. (Or the frybread can be the basis of a main course: top it with ground beef, chopped lettuce, and grated cheese.)

MARCH

FOOD FOR THOUGHT

Saint Katharine inherited a fortune from her parents, but the greatest gift she received from her family was the faith that called her to religious life. Consider what gift you received from your parents, and what gift you will give to your children. Will it be something material, something that will break or go out of style? Or will it be something spiritual, like faith, the gift that keeps on giving?

MARCH 7 *(JANUARY 28)*
SAINT THOMAS AQUINAS

Thomas (1225–1274) was born into a noble family who had him educated by the Benedictines at Monte Cassino from the age of five and who expected him to enter that prestigious and influential monastery when he came of age. Thomas shocked them, however, with his determination to join the Dominicans, an order of—gulp—mendicants (beggars and itinerant preachers). They locked him in a tower of the family castle in an attempt to break his will, and his brothers even put a loose woman in his room. Thomas promptly chased her out with a firebrand. Eventually he escaped with the help of his sisters, and Thomas Aquinas went on to be a Dominican priest, a professor at the University of Paris, a Doctor of the Church, and arguably the greatest theologian of all time.

Aquinas's nickname in school was "the Dumb Ox" because he spoke little and was physically imposing. What exactly that means is uncertain: There was a rumor, probably spread by his puritanical detractors, that the saint was so fat that they had to cut a crescent into the dinner table in order for him to dine. His early biographers, on the other hand, insist that he was very tall and well proportioned. Whatever the truth about his girth, Aquinas is sometimes invoked today for people suffering from body-size issues.

Saint Thomas Aquinas was not the ideal dining companion. At a banquet with King Saint Louis IX of France, the absent-minded college professor became so lost in thought that he slammed his fist on the table and shouted, "And that will settle the Manicheans!" The dinner party went dead silent, but the gracious king instructed a secretary to approach Aquinas with a notepad, lest his important insight be forgotten.

Thomas's masterpiece, the *Summa Theologiae*, covers just about every topic you can imagine from a theological perspective, including food. Among some of his insights: meat is delicious (in general, more so than fish) and nutritious, but it also stimulates lust, which is one of the reasons that we fast from it during Lent.[1] Strange as that sounds, it may be true: meat is high in zinc, which raises testosterone levels.[2]

Coincidentally, the miracles that are attributed to Saint Thomas's intercession and that involve food are about fish. A Master Matthew of Viterbo had had a violent reaction to fish ever since he was a baby. Even if he ate a small amount, he either vomited it up or got a fever; as a result, he could not stand the taste or smell of fish. This presented a problem during Lent, when non-meat alternatives were few and far between, and so at the start of one Lent Matthew prayed to Saint Thomas for help so that he could have meals with his companions. The next night he dreamed that he saw a Dominican friar presenting him a fish and saying to him: "Master Matthew, eat this fish that Brother Thomas sends to you."[3] From that moment on, Matthew never had an adverse reaction to the scaly creatures.

Similarly, a man had a small son who reacted to a certain fish by going into a fit of hiccupping; this happened so often that the poor lad went mad. (Did it not occur to them to keep the offending fish away from his dinner plate?) In any event, the father prayed at the tomb of Saint Thomas, and the boy was cured.[4] Saint Thomas Aquinas is the patron saint of many causes, including Catholic schools, students, apologists, and booksellers, but with the meteoric rise in food allergies over the past few decades, we think that we should add this cause to the list.

Allow us to recount one more food miracle involving fish and Saint Thomas. As he was journeying through Italy to attend the Council of Lyons, Aquinas grew gravely ill and lost all appetite. His anxious doctor asked him if there was anything he could get him. Aquinas replied that he had a hankering for herring, but the fish, though common in France where he had been teaching, was unavailable in that part of Italy. The doctor left sad but decided to check the market anyway; to his amazement, there was one crate of fresh herrings coming in from the docks. He returned to Aquinas's bedside with the coveted dish. Saint Thomas realized that this was a miracle which God's mercy had conceded to his appetite. "Sir," he said, "it is better that I entrust myself to Providence than to dare eat these fishes which a divine power has given to me and which I wanted out of an excessive desire." In other words, Saint Thomas took this opportunity to mortify himself, even on his deathbed.[5] Normally we would not praise somebody for refusing to eat the very thing that he had ordered (especially if we were waiters), but these were special circumstances.

Aquinas never finished composing the *Summa Theologiae*. About six months before his death, he had a mystical vision so glorious that, he later said, it made everything he had written now seem like straw. He never wrote again.

We have combined this story with Thomas's fish connections in a magnificent dish called Paglia e Fieno e Pesce, or green and white pasta and cod. The pasta represents the straw.

Paglia e Fieno e Pesce (Straw and Hay and Fish Pasta)
Serves: 4–6   **Cooking time: 30 minutes**

1 lb. paglia e fieno (green and white pasta—or combine ½ pound of green spaghetti with ½ pound of regular spaghetti)

1 shallot, minced

2 cloves garlic, minced

¼ lb. cod, cut into ½-inch cubes

2 Tbsps. olive oil

1½ cups heavy cream

½ cup dry white wine

1 tsp. salt, plus 2 Tbsps. more for the pasta water

1 tsp. black pepper

2 Tbsps. parsley, finely chopped

1. Fill a large pot with water and bring to a boil. Add 2 Tbsps. of salt and then the pasta and swirl it to keep it from sticking together.
2. To a sauté pan, heat olive oil over medium-high heat, add the cod, and cook until it begins to caramelize, about 3–5 minutes on each side. Use a slotted spoon to remove the cod and set it aside.
3. In the same pan, sauté the garlic and shallots for 2 minutes.
4. Add the white wine and cook for another 2 minutes.
5. Add the heavy cream, ½ tsp. salt, and pepper and cook until the mixture begins to bubble and thicken.
6. When the pasta is cooked, reserve one cup of starchy water. Drain the rest of the water and immediately place the pasta into the cream sauce. Add 1–2 Tbsps. of starchy pasta water at a time to loosen the sauce to the desired consistency.
7. Add the cod to the pan and mix all the ingredients together.
8. Garnish with fresh minced parsley and serve immediately.

MARCH

FOOD FOR THOUGHT

Educated people should seek humility in order to become truly wise. Saint Thomas Aquinas shows us that all the education in the world means little without a humble faith.

MARCH 12 *(SEPTEMBER 3)*
SAINT GREGORY THE GREAT

The son of a Roman senator and a Christian saint (Celia), Pope Saint Gregory the Great is known for many things. He was the first monk ever to become pope. After his election, he coined the title "Servant of the Servants of God" for himself and his successors. He organized and contributed to the sacred Church music that now bears his name, Gregorian chant. And last but not least, he codified the Roman liturgy, which is why the Traditional Latin Mass, when it is not called the Extraordinary Form of the Roman Rite, is sometimes referred to as the Gregorian Rite.

There is a charming yarn about Saint Gregory and cherries. On Saint Mark's Day (April 25), the ascetical pontiff was overwhelmed by a hankering for cherries and commanded his servants to find some—a tall order given that the cherry trees along the hills of Trastevere were only just in bloom. One disconsolate gardener was searching the area when Saint Mark appeared to him and granted his petition by blessing a tree and making it heavy with fruit. When the cherries were brought to the pope, the story goes, the Servant of the Servants of God "wolfed down a bellyful." Ever since then, it is customary for the pope to enjoy a bowl of cherries on Saint Mark's Day.

Gregory is the fellow who sent Saint Augustine of Canterbury to England to convert the Anglo-Saxons after seeing captured slaves from that land paraded through the streets of Rome. Marveling at their fair skin, he asked, "Who are they?" "Angles," came the reply. "Not Angles but Angels," the pope corrected, showing his kindness but also his total ignorance of Englishmen (grin). Gregory was also a master of what today is called "inculturation," the art of evangelizing in such a way that you only uproot the parts of the native culture that are bad and leave the rest alone, baptizing it for the greater glory of God. We are confident that Gregory would approve of this English-esque comfort food made in his honor from both Roman and British ingredients. And for dessert, enjoy a bowl of cherries, of course.

Sausage with Onion Gravy

Serves: 4   **Cooking time: 1½ hours**

4 link sausages

2 Tbsps. (ordinary salted) butter

2 yellow onions, thinly sliced (about 4 cups)

½ cup dry red wine

2 sprigs fresh thyme

2 sprigs fresh sage

2 cups beef broth

2 tsps. Worcestershire sauce

1 tsp. salt

1 tsp. black pepper

1 Tbsp. yellow mustard

1 Tbsp. balsamic vinegar

1 Tbsp. cornstarch

2 Tbsps. water

2 Tbsps. unsalted butter, kept cold and cubed

nonstick cooking spray

1. Preheat oven to 350°F and prepare an oven-safe baking dish with nonstick cooking spray.
2. In a large frying pan, cook the sausages whole, a few minutes on each side until they begin to brown.
3. Remove partially cooked sausages from the pan, place them in the oven-safe baking dish, and cook for 10–12 minutes.
4. To the frying pan, add the 2 Tbsps. of salted butter and melt over medium heat.
5. Add the onions and stir occasionally until the onions become caramelized.
6. Add the red wine, thyme, and sage and cook for 2–3 minutes.
7. Turn the burner down to low.
8. Add the broth, salt, pepper, mustard, and balsamic vinegar and simmer for 10–15 minutes, stirring occasionally.
9. Add the cornstarch and water, continually whisking to avoid lumps. Cook for another 1–2 minutes until the sauce thickens.
10. Remove from heat, add the cubes of cold butter, and whisk to dissolve the butter and make the sauce creamy.
11. Serve the sausage with a ladle of the onion sauce, accompanied with potatoes, rice, or bread.

MARCH

FOOD FOR THOUGHT

As Gregory understood, evangelizing requires fellowship with people of different cultures, becoming a part of other people's lives, and sharing a meal with them, even when it is not the kind of food with which you are familiar. Breaking bread together creates a sense of communion, and the bread will taste even better when dipped in our onion gravy.

MARCH 17
SAINT PATRICK

Saint Patrick, the Apostle of Ireland (387–460), first came to the Emerald Isle under less than auspicious circumstances: he was brought as a slave, having been abducted from his family at the age of sixteen by Irish pirates. For six years he labored as a shepherd, treating the time as an opportunity to become more deeply converted to Christ and to pray. He escaped, but after being ordained he answered a mystical call to return to his former home of captivity, this time as a shepherd of men. He encountered resistance from local chieftains and the Druids and was beaten, robbed, and enchained, but he persevered. Before his death, Patrick had baptized thousands, ordained numerous priests, and helped several noble women enter the religious life.

Irish Americans typically have corned beef and cabbage on Saint Patrick's Day, in large part because both items were inexpensive in the nineteenth century when the Irish were poor immigrants. Back in the old country, the traditional dinner for the feast consists of some kind of meat, a potato dish called colcannon, and Irish soda bread. Here we include a delicious twist on an old favorite. And it is easier to make!

MARCH

Corned Beef and Cabbage Sandwich
Serves: 4   **Cooking time: 20 minutes**

8 slices marble rye bread

16 slices corned beef deli meat

4 Tbsps. butter, divided

4 slices Irish cheddar cheese

¼ cup mayonnaise

2 Tbsps. mustard

1 tsp. paprika

1 Tbsp. white vinegar

2 cups cabbage, thinly shredded

¼ cup Guinness beer

1 Tbsp. sugar

2 tsps. salt

2 tsps. black pepper

1. Preheat oven to 400°F.
2. Melt 2 Tbsps. of the butter in a pan over medium heat.
3. Add the cabbage and cook for 3–5 minutes, stirring occasionally, until the cabbage softens.
4. Add beer and cook until reduced by half.
5. Add sugar, salt, and pepper and stir.
6. Strain cabbage and discard liquid.
7. In a bowl, mix mayonnaise, mustard, vinegar, and paprika until thoroughly combined.
8. Lay out all 8 pieces of bread on an oven-safe baking sheet and spread mayonnaise mixture on each piece.
9. Add one slice of meat to 4 of the pieces of bread.
10. Add a slice of cheese to all 4.
11. Add a small amount of the cabbage mixture to all 4.
12. Add another slice of the meat to each.
13. Use the other slice of bread to top off the sandwich, pressing each sandwich firmly together.
14. Melt the remaining 2 Tbsps. butter in a small saucepan or microwavable bowl. Brush both sides of the sandwich with the melted butter.
15. Place the baking sheet of the sandwiches in the oven and cook for 10–12 minutes, until the bread is toasted and the cheese is melted.
16. Remove the sandwiches from the oven and allow to rest 1–2 minutes before cutting in half.

MARCH

FOOD FOR THOUGHT

While Saint Patrick's feast day has become a day of revelry, it should above all be a day of holiness and prayer. The saint was known for his devotion, his clear teaching, and his courageous and persevering faith. Celebrate the day with good food, good drink, family, and friends—and a sincere prayer that his evangelization efforts may continue to bear fruit in Ireland and around the world.

MARCH 19
SAINT JOSEPH

Saint Joseph, the husband of the Blessed Virgin Mary and the foster father of Our Lord, receives rare praise in the Bible: he is described as "a just man" (Matthew 1:19, Luke 23:50). In the thousands of pages of Sacred Scripture, you can probably count on one hand the number of times this happens. Noah, by contrast, is called "just in his generations" (Genesis 6:9), probably—judging from his checkered record—a euphemistic way of saying that he was the best of a bad lot.

Despite its location in Lent, Saint Joseph's Day—which is also Father's Day in Spain, Portugal, and Italy—is a time of great festivity. In Italy and some parts of the United States the faithful give thanks to Saint Joseph for delivering Sicily from a famine long ago. Elaborate three-tiered "Saint Joseph tables" (*tavole di San Giuseppe*) are set up at church and loaded with various dishes, many of which include bread crumbs to symbolize the sawdust of a carpenter. Also included are fava beans, which sustained the Sicilians during the famine; often they are blessed by the priest to be taken home as a protection from evil and misfortune. The celebration typically begins with a cry of *Viva la tavola di San Giuseppe!* and ends with everyone (including the poor) taking home food and a "lucky" blessed bean. New Orleans has added to these festivities an annual parade through the French Quarter. On the more domestic side is a custom from the seventeenth century in which a statue of Joseph is placed on the table during dinner and "served" generous portions, all of which then go to the poor.[6]

In the old, old days, Lent was a time of fasting and total abstinence from flesh meat, and not even the high rank of Saint Joseph's Day changed that. As a result, the traditional dishes for this feast are meatless. They include: minestrone and dried bread crumbs, Ravioli di San Giuseppe, Sfingi di San Giuseppe (Saint Joseph's Pastries), Zeppole or Saint Joseph's Day Cake (a kind of fritter), and various kinds of Saint Joseph's Bread. We include here an excellent version whose simple dough provides a crusty outer texture with a hint of sweetness and licorice anise flavor.

Saint Joseph's Bread

Serves: 4   **Cooking time: 1 hour**

1⅓ cups lukewarm milk (110°F)	½ cup sugar	5 large eggs, divided
2 packages active dry yeast	2 tsps. salt	1 Tbsp. water
6 cups bread flour, divided	4 Tbsps. melted butter, at room temperature	1 tsp. anise seeds
		2 Tbsps. sesame seeds

1. Combine lukewarm milk and yeast in the bowl of a stand mixer. Stir together and rest for 10 minutes until yeast blooms.
2. Add melted butter, sugar, and 1 cup of the flour and beat with the regular paddle attachment of the mixer for about 2 minutes.
3. Add 4 of the eggs, the anise seeds, and 1 more cup of flour and beat for 2 more minutes.
4. Switch out the regular paddle attachment on the mixer for the dough hook and add the remaining flour ½ cup at a time until the dough starts to tighten up. (Depending on the size of the eggs, you may not need all the flour.) Continue to knead the dough for about 3–4 minutes.
5. Transfer dough to a greased bowl, cover with a cloth towel, and allow to rise in a warm place until doubled, about 1 hour.
6. Punch the dough and divide it into 3 equal pieces.
7. Roll each piece of dough into the shape of a thick noodle, about ½–1 inch thick and 20–22 inches long. Braid the dough together loosely and tuck the ends of the braids under the dough. Place the braided loaf on a baking sheet lined with parchment paper.
8. Preheat oven to 350°F.
9. Combine the water and the remaining egg to make an egg wash, and use it to brush the loaf.
10. Generously sprinkle the top of the dough with sesame seeds.
11. Bake for 30–35 minutes, or until golden brown.
12. Transfer dough to wire rack and rest for 10–15 minutes before cutting and serving.

FOOD FOR THOUGHT

As a father, Saint Joseph had to provide daily bread to his Son, who would give His flesh and blood as the Bread of Life and the Cup of Eternal Salvation. In other words, Joseph provided bread to Bread: the bread he gave became the flesh of his foster Son, and that flesh has become our Bread in the Eucharist. Pretty cool.

MARCH 21 *(JULY 11)*
SAINT BENEDICT

Benedict of Nursia (480–543 or 547) was born in the Umbrian region of Italy. The son of a noble family, he was receiving a liberal arts education in Rome when he decided to dedicate his life entirely to Christ and become a hermit, which he did by living alone in a cave for three years. Others heard of Benedict's holiness and asked him to become their abbot, but when he rebuked them for their wicked lives, they tried to murder him by putting poison in his drink. Saint Benedict, however, foiled their plot by making the sign of the cross over the cup, which then broke. Having had enough of those fellows, Benedict went on to found thirteen monasteries, including the great Abbey of Monte Cassino in Italy.

To help his fledgling monasteries, Benedict wrote his masterpiece *The Rule of Saint Benedict,* a simple yet comprehensive set of instructions on how to be a good monk. Several chapters concern food and meals, highlighting the importance of eating together as a communal bond. Benedict anticipates one meal per day, with two cooked dishes as the menu. However, he adds, if there are fruit or fresh vegetables, those can be added, too.[7] From the Ides of September (September 13) until the beginning of Lent, the monks should dine at 3:00 p.m., but from Lent to Easter they should dine in the evening so long as they do not need lamplight during their meal.[8] In general, unless the monks need extra protein for their manual labors or are "very weak or ill," they should not eat the flesh of four-footed animals. A pound of bread, measured by the cellarer, should be sufficient for the day. But if a monk is misbehaving, he must have his meal *after* the rest of the community.[9] An early form of detention?

Eggs Benedict is not named after our saint of the day (it is reputed to take its name from Pope Benedict XIII, who usually had it for breakfast during his six-year reign from 1724 to 1730), but who cares? This Italianized version is a triumph that will help you celebrate the founder of Western monasticism's encouragement to work and pray—and eat. The creaminess of the poached egg contrasts with the crispiness of toasted brioche bun and is complemented by the savory quality of the ham and the delicate subtle flavor of the hollandaise.

MARCH

Italian Eggs Benedict with Basil Hollandaise
Serves: 2   Cooking time: 30 minutes

2 whole eggs

4 egg yolks

1 Tbsp. vinegar

4–5 cups water

1 brioche bun, halved and lightly toasted with butter

2–4 slices prosciutto, slightly toasted in a nonstick pan until it becomes a little crispy

½ cup butter, melted

1 Tbsp. lemon juice

2 tsps. fresh basil leaves, finely minced

2–4 slices Roma tomatoes

½ tsp. salt

¼ tsp. white pepper

½ tsp. garlic powder

1. Boil the water in a small saucepan, then reduce to low heat.
2. When the water is simmering, add the vinegar and stir to create a swirl effect.
3. Break one egg into a small bowl, then gently add it to the swirling water.
4. Cook the egg in the lightly simmering and swirling water for 2–3 minutes.
5. Use a slotted spoon to remove the egg and place it on a plate lined with paper towel. Repeat the process with the other egg.
6. Prepare the hollandaise sauce. Place a small glass or metal bowl on top of the saucepan to create a double boiler, making sure the boiling water doesn't touch the bowl.
7. Add the egg yolks and the lemon juice to the bowl and whisk together until the mixture thickens slightly.
8. Drizzle the melted butter slowly into the bowl, continuing to whisk until the sauce is thick.
9. Add the basil, salt, white pepper, and garlic powder and continue to whisk until all the ingredients are fully incorporated.
10. When the hollandaise sauce is made, set aside for the rest of the assembly.
11. Place a few slices of the tomato on each buttered and toasted brioche half, add crispy prosciutto, followed by the poached egg and topped off with a dollop of the basil hollandaise.

FOOD FOR THOUGHT

The motto *Ora et Labora*—"Work and Pray"—is an effective rule not just for Benedictine monks but for everyone. Ask yourself how you work and pray in your daily life. If you discover room for improvement, consider making a retreat to a Benedictine monastery or abbey and allowing yourself to be inspired by the monks' example.

MARCH

MARCH 22
SAINT CATHERINE OF SWEDEN

Catherine (1331–1381) was the fourth child of Saint Bridget, Queen of Sweden. Saint Catherine was required by her father to marry a German nobleman at the age of thirteen or fourteen, but she persuaded her new husband to join her in taking a vow of celibacy, which freed the couple to devote themselves wholeheartedly to the spiritual life and works of charity. Catherine accompanied her saintly mother to Rome, refused all offers of marriage when her husband died, and became the head of her mother's religious order (the Brigittines) after her mother died. The patron saint of miscarriage prevention, Catherine is often portrayed in Christian art with a hind at her side, for according to the story a deer came to her aid "when unchaste youths sought to ensnare her."

We will spare Saint Catherine's furry friends and pass on venison tonight, but what about a favorite from her homeland? This recipe for Swedish Meatballs and Gravy has international appeal. The creamy sauce pairs perfectly with the savory meatballs, and it is a perfect dish for families and larger gatherings with friends. We also imagine that it is the kind of thing that Saint Catherine would serve at her dinner parties, which always included the rich, the poor, and the forgotten. For a saint, everyone deserves something delicious like these meatballs.

MARCH

Swedish Meatballs and Gravy
Serves: 8   Cooking time: 1½ hours

THE MEATBALLS

½ cup bread crumbs, Italian-seasoned or plain

½ cup milk

1 egg, beaten

1 clove garlic

½ tsp. salt

½ tsp. black pepper

½ tsp. allspice

½ onion, finely chopped

1 lb. ground beef

½ lb. ground pork

2 Tbsps. parsley, finely chopped

2 Tbsps. butter

1 Tbsp. olive oil

1. In a large bowl, combine bread crumbs with milk, egg, garlic, salt, pepper, and allspice and allow the milk to be absorbed into the bread crumbs.
2. Add the ground beef, pork, onions, and parsley and mix together, using your hands to fully incorporate all the ingredients.
3. Using a measuring cup or ice cream scoop, portion out either 20 small or 8 large meatballs, place them on a tray, and set aside.
4. Heat the butter and olive oil in a large frying pan over a burner on medium.
5. When the oil is hot, add the meatballs to the pan, about 5–6 at a time, being careful not to overcrowd the pan. Cook the meatballs about 1–2 minutes on each side, using a spoon to turn them carefully without breaking them apart.
6. When the meatballs are browned on all sides, carefully place them in a large cooking pot.

THE GRAVY

½ cup butter

2 Tbsps. all-purpose flour

1 cup beef broth (or you can substitute chicken or vegetable broth)

1 cup heavy whipping cream

2 tsps. soy sauce

2 Tbsps. ground mustard

1 tsp. garlic powder

½ tsp. salt

½ tsp. black pepper

1. To the frying pan you browned the meatballs in, add the butter and melt it.
2. Add the all-purpose flour and whisk it together with the melted butter to create a smooth paste. Cook for about 1–2 minutes, continuing to whisk.
3. Add the broth a little at a time to the pan, whisking to break up any lumps. Continue to add the broth so that all of the flour is fully incorporated and the sauce begins to thicken.
4. Add the heavy cream, soy sauce, mustard, salt, pepper, and garlic powder and cook for another 3–5 minutes over medium heat, until the sauce is thick and creamy.
5. Pour the sauce into the large pot with the meatballs and the juices. Cover the pot and cook over low heat, simmering for another 5–10 minutes.
6. Serve over mashed potatoes or rice and sprinkle with parsley for garnish.

MARCH

FOOD FOR THOUGHT

Have you ever pondered the international versatility of the humble meatball? A minor change in ingredients can turn a meatball into an Italian, French, Swedish, or even Asian dish. The saints, too, knew how to take the universal Good News and make it feel right at home in every age and culture.

MARCH 25
FEAST OF THE ANNUNCIATION OF THE BLESSED VIRGIN MARY

The Annunciation, one of the oldest and greatest Marian feasts that we have, is filled with meaning. First, it marks the beginning of the end of Satan's rule over mankind. Just as the first Eve's *no* to God led to our slavery under sin, the New Eve's *fiat* to God opened the way to our salvation.[10] Pope Benedict XVI beautifully describes this *fiat* as saying yes to a marriage proposal: "As Mary stood before the Lord, she represented the whole of humanity. In the angel's message, it was as if God made a marriage proposal to the human race. And in our name, Mary said yes."[11]

And just as the Annunciation is a kind of wedding between God and man, it is also a kind of wedding between Mary and the Third Person of the Blessed Trinity. The Mother of God is hailed as the Spouse of the Holy Spirit because on this day the power of the Holy Ghost overshadowed her (see Luke 1:35).

As if that weren't enough, the Annunciation is, like Christmas, a great feast of the Incarnation. This is the day that the Second Person of the Holy Trinity united Himself to our humanity by humbly becoming a zygote, a single eukaryotic cell, in Our Lady's womb. Or to put it more plainly, this is the day that the Word first became flesh and dwelt among us (see John 1:14). The place where He first chose to dwell (or, to translate the original Greek more literally, to pitch His tent) was within this maiden of Nazareth, making her a holy tabernacle and a new and truer Ark of

49

the Covenant. This is the day, as the Maronite liturgy proclaims, that "the peace of God is planted, and the heights and depths cry out: 'O come, Lord Jesus!'"[12]

In a few countries, bread or something like it was used to celebrate the occasion, perhaps because of its connotation with the Eucharist (which also makes the Word flesh), perhaps because Our Lady now has "a loaf in the oven." That's not just a modern phrase, by the way: Jesus's contemporaries also thought of the womb as an oven and of bread as life.

In old Russia, blessed unconsecrated wheat wafers were distributed by the priest after the Divine Liturgy. The father of the house took them home and gave them to his family and servants, who received them with a deep bow and ate them in silence. Leftover "Annunciation bread" would be buried in the fields as protection against frost, hail, blight, and drought.[13]

In Sweden, the feast was nicknamed Waffle Day (Vaffeldagen). We'll give you three guesses what they ate. Our Pancakes with Macerated Strawberries are close enough, and the strawberries are a classic symbol of Our Lady (see August 15).

....

Pancakes with Macerated Strawberries
Serves: 4　　　　　　　**Cooking time: 2½ hours**

1½ cups flour
2 cups sour cream
½ tsp. salt
3–4 Tbsps. ice-cold water

½ cup melted butter, divided
¼ cup lemon juice
2 Tbsps. sugar

2 tsps. cinnamon
¼ cup fresh strawberries, sliced into thin pieces

1. Mix together flour, sour cream, and water until ingredients are fully combined to make pancake batter.
2. Set aside in refrigerator for at least 1 hour.
3. Coat a nonstick pan with 1–2 Tbsps. melted butter, and heat over medium heat.
4. Ladle ¼ cup of the chilled batter into the pan and cook until bubbles start to form on top of the batter.
5. Use a spatula to flip the pancake and cook for about 2 more minutes, or until the batter is fully cooked.
6. Repeat until you have used all the batter.
7. To make the macerated strawberries, combine the lemon juice, sugar, cinnamon, and fresh strawberries in a bowl and mix until sugar is dissolved.
8. Use a potato masher to crush the strawberries into smaller pieces.
9. When the pancakes are done, drizzle some of the strawberries and juices onto each pancake.

FOOD FOR THOUGHT

Saying yes to God's plan isn't easy because we don't always know what God's plan is for us. But we do know the basics, like saying our prayers, going to church, practicing consistent acts of kindness and patience, and being generous with our love to those in need. These are the basics of our faith, which open us up to a discernment of God's plan. Practice saying yes to these basics as you give thanks to Our Lady, who with one yes changed the world when she agreed to bring the Word into it.

MARCH

CHAPTER 4

April Saints

APRIL 2
SAINT FRANCIS OF PAOLA

Francis of Paola (1416–1507) was the founder of the Order of Minims. He had the gift of prophecy and the ability to read consciences. No respecter of persons, he openly chided the king of Naples for his ill-doings and suffered persecution as a result. When French king Louis XI begged him to visit his court, the saint refused until ordered to by the pope. Saint Francis died on Good Friday 1507; when the Huguenots destroyed his tomb in 1562, they found his body incorrupt.

In France, Saint Francis is also remembered for a gift he brought to King Louis XI from his native home of Calabria, Italy: Bartlett pears. The saint's nickname at court was *le Bon Chrétien*, or "the Good Christian," and this moniker was applied to the pear he had introduced to the country. To this day, what is called a Bartlett pear in the United States and a Williams pear in Great Britain is known in France as a *poire bon chrétien*.

Even if there are no Bartlett pears available in your area, you can celebrate the saint's good Christian faith with any pears you can find: enjoy them for dessert.

APRIL 4
SAINT ISIDORE

Isidore of Seville (560–636) is a Doctor of the Church who is often called the "last scholar of the ancient world," but he did not start out that way. A poor student, Isidore eventually put his entire trust in God and went on to become the most learned man of his day. In his encyclopedic *Etymologies*, Isidore preserved all of the ancient learning he could find,

successfully synthesizing the remnants of Roman civilization and the ascendent Visigothic culture of ancient Spain.

Most of what Isidore has to say about food in the *Etymologies* concerns the origin of terms, although he offers some practical advice along the way. The saint, for example, highly recommends grace before meals. "Food should not be consumed before saying a prayer," he writes. "Refreshment of the spirit should be considered more important, because heavenly things are more important than earthly."[1] On the subject of moderation, Isidore recalls an old story: "A certain Apicius was the first to devise cookware. He died by a voluntary death, after stuffing himself with good things—and rightly so, because he who is a slave to his maw and to his gluttony kills both the soul and the body."[2]

Sopa Fideos, or vegetable noodle soup, pays tribute to Saint Isidore's earthly homeland as well as to his interest in bodily health and moderation.

Saint Isidore Soup, a.k.a. Sopa Fideos
Serves: 4   **Cooking time: 30 minutes**

2 Tbsps. olive oil
½ onion, chopped
4 cloves garlic, chopped
1 carrot, diced (about ¼ cup)
2 stalks celery, diced

15-oz. can chickpeas, drained
½ tsp thyme (dry or fresh), minced
5 cups vegetable broth
½ tsp. saffron thread

1 cup Spanish *fideos* (or substitute elbow macaroni, orzo, or short pasta)
1–2 tsps. kosher salt or sea salt
1–2 tsps. black pepper
2–3 Tbsps. fresh parsley, finely minced

1. Heat the olive oil in a large stockpot over medium-high heat.
2. When the oil is hot (1–2 minutes), add the onion, carrot, celery, and garlic and sauté for 2–3 minutes.
3. Add the chickpeas, thyme, salt, pepper, saffron, and thyme and cook together 2–3 minutes, stirring occasionally.

APRIL

55

4. Add the vegetable broth and turn the heat up to high. Stir ingredients together and allow broth to come to a boil.

5. When the broth boils, add the *fideos* (or the substitute pasta) and cook according to the instructions on the box, around 10 minutes. Keep the lid on the pot to retain the liquids and stir occasionally. Be careful not to let the soup boil over.

6. When the *fideos* are tender but slightly chewy, turn off the heat and fill individual bowls with a large ladle of the soup.

7. Garnish with a sprinkle of fresh parsley and serve.

FOOD FOR THOUGHT

Draw from the wisdom of today's saint: bless your food first, and then enjoy it without killing your soul or body.

APRIL 14 *(JUNE 1)*
SAINT JUSTIN MARTYR

Justin (103–165) was born in what is now the city of Nablus on the northern West Bank of Palestine. It is somewhat ironic that he is most famous for his prolonged encounter with philosophy: after defeating the Cynic philosopher Crescens in a debate, Justin was flogged and beheaded during the reign of the Stoic philosopher Emperor Marcus Aurelius. Justin had studied in a number of different philosophical schools until one day he met a mysterious old man on the beach who convinced him that the mind cannot arrive at the fullness of truth without divine assistance. The man went on to tell Justin about the Hebrew prophets who were inspired by the Holy Spirit.

Justin converted, but he did not completely leave Greek philosophy behind. Indeed, he wore the distinctive

cloak of the philosophers and opened a philosophical school in Rome where he taught students for free about Christianity, the "true philosophy."

Musakhan is a sumac-spiced chicken that combines savory Middle Eastern flavors with the bright essence of lemon. Sumac has been used as a spice, a dye for decorations, and a medicine. Similarly, Saint Justin's teachings bring a freshness to the faith, highlight its beauty, and show its healing quality. And sumac's signature color (*summāq* is Arabic for red) recalls Justin's glorious martyrdom.

Sumac-Spiced Chicken (Musakhan)
Serves: 4 **Cooking time: 1 hour**

4 chicken thighs and 4 drumsticks

4 tsps. allspice

4 tsps. salt

2 tsps. black pepper

4 tsps. cardamom

4 tsps. cumin

4 tsps. sumac (or substitute lemon zest)

¼ cup olive oil

2 medium white onions, thinly sliced

1 cup pine nuts (or substitute shaved almonds)

2 lemons, cut into 8 slices

½ cup water

4 pieces pita bread

2–3 Tbsps. parsley, finely minced

1. Set oven to 350°F.
2. Wash chicken, dry with paper towel, and place in a bowl to season and marinate.
3. Rub the allspice, cardamom, cumin, sumac (or lemon zest), salt, and pepper into the meat, pressing the seasoning onto all parts of the chicken.
4. Heat the olive oil in a skillet or oven-safe frying pan over medium-high heat and sear chicken for about 4 minutes on each side, until golden brown. Remove the chicken from the pan and set aside on a plate.
5. Add the onions to the pan and sauté them until they turn translucent, 4–5 minutes on medium heat, stirring occasionally.
6. Add the pine nuts and water to the pan and mix all together.
7. Add the lemon slices to the pan, spreading them out evenly on top of the onion mixture.
8. Add the chicken pieces to the pan, skin-side down, immersing them in the water and nestling them into the lemons and onions.
9. Cover the pan with aluminum foil, put it in the oven, and cook the chicken for 30 minutes.

APRIL

10. When the chicken is cooked to an internal temperature of 165°F, carefully remove the foil.

11. Turn the oven to broil and put the chicken back in the oven for another 3–5 minutes, or until it becomes golden brown and crispy, with most of the water evaporated.

12. Warm the pita bread in the oven for a few minutes and place one piece of the bread on a plate; scoop out some of the onions and pine nuts and put them on top of the pita, and place one chicken thigh and drumstick on top of the onions. Place lemon slices on the chicken. Repeat to create three more servings. Garnish with fresh parsley.

FOOD FOR THOUGHT

The multipurpose uses of plants such as sumac remind us to be versatile servants of God. We are called to be "food" or a refreshment for others by our charity, to bring beauty into this world with our skills and talents, and to bring healing to people through our hospitality and friendship.

APRIL 17 *(APRIL 20)*
SAINT ANICETUS

Pope Saint Anicetus (d. 168) was the eleventh successor of Saint Peter and governed the Church during the reign of Emperor Marcus Aurelius. He was a Syrian from the city of Emesa (modern-day Homs). We don't know a great deal about this pope except that he was the first bishop of Rome to condemn heresy, by forbidding Montanism and opposing Gnosticism and Marcionism. According to the old Roman Breviary, he also "passed a decree which forbade clerics to nourish their hair," meaning not that he was prohibiting shampoo but that he was

APRIL

outlawing long hair, the fashion of the Gnostics. (Didn't you always suspect a connection between the Gnostics and the hippies?)

In culinary terms, the word "anicette" is anethole, with a flavor profile similar to licorice, star anise, and fennel. It has a unique sweetness with the depth of a bitter licorice. This pope and saint had a great responsibility to bring healing and unity to the Church. His life was one of holiness, and his death by martyrdom was bittersweet. Honor him tonight with a delicious dish that celebrates his shepherding skills and healing role.

Roasted Lamb Chops & Fennel with Anicette Gremolata
Serves: 4   Cooking time: 40 minutes

8–12 frenched lamb chops (2–3 per person)

3 Tbsps. garlic, minced

5–6 Tbsps. olive oil, divided

2 Tbsps. mustard

1 whole fennel stalk and bulb, cut into pieces ½-inch thick

1 cup fennel fronds (removed from the fennel stalk)

2 tsps. salt

2 tsps. black pepper

1 whole orange, zested and juiced

1 Tbsp. balsamic vinegar

3–4 Tbsps. Italian-seasoned bread crumbs

1 clove garlic, minced

½ tsp. salt

½ tsp. black pepper

1. Prepare the gremolata: Put the fennel fronds, garlic, orange zest, orange juice, balsamic vinegar, salt, pepper, and 4 Tbsps. olive oil into a food processor or blender. Pulse to combine, creating a thick and oily paste. Remove the mixture and place it into a bowl with the bread crumbs. Stir together the bread crumbs and fennel-frond mix. Add more olive oil if necessary.
2. Preheat oven to 450°F.
3. Season the lamb chops with salt, pepper, mustard, and remaining 2 Tbsps. olive oil.
4. Layer the pieces of fennel stalk and bulb on the bottom of an oven-safe baking dish and cook in the oven for 8 minutes, then flip and cook for another 8 minutes.
5. Place the lamb chops on top of the fennel and cook in the oven for 3–6 minutes, or until the bottom of the lamb chops start to caramelize.
6. Flip the lamb chops and return to the oven to cook for another 3–6 minutes.
7. Remove the pan from the oven and allow meat to rest before serving with a drizzle of the gremolata.

APRIL

FOOD FOR THOUGHT

Popes in the early Christian era had to protect the deposit of faith, bring unity to a growing body of believers, evangelize the nations, and build the foundations of an international organization. Consider learning more about apostolic succession, and be grateful for the gift of a continuous line of supreme pontiffs from Peter to Anicetus to our current pope.

APRIL 21
SAINT ANSELM

Anselm of Canterbury (1033–1109), the founder of scholasticism and a Doctor of the Church, was born in Aosta in northern Italy. Although Anselm relished life in the monastery as an abbot in Normandy, he was called to cross the English Channel and become the archbishop of Canterbury. Before and after his consecration, he struggled constantly, first with King William II and then King Henry I, over the Investiture Controversy raging at the time.

It is as a theologian, however, that Anselm ranks, in the words of Pope Benedict XVI, as "one of the most luminous figures in the tradition of the Church and in the history of Western European thought itself."[3] Anselm's emphasis on belief as the condition of understanding provided what is now the classical definition of theology: *fides quaerens intellectum*, faith seeking understanding. Anselm even goes so far as to suggest that the understanding we enjoy in this life is "a middle state between faith and that Beauty which is grasped by the intellect" alone. "The more someone attains understanding," he concludes, "the closer he approaches that Beauty to which we all aspire."[4] What a beautiful sentiment! Rightly, Saint Anselm's title is *Doctor Magnificus*, the Magnificent Doctor.

When we think of Italian cuisine, we think of tomato sauce and pasta. And when we think of English cuisine, we think of fish and chips, bangers and mash, and, thanks to recent immigration patterns, Indian-spiced curry. This dish celebrates Anselm's Italian heritage as well as his episcopal activities in England with a fusion dish of Italian tomato sauce, English cream, and Indian curry. It's a chicken tikka masala, than which nothing greater of its kind can be cooked.

APRIL

Chicken Tikka Masala

Serves: 4   **Cooking time: 1 hour**

THE CHICKEN AND MARINADE

4–5 chicken thighs, skinned and deboned, cut into ¼-inch pieces

1 cup plain yogurt

2 tsps. fresh garlic, minced

1 Tbsp. fresh ginger, minced

2 tsps. garam masala

1 tsp. turmeric

1 tsp. cumin

1 tsp. chili powder

1 tsp. salt

1 tsp. black pepper

1 tsp. onion powder

2 Tbsps. canola or vegetable oil

1. Wash the chicken pieces, pat them dry with a paper towel, and place them in a large bowl.
2. In another bowl, mix the garlic, ginger, garam masala, turmeric, cumin, chili powder, salt, pepper, and onion powder into the yogurt to create the marinade.
3. Pour the marinade onto the chicken, mix thoroughly, put the bowl in the refrigerator, and allow the chicken to marinate for at least 1–2 hours (preferably overnight).
4. Heat the oil to medium in a large skillet or pot.
5. Add a few pieces of chicken at a time, not overcrowding the pan, and cook for 3 minutes on each side. Remove and repeat the process in small batches to ensure each piece of chicken is properly seared on the outside. (Note, the chicken is not fully cooked at this time, so do not taste it.)
6. Remove the chicken from the pot to a covered dish where it will stay warm.

THE MASALA SAUCE

2 Tbsps. butter

2 shallots, minced

1 Tbsp. fresh ginger, minced

2 tsps. garam masala

1 tsp. turmeric

14–15 oz. tomato sauce

1 tsp. chili powder

2 tsps. sweet paprika

1 tsp. salt

2 cups heavy cream

2 tsps. brown sugar

1 cup cilantro leaves

½ cup water (if needed to loosen the sauce)

1. To the oil in the pot you cooked the chicken in, add the butter and melt over medium heat.
2. Add the shallots, garlic, and ginger and sauté for 2–3 minutes.

APRIL

3. Add the garam masala, cumin, turmeric, coriander, chili powder, paprika, brown sugar, and salt and stir all together until the butter (along with the oil left over from cooking the chicken) is fragrant and all the spices are fully incorporated.
4. Return the chicken to the pot and stir.
5. Add the tomato sauce and cream and cook for 10–15 minutes, uncovered, stirring occasionally, until the sauce becomes thick, deep red, and creamy.
6. If it gets too thick, add water a little at a time and keep stirring until the proper consistency is reached.
7. When chicken is cooked and sauce is thick and creamy, ladle some of the chicken and sauce over some rice or naan bread and garnish with a sprinkle of cilantro leaves.

FOOD FOR THOUGHT

Allow your taste buds to travel to different places by trying different foods. Compare how ingredients are mixed or interchanged in different cooking traditions. Consider creating your own "fusion" dish with different ingredients from different countries. It's a very "Catholic" thing to do—creating connections between different cultures and people.

APRIL 23
SAINT GEORGE

George (ca. 275–303) was a native of Lydda in Palestine and a Roman soldier who received the crown of martyrdom by being beheaded after several unsuccessful attempts to execute him. According to one legend, his persecutors gave him poison to drink but he made the sign of the cross over it and remained unharmed. In the West Saint George is one of the Fourteen Holy Helpers invoked for the protection of domestic animals, and in the Christian East he is called "the Great Martyr."

George is also the patron saint of an astonishing number of countries, cities, organizations, occupations, and causes, too numerous to mention here. In the English-speaking world, he is perhaps best known as the patron saint of England: the flag of England bears his "+"-shaped red cross on a white background, and the same cross appears—along with the "X"-shaped crosses of Saint Andrew and Saint Patrick—on the Union Jack, the flag of the United Kingdom.

English armies once used the saint's name as a battle cry, shouting "Montjoie! Saint George!" (A *montjoie* was a milestone for soldiers, and later a standard that showed the troops the way into battle.) George is also the patron saint of chivalry, Boy Scouts, and soldiers.

And let us not forget the Republic of Georgia. This ancient nation and former part of the Soviet Union is believed to have been named for Saint George, which is why he is the patron saint of the country and why its flag consists of five of the red Saint George crosses.

And, of course, there is the medieval story of how George rescued a princess named Alexandra from a dragon who had been terrorizing a town in Libya or Syria. The princess had been chosen by lot to be the dragon's next meal; after making the sign of the cross, George fought the dragon, pinning it to the earth with his lance. He led the defeated monster into the city and told the twenty thousand townsfolk that he would kill it if they all converted to Christianity, which they did. George then beheaded the dragon with his sword.

Unless you live in Hogsmeade, dragon meat will be hard to find. Turn instead to this marvelous recipe. The asparagus represents Saint George's sword, the mushrooms his time in the wilderness, and the chili pepper the fiery breath of the dragon he slayed.

Saint George's Asparagus Spears and Mushrooms
Serves: 4 (as a side dish)   **Cooking time: 30 minutes**

1 lb. of thin asparagus spears, trimmed (break off the bottom ½–1 inch of each spear and discard it)

1 lb. mushrooms, washed clean and dried with a paper towel

2 cloves garlic, minced

2 Tbsps. olive oil

1–2 tsps. chili pepper flakes

1 tsp. salt

1 Tbsp. red wine vinegar

1. Preheat oven to 450°F.
2. Prepare an oven-safe sheet pan or baking dish with parchment paper.
3. Combine all of the ingredients together in the pan or dish and toss them with your hands.
4. Separate the asparagus and mushrooms, making sure to leave a little room between the vegetables in the pan.

APRIL

5. Roast in the oven for 8–10 minutes.
6. Remove immediately from the oven, put the mushrooms on a rack, let them drain, and return them to the pan.
7. Serve as a side dish to your favorite meat.

FOOD FOR THOUGHT

Whatever you feast upon, bless it, raise high a glass, and cry out: "Montjoie! Saint George!" or "Vive Monsieur Saint Georges!" Traditional Georgian toasts include *Gagimardschoss* and *Vakhtanguri*—which are easier to pronounce after the second round of strong drink. And don't forget to pray for all of Saint George's clients—all the countries, clubs, and causes.

APRIL 28
SAINT LOUIS DE MONTFORT

Louis-Marie Grignion de Montfort (1673–1716) was a French priest best known for his preaching, his theological writings on the Blessed Virgin Mary, and his promotion of consecrating one's life to Mary. What is less known is that he had a short fuse.

Apparently, during an outdoor sermon in the village of Roussay, a group of men deep in their cups heckled the saint with vulgar shouts and songs from a nearby café. After finishing the sermon and blessing the congregation, Saint Louis marched over to the hecklers. Here is what happened next, in the words of Father Bryce Sibley:

They greeted Saint Louis, who was a massive man, with a few derisive yet humorous comments. Saint Louis however responded with his fists. He struck each of the men, knocking them unconscious. Then just as Our Lord drove the moneychangers out of the temple, Saint Louis began tearing up the café, overturning tables, throwing chairs, smashing glasses and breaking bottles. He then walked out of the café, over the bodies of the drunken hoodlums, and back up the street. Needless to say, he never had a problem with disruptive behavior during his homilies for the rest of his stay in that town.[5]

Louis's two-fisted tantrum may have been due to the fact that he was from France's only Celtic region, Brittany (you know, the Celts: Irish brawlers and Scottish soccer hooligans). Ratatouille may be from the opposite side of the country (it originated in Nice on the Mediterranean coast), but as a coarse stew with wholesome vegetables, it recalls Saint Louis's childhood growing up on a farm (until the age of twelve). And like the Blessed Virgin Mary, whose devotion Saint Louis promoted, it is humble, elegant, and memorable. Finally, think of the red pepper flakes as a nod to Saint Louis's fiery temper.

Rustic Ratatouille

Feeds: 4–6   **Cooking time: 1½ hours**

1 medium eggplant (peeled or not, according to your preference), cut into large cubes

1 tsp. salt

¼ cup olive oil, divided

1 medium red onion, diced

2 medium zucchini, cut into ½-inch cubes

2 medium yellow squash, cut into ½-inch cubes

1 red pepper and 1 yellow pepper, cut into ½-inch pieces

4 cloves garlic, minced

½ cup dry white wine

15-oz. can crushed tomatoes

1–2 bay leaves

1–2 tsps. dried oregano

1 tsp. red pepper flakes

½–1 tsp. black pepper (to taste)

4–5 leaves fresh basil

1. Salt the eggplant cubes and put them in a colander for 20–30 minutes to drain some of the eggplant's excess bitter liquid. Pat the eggplant with a paper towel.
2. Heat 1 Tbsp. of olive oil in a large pot or Dutch oven over medium-high heat.
3. Add the eggplant and stir occasionally, cooking for 3–5 minutes, until the eggplant softens and is slightly browned, and then remove it from the pot and set aside.
4. Add a little more olive oil to the pot and cook the squash, zucchini, and onions for 3–5 minutes, or until the vegetables are soft and slightly browned. Remove and set aside.

APRIL

5. Add a little more oil to the pot, and cook the bell peppers for 3–5 minutes or until soft and slightly caramelized. Remove and set aside.

6. Add the garlic, crushed tomatoes, bay leaves, oregano, red pepper flakes, and wine to the pot, and cook for 2–3 minutes, stirring occasionally, until the sauce starts to bubble.

7. Return the cooked eggplant, zucchini, yellow squash, onions, and bell peppers to the pot and gently mix the ingredients together.

8. Turn the heat to low, put the lid or foil on top of the pot, and cook for 20 minutes, simmering all the ingredients together. Do not stir, but make sure there is enough liquid to avoid burning the bottom of the pot.

9. After 20 minutes, carefully remove the lid and discard the bay leaves.

10. Ladle or spoon into a bowl or over a plate of rice or potatoes.

11. Tear the basil leaves and use them as garnish on top of the ratatouille. Drizzle a little olive oil over the vegetables and serve.

FOOD FOR THOUGHT

The rustic and wholesome ingredients of ratatouille put us in mind of the farm-to-table movement. It is a very Catholic approach to eating, connecting us to the local sources of our food, increasing our gratitude for our farmers, and encouraging a return to simplicity and authenticity in our food and in ourselves. Saint Louis de Montfort strikes us as the kind of simple and authentic man we should all strive to be—ideally without all the destruction of private property and head-bashing.

APRIL 30 *(APRIL 29)*
SAINT CATHERINE OF SIENA

Catherine of Siena (1347–1380) was the youngest of twenty-five children. She was so cheerful as a child that her family nicknamed her "Euphrosyne," the Greek word for "joy" and the name of an early saint. Catherine began receiving visions at an early age and consecrated her life to God at the age of seven. She resisted her parents' efforts to have her married, cutting off her beautiful hair to make herself a less desirable prospect. As punishment and to rob her of the solitude she desired, her parents made her do menial jobs

APRIL

around the house. Catherine turned these lemons into lemonade, for during this time God showed her how to build a private monastic cell in her soul where no trouble could enter. This divine lesson would become one of the themes in her most famous work, *The Dialogue of Saint Catherine.*

Catherine eventually became a tertiary in the Dominican Order and practiced extraordinary asceticism. On Mardi Gras of 1266, while the townsfolk were living it up outside, she had a vision in which Jesus Christ mystically married her, placing a wedding ring on her finger that only she could see. Catherine assisted plague victims, arbitrated high-level disputes, and counseled and even chided popes, convincing Gregory XI to end the "Babylonian Captivity," the period when the popes resided in Avignon, France, instead of Rome. In 1970 she was declared a Doctor of the Church.

Saint Catherine's dietary habits are rather controversial; some folks suspect that she suffered from anorexia. Miraculously, she lived for several years on nothing but daily Holy Communion. Her confessor eventually ordered her to eat properly, but by that time it was too late: by January of 1380, she had lost the ability to eat or swallow, and on April 29 of that year she died at the age of thirty-three.

Okay, that is depressing, but Saint Catherine had a heart of gold, especially where the poor were concerned. It was her custom to bake bread daily for them. In honor of this custom, bake or buy a loaf in her honor and pair it with this delicious dish. Pici pasta was invented by Sienese *pastaii* (pasta makers), and the spicy sausage betokens Catherine's holy boldness. And let's say that the pumpkin symbolizes her Cinderella story—transformed from being a housemaid abused by her own family to a bride of the ultimate Prince Charming, the Prince of Peace.

Pici Pasta with Pumpkin and Spicy Sausage
Serves: 4–6   Cooking time: 30 minutes

1 lb. pici pasta

2 cups pumpkin (or butternut squash), cut into ½-inch cubes

2 links spicy Italian sausage, casings removed

2 Tbsps. olive oil, plus more to drizzle the pasta

2 cloves garlic, minced

1 medium yellow onion, minced

1–2 tsps. finely minced fresh rosemary

1 tsp. black pepper

½ cup dry white wine

2 Tbsps. parmesan cheese, finely grated

1. Boil pici pasta in water with salt. Cook al dente: cook according to the instructions on the package, but shorten the cooking time by 2–3 minutes. (Note: pici pasta takes longer to cook than other noodles.) Drain the pasta, reserving 1 cup of the starchy water.

2. While the pasta is cooking, heat the olive oil in a large sauté pan and add the sausage. Use two wooden spatulas to break up the sausage into smaller pieces.

3. Add the pumpkin, onion, and garlic and cook until the pumpkin is soft.

4. Season with pepper and rosemary.

5. Add white wine to deglaze the pan. Mix ingredients together.

6. When the pasta is cooked, add 2 Tbsps. of the starchy water. Mix all of the ingredients together, adding a little more starchy water to reach your desired consistency, about ½ inch of water and oil in the pan.

7. Add the pasta and 1 Tbsp. of the parmesan cheese and mix all the ingredients together.

8. Plate the pasta with an extra drizzle of olive oil and a light dusting of parmesan cheese.

FOOD FOR THOUGHT

Spiritual authors are right to warn us about the evils of gluttony, but the life of Saint Catherine of Siena reminds us that it is possible to err on the opposite extreme, especially in a body-conscious age such as ours. Tonight, remember the old adage: moderation in all things.

APRIL

CHAPTER 5

May Saints

MAY

MAY 1
SAINT JOSEPH THE WORKER

Just as the early Church co-opted various pagan festivals and converted them to good use, so too in 1955 did Pope Pius XII co-opt the Communist holiday of International Workers' Day by instituting the feast of Saint Joseph the Worker. Well, he almost did: Italians jokingly refer to the day as *San Giuseppe Comunista*. At any rate, Saint Joseph was certainly a model worker: although he was from the royal House of David, he did not hesitate to work at a blue-collar job in order to provide for the Holy Family.

May 1 was also a famous pagan holiday. On "May Day" folks danced around the maypole and did other festive things to celebrate the coming of spring, such as planting trees and hiding eggs, sausages, and cakes in the branches. Others (more wisely in our opinion) preferred to hide food items in their stomachs by feasting on a hearty *Bauernfrühstück*, or Peasant Breakfast, a traditional brunch made of bacon, eggs, potato, and chives that will satisfy any worker's appetite.[1]

An even better tribute to the patron of workers is a Not-So-Sloppy Joe. We have taken this American favorite and cleaned it up to represent Joseph's tidy work habits. And the sauce makes this sloppy joe the best that you will ever have, a tribute to the high quality of Joseph's work.

Not-So-Sloppy Joe
Serves: 4–5   **Cooking time: 30 minutes**

1 Tbsp. butter
1 tsp. olive oil
1 lb. ground beef
½ bell pepper (red or green), diced
½ yellow onion, diced

3 cloves garlic, minced
1 Tbsp. tomato paste
⅔ cup ketchup
⅓ cup water

1 Tbsp. brown sugar (or less, if you prefer) 2 tsps. kosher salt

1 tsp. yellow mustard 1 tsp. black pepper

¾ tsp. chili powder ¼ tsp. red pepper flakes (optional)

½ tsp. Worcestershire sauce 1–2 dashes hot sauce (optional)

1. Heat butter and oil in a large skillet over medium-high heat. Add garlic and onion and cook until caramelized, approximately 2 minutes.

2. Add bell peppers and cook for 1–2 minutes.

3. Add and brown the ground beef, about 5 minutes, breaking it apart into crumbles as it cooks.

4. Add tomato paste, ketchup, water, brown sugar, mustard, chili powder, Worcestershire sauce, salt, black pepper, and optional red pepper flakes and hot sauce. Stir well to combine.

5. Cook over medium heat for 10–15 minutes, stirring occasionally, until mixture has thickened to your liking.

6. Remove from heat and serve over toasted buns or pita bread.

FOOD FOR THOUGHT

There is a saying that cleanliness is next to godliness. This coming week, ask yourself what sloppiness in your life needs cleaning up, both in your professional and personal life. And using the example of Saint Joseph's silence, take small, silent, and drama-free steps to clean up those areas of your life.

This feast is also a good opportunity to reboot your understanding of work, using Saint Joseph as your guide. For the devout Christian, free enterprise and work are good things—for the sake not of wealth or power but of exercising generosity and holiness. According to a mystical vision by Mary of Agreda, after Joseph and Mary were espoused, Joseph asked his young bride if he should continue his trade as a carpenter in order "to serve her and to gain something for distribution among the poor."[2] Note the two reasons: Joseph wished to make money not in order to hoard it (or to spend it on that bass boat with the new fish-finder he'd been eyeing), but in order to provide for his family and the poor. Imagine if every wage earner in the world thought and acted the same way!

MAY 1
SAINT PEREGRINE

We know that we already have a saint to celebrate on May 1, but we cannot overlook the patron saint of open sores, cancer, AIDS, and other life-threatening diseases. Saint Peregrine Laziosi (1260–1345) started his journey to holiness in an interesting way, by smacking a saint. Peregrine belonged to an anti-papal faction in the Papal States, and when the pope sent Saint Philip Benizi to talk some sense to them, the agitated eighteen-year-old Peregrine heckled and struck the saint on the face. But when Philip Benizi's only reaction was to turn and offer the other cheek, Peregrine immediately repented. From then on, he avoided his worldly friends and spent hours on his knees in prayer. When the Blessed Virgin Mary told him to join Philip Benizi's order (the Servites), Peregrine obeyed and became a model priest. He was so tireless in his work that it is said that for thirty years he never sat down.

Peregrine is the patron saint of cancer and open sores for good reason. Because of his mortifications (such as standing all the time), at the age of sixty he developed varicose veins that turned into cancer in his right leg. The open sore was not only excruciating for him but repulsive to everyone around him. Peregrine bore this trial without complaint, and when the doctors told him they would have to amputate his leg, he spent the night before the operation in prayer. During this vigil he went into a kind of trance and saw Jesus touch his leg. The next morning, when the doctors came to operate, they were astonished to find no trace of the disease.

Kale is known to be a cancer-fighting leafy vegetable. This Tuscan soup made with kale, potatoes, and savory sausage is a way to court health in both body and soul. And Tuscany is in between Philip's home region of Emilia-Romagna and Umbria, where the Servites were located. Perhaps Saint Philip had a cup of this soup on his way to becoming a Servite.

Pilgrim's Zuppa Toscana
Serves: 4   **Cooking time: 30 minutes**

2 Italian sausages, hot or mild, casings removed

2 tsps. olive oil

¼ cup dry white wine

1 clove garlic, minced

3–4 smooth-skinned potatoes, cut into small pieces

2 cups kale, with the center stems removed and the leaves cut into small pieces

1 shallot, minced

1 carrot, diced

2 stalks celery, diced

2–3 tsps. parmesan cheese

6 cups chicken, beef, or vegetable broth

1. In a large pot, heat the olive oil over medium heat.
2. Add the Italian sausages and use two wooden spoons or spatulas to break them into smaller pieces as they brown.
3. Add the potatoes and cook for 3–4 minutes, stirring occasionally.
4. Add the garlic, shallots, carrots, celery, and kale and sauté until the kale leaves have softened.
5. Add the white wine to deglaze the pan, and use a wooden spoon to scrape any of the caramelized pieces off the bottom of the pot.
6. Add the broth, stir the ingredients together, and cook until the soup simmers, 10–15 minutes.
7. Serve with a crusty piece of bread.

FOOD FOR THOUGHT

Saint Peregrine had a special love for the poor, especially where food was concerned. On one occasion, he miraculously multiplied grain and wine during a severe shortage. Although we cannot do the same, we can imitate his charity for the less fortunate—and pray for cancer patients.

MAY 2
SAINT ATHANASIUS

Catholicae religionis propugnator acerrimus—"a most vigorous defender of the Catholic religion"—is what the Roman Breviary calls the great Saint Athanasius (ca. 296–373), bishop of Alexandria, author of beautiful writings such as *On the Incarnation*, and scourge of the Arians. Dom Prosper Guéranger was probably not exaggerating when he wrote that "never did our holy faith go through a greater ordeal than in the sad times immediately following the peace of the Church," when after three centuries of Roman persecution, a frustrated Satan cleverly unleashed from Hell "a heresy which threatened to blight the fruit of three hundred years of martyrdom."[3] The Arians taught that Jesus Christ was *homoiousios*, or "like the Father," whereas the Council of Nicea defined Jesus Christ as being *homoousios*, "consubstantial with," or of "the same stuff," as the Father. Thus, there is literally one iota of difference between orthodoxy and heresy—a sober reminder of how the smallest deviation can lead to the greatest error.

Against all odds, Athanasius stood up to a vast conspiracy of devious Arian heretics and imperial bootlickers and thus earned the epithet *Athanasius contra mundum*, or "Athanasius against the world." He was sent into exile several times. He had to hide in a dry well for five years, where he was fed by the only person who knew his location. On another occasion he had to take refuge in his father's sepulcher for four months.

These Tamiya Fava Bean Fritters are similar to falafel and an old Egyptian favorite: we picture Saint Athanasius snacking on them while he was on the lam from the imperial authorities. The fava beans (which we saw on Saint Joseph's Day, but not as food!) make this meal extra special, since the fava bean is considered a superfood. Saint Athanasius's writings are like that: his defense of Our Lord's divinity is a superfood for the soul.

Tamiya Fava Bean Fritters

Serves: 4   **Cooking time: 1 hour**

16-oz. can of fava beans, drained and patted dry with a paper towel

6–8 scallions, minced

3–5 cloves garlic, minced

¼ cup fresh cilantro, minced

2 tsps. cumin

1 tsp. baking powder

½ tsp. cayenne

2 tsps. salt

1 tsp. black pepper

1 tsp. ground coriander

2 cups all-purpose flour

2–3 cups vegetable oil

1. Grind fava beans in a food processor until they form a grainy paste.
2. Add scallions, garlic, cilantro, cumin, baking powder, cayenne, salt, pepper, and coriander, and mix all the ingredients together until they're fully incorporated.
3. Refrigerate for at least 30 minutes.
4. Use a melon baller to form 1-inch balls. Slightly flatten each fritter to form a thick disk shape.
5. Dredge each fritter in flour and shake off the excess flour.
6. Heat oil in a large frying pan over medium heat.
7. When frying oil reaches 360°F, carefully place 4–5 fritters into the oil at a time. Do not overcrowd.
8. Cook for 3–5 minutes and carefully flip and cook for another 3–5 minutes, until golden brown.
9. Remove the fritters using a slotted spoon or meshed skimmer and place them on a plate lined with a paper towel or on a baking sheet with a wire rack.
10. Immediately sprinkle a little salt over the fritters.
11. Serve with a dipping sauce of your choice.

FOOD FOR THOUGHT

Theology and history help the modern Christian to be more faithful and orthodox in his or her practice of the faith. Consider reading one of the writings from Saint Athanasius as a way of avoiding heresy and getting excited about sound doctrine. His book *On the Incarnation* was praised by C. S. Lewis as a clearly written masterpiece.

MAY 4
SAINT FLORIAN

Saint Florian (ca. 250) was a Roman soldier whose duties included training an elite group of soldiers to fight fires. Condemned for his Christian faith to be burned at the stake, he egged on the soldiers to light the wood by saying that he would ascend to Heaven on top of the flames. Frightened, the soldiers instead drowned him. Florian's body was recovered, and he went on to become a popular saint in German-speaking areas and the patron saint of firefighters. To this day, Saint Florian's Cross is part of the emblem for fire departments around the world, and in southern Germany and Austria fire services use the word "Florian" to refer to fire stations and fire trucks.

Tafelspitz is a Viennese classic that can help you remember a saint who was supposed to be burned but was drowned instead. Rather than grilling the tri-tip beef, this recipe calls for immersing the meat in water and boiling the Heaven into it. And the Viennese provenance of this dish ties us into the Austrian devotion to the saint.

....

Tafelspitz: Boiled Beef Tri-Tip with Apple and Horseradish Sauce
Serves: 4–6   **Cooking time: 3½ hours**

3–4 lbs. tri-tip beef

2–3 marrow bones—ask your local butcher, or substitute ½ cup of tallow (beef fat)

3 carrots, peeled and cut into 1-inch cubes

3 turnips or parsnips, peeled and cut into 1-inch cubes

2 stalks celery, washed and cut into 1-inch pieces

1 large onion, peeled and cut into 1-inch cubes

2 bay leaves

1 Tbsp. black pepper

1 Tbsp. allspice

1 tsp. juniper berries (or substitute a sprig of fresh rosemary)
1 Tbsp. salt
1–2 Tbsps. butter

1 Tbsp. flour
water

THE SAUCE

¼ cup chives, finely minced
1 cup sour cream
2 Tbsps. fresh horseradish, finely grated

1 cup heavy whipping cream
1 tsp. lemon juice
1 tsp. salt

1. Prepare the tri-tip by washing it clean. (The tri-tip may have a layer of fat on it, which can be broiled in the oven for extra flavor and then removed before serving.)
2. Place the marrow bone (or layer of beef fat) in the bottom of a large pot. Put the tri-tip on top of the marrow bones.
3. Add half of the carrots, turnips, and celery to the pot, being sure to reserve the other half of these vegetables.
4. Add the bay leaves, black pepper, allspice, juniper berry (or rosemary), and salt.
5. Cut the onion in half and char it by putting it on an ungreased pan and turning up the heat until it begins to "burn" and turn very dark gray, almost burnt black. Add it to the pot.
6. Add water to the pot until the meat is covered.
7. Put a lid on the pot and boil over medium heat. Skim the frothy residue that floats to the top of the boiling water and discard.
8. After 2–2½ hours, check to see if the beef is fork-tender (if a fork easily pierces the meat).
9. Remove the meat and the bones. Strain the vegetables and broth in a colander or sieve, retaining the broth and discarding the boiled vegetables and spices. Return the meat back to the broth.
10. Add the reserved half of the uncooked vegetables (carrots, celery, turnips), cover the pot, and cook for another 30–60 minutes over medium heat, until it is very tender.
11. While it cooks, prepare the sauce by combining the sour cream, chives, horseradish, whipping cream, lemon juice, and salt to a bowl and mixing together.
12. Remove the meat from the broth, rest for 10–15 minutes, and cut into ½-inch slices.
13. In a bowl, combine 1 Tbsp. of flour with 2 Tbsps. of water and mix into a slurry.
14. Add the flour slurry and butter to the broth and whisk while cooking over medium heat. The sauce will thicken into a light gravy.
15. Serve each guest with a few slices of meat, a few of the vegetables, and a ladle of the sour cream sauce. This can be accompanied with boiled potatoes, rice, or spaetzle.

MAY

FOOD FOR THOUGHT

A tough piece of meat can be tenderized after a long period of cooking. Perhaps, if we find ourselves in hot water, we can reflect on how God may be using this time to make us a little more tender. The traditional prayer "Jesus, meek and humble of heart, make our hearts like unto thine" is a good one to recite, for we all need to tenderize our hearts.

MAY 10/APRIL 15
SAINT DAMIEN DE VEUSTER

Father Damien of Molokai (1840–1889) was a "martyr of charity" who succumbed to leprosy after sixteen years of caring for the spiritual and temporal needs of lepers on the state-quarantined island of Molokai in Hawaii. The lepers had been forced there by the government of what was then the Kingdom of Hawaii (under British rule), and there was no one there to assist them. When the local bishop received a desperate plea for a pastor, he asked his priests for a volunteer. Four of them courageously accepted, and the bishop chose Damien. Damien explained that he did not fear death because, as a member of the Congregation of the Sacred Hearts of Jesus and Mary, he was already dead to the world—a funeral pall having been placed over him during his ordination to the priesthood.

Tough as nails, Damien built a chapel on the island with his own hands, instituted order and agriculture, and administered tender mercy to the suffering and dying despite the utterly deplorable things he saw, touched, and smelled—which, if we relayed them here, would spoil

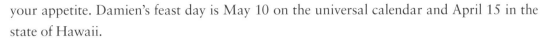

your appetite. Damien's feast day is May 10 on the universal calendar and April 15 in the state of Hawaii.

Damien was not fussy when it came to food. He ate what his lepers ate, which was meager indeed: paltry supplies from a stingy government and what could be grown on the island. Having been a friend, pastor, caregiver, and advocate for the lepers, he likely learned to cook or enjoy their native dishes. Kalua Pork is a favorite Hawaiian dish, and this recipe celebrates the fusion of a Flemish missionary with Hawaii's remote and quarantined lepers. If you can't find banana leaves, then cabbage leaves will also work, especially since Saint Damien would have eaten cabbage when he still lived in Europe.

Kalua Pork with Banana (or Cabbage) Leaves

2½–3 lbs. boneless pork shoulder

10 cloves garlic, peeled and cut in half lengthwise

2 Tbsps. olive or avocado oil

1 large banana leaf cut into 3 small pieces (or substitute 4–5 leaves from the outer layers of a head of green cabbage, lightly soaked in hot water, with the center ribs removed for easy wrapping)

2 Tbsps. Hawaiian sea salt (or substitute kosher salt)

2–3 tsps. liquid smoke

2 cups water or chicken broth

1. Preheat oven to 325°F and prepare center rack so that a large Dutch oven will fit.
2. Cut the pork shoulder into 3 equal pieces, trimming off excessive fat caps.
3. Use a paring knife and cut deep slits into the pork, 4–5 per piece, and insert sliced garlic into each slit.
4. In a Dutch oven, heat the oil over medium-high heat. Once the oil is hot, sear the pork, one piece at a time, on all sides of each cut of the pork. Remove the pork from the Dutch oven and set aside.
5. When the pork is cool enough to touch, season it with the salt and liquid smoke, using your hands to cover all sides of the pork.
6. Wrap the pork in the banana or cabbage leaves: place each piece of pork on a leaf, wrap it tightly, and place it in the Dutch oven.
7. Add the water or broth.
8. Place the lid on the Dutch oven and put it in the middle of the oven. Cook for 1 hour, remove the Dutch oven from the oven, carefully remove the banana or cabbage leaves, and test the pork's tenderness. If it does not easily separate with a fork, return it to the oven for another 30–40 minutes.

9. Once the pork is fork-tender, carefully remove the banana or cabbage leaves. Discard the banana leaves. Or, if you used cabbage, cut the leaves into smaller pieces to serve with the pork.
10. Shred the pork with two forks or cut into big chunks, knowing it will be so tender it will fall apart as it's cut.
11. Serve with rice, plantains, or pickled vegetables.

FOOD FOR THOUGHT

Spending time with people who are rejected or marginalized is a great way to test our patience, compassion, and desire to serve the least of our brothers and sisters, who, Jesus promised, will inherit the Kingdom of Heaven.

MAY 16

SAINT BRENDAN

Move over, Christopher Columbus, and take a backseat, Leif Erikson: Irishmen know who *really* discovered America. It was one of their own, Saint Brendan the Navigator (ca. 484–577).

Well, maybe. Saint Brendan was an Irish monk who was educated by the nun Saint Ita and the bishop Saint Erc and who after his ordination journeyed throughout Ireland founding monastic cells, but he is chiefly remembered for a seven-year voyage allegedly taken with other monks, one of them being Saint Columba. Brendan's adventures are recorded in later documents such as *The Voyage of Saint Brendan the Abbot*—a highly entertaining collection of fanciful episodes that culminate in the discovery of an "Isle of the Blessed" somewhere in the west Atlantic. In an earlier chapter, the seafarers discover a monastic island where the monks never age. In another, they meet Judas Iscariot on an island and learn that he is allowed to vacation there on Sundays and feast days. In another, the group lands on an island and starts a bonfire, only to have the island sink: it turns out that they had alighted on the back of a whale.

Saint Brendan's voyage is a classic of Irish and world literature (think Sinbad the Sailor), but some folks see in it the possibility that the saint really did discover North America. In 1976–1977 British explorer Timothy Severin put this theory to the test by reconstructing a *currach*, an Irish sailboat made of wood and leather, and sailing it 4,500 miles from Ireland to Newfoundland. In 1983 an amateur linguist named Barry Fell claimed that rock inscriptions found in West Virginia were written in an old Irish language called ogam sometime in the sixth, seventh, or eighth century and that they tell the story of Christ's nativity. Fell's work, however, has received withering criticism from the academy.

And so the mystery continues; at least there will be something to talk about as you and your friends or family break bread together on Saint Brendan's Day.

Saint Brendan is the Irish patron of seafarers, sailors, and coastal communities. This delicious Irish Seafood Chowder, often made of leftovers and fish scraps, is a medley prepared with Irish cooking methods and spices, paying homage to Saint Brendan's home country and cuisine.

Irish Seafood Chowder
Serves: 4   **Cooking time: 40 minutes**

1 small onion, diced

2 slices thick-cut bacon, diced

4 thin-skinned potatoes, cut into ¼-inch cubes

1 Tbsp. Irish butter

½ tsp. dried thyme

1 bay leaf

½ tsp. salt

½ tsp. pepper

3 cups seafood stock (or substitute vegetable stock)

4–6 oz. haddock, cut into small chunks

4–6 oz. salmon, with the skin removed, cut into small chunks

8 mussels still in their shells, cleaned with a brush

½ cup heavy cream

1 lemon, cut into quarters

2 Tbsps. fresh parsley, chopped

Crusty bread

1. Melt butter into a pot over medium heat.
2. Add bacon and potatoes and cook for 4–5 minutes.
3. When the bacon is rendered and the potatoes have softened, add the onions and cook, stirring occasionally, for 2–3 minutes, or until they are translucent.
4. Add the thyme, bay leaf, and seafood stock or vegetable broth.
5. Cook for 10 minutes, or until the stock starts to simmer.
6. Add the haddock, salmon, and mussels and carefully stir all the ingredients together.
7. Cook for 3–5 minutes, or until the mussels open up. (Discard any unopened mussels).
8. Remove the pot from the heat and discard the bay leaf.
9. Add the cream and stir.
10. Garnish with a sprinkle of parsley and serve with a lemon wedge and a piece of crusty bread.

FOOD FOR THOUGHT

Exploring can help us be humble, for it requires us to be willing to learn something new. Think about where you want to go and ask yourself why. Then take some steps to fulfill your desires, with a prayer that your explorations will expand and deepen your faith.

MAY 16
SAINT HONORATUS

May 16 is also the day that the Church honors a great patron saint of pastry chefs. Honoré or Honoratus of Amiens (d. ca 600) was born in Port-le-Grand, France, to a noble family. His parents, noting the lad's piety, had him educated by Saint Beatus, the sixth bishop of Amiens, France. After Beatus's death, Honoratus was chosen to become his successor. Being a humble man, Honoratus felt unworthy of the job, but according to tradition, God confirmed the decision through several signs: a ray of light descended upon him, and holy oil miraculously appeared on his forehead.

But the most famous miracle about Honoratus's election is that when news of his election reached his family, his old nursemaid, who was baking bread at the time, said that she would not believe what she had heard unless the baker's peel she was using turned into a tree. Sure enough, when she stuck the end of the peel into the ground, it sprouted roots and turned into a mulberry tree.

Why, we wonder, did the nursemaid refuse to believe the news? Did she think, like Honoratus himself, that he was unworthy of the job? Maybe it was her own shortsightedness. There is a saying attributed to the German philosopher Hegel: "No man is a hero to his valet. This is not because the hero is not a hero, but because the valet is a valet." That is, the job of a domestic servant is not to recognize greatness but to focus on the weeds and how to deal with them. Or perhaps the nursemaid had the opposite reaction: knowing how holy Honoratus was and how rare good episcopal appointments are (!?), the news was simply too good to be true.

Whatever the reason behind the nursemaid's incredulity, we can credit her for helping to make Saint Honoratus the patron saint of bakers, and for that we should be grateful.

Gâteau Honoré, or the Saint Honoratus Cake, is a magnificent confection, but it is difficult to make in its original form, requiring puff pastries, profiteroles, caramel, and Chantilly cream. Instead, enjoy this simple hack to help get the flavors without the fuss.

Simple Saint Honoratus Cake

5 puff pastry sheets, cut into 3 x 6–inch rectangles

2 Tbsps. butter, melted

3 Tbsps. confectioner's sugar

1 tsp. cinnamon

THE LAYERS

1. Preheat oven to 375°F.
2. Place the puff pastry sheets 1 inch apart on a baking sheet lined with parchment paper.
3. Combine melted butter, sugar, and cinnamon in a bowl and mix until the ingredients are thoroughly combined.
4. Brush the butter mixture onto the top of each of the puff pastry pieces.
5. Cook for 15–20 minutes, or until the puff pastry is golden brown.
6. Remove the baking sheet from the oven and allow the puff pastries to cool for about 15 minutes.
7. Carefully cut each piece of pastry in half lengthwise to make 10 separate rectangular pieces.

FILLING #1: CHANTILLY CREAM

2 cups heavy whipping cream, refrigerated

2 tsps. vanilla extract

¼ cup confectioners' sugar

½ tsp. salt

1. Refrigerate a large bowl for 30 minutes.
2. Combine the heavy cream, vanilla extract, confectioners' sugar, and salt in the bowl and use a hand mixer to whip them together until the cream begins to thicken and peaks form.
3. Refrigerate until you are ready to assemble the cake.

FILLING #2: CARAMEL SAUCE

1 cup sugar

2 Tbsps. water

4 Tbsps. unsalted butter, cubed and kept cold

1 tsp. vanilla extract

½ tsp. salt

1. Add the sugar and water to a nonstick sauté pan and cook over medium heat, using a high-heat spatula to stir, scraping the bottom and sides of the pan.
2. Continue cooking until the sugar begins to bubble, lower the heat, and stop stirring, but continue to scrape the sides to avoid crystallization.

MAY

3. Cook 5–8 minutes, as the caramel turns an amber color, keeping an eye on the sugar so that it doesn't burn.
4. Remove from the heat, carefully add the butter, and whisk together until the butter is fully incorporated.
5. Add the vanilla extract and salt and continue to whisk together.
6. Set aside to cool for 10–15 minutes.

ASSEMBLING THE CAKE

¼ cup confectioners' sugar, sifted   6–8 fresh strawberries, stems removed and halved

1. Put one rectangle of the puff pastry on a plate and drizzle with a little caramel.
2. Put another rectangle of pastry on top of the caramel.
3. Spread a little of the Chantilly cream on top of the puff pastry.
4. Put another rectangle of pastry on top of the Chantilly cream.
5. Repeat the process to make a 10-layer cake with interspersed caramel and Chantilly cream layers between the puff pastry.
6. Top off with strawberries and a dusting of confectioners' sugar.

FOOD FOR THOUGHT

It is easy to be distrustful in this cynical world filled with misinformation and fake news. But rather than give in to incredulity and skepticism, let us pray for the virtues of discernment and sound judgment, that God may illumine our minds without having to turn kitchen utensils into mulberry trees.

MAY 22
SAINT RITA

Saint Rita of Cascia (1386–1456) was a remarkable woman. As a girl she greatly desired to become a nun, but when she was twelve her parents married her off to a cruel and ill-tempered man. Despite this, Rita was a model wife and mother for eighteen years. When her husband was murdered, her twin sons vowed revenge. Unable to dissuade them, Rita prayed that God take their lives rather than allow them to commit a mortal sin. Both sons died a year later, fully reconciled to the Church.

Rita then wished to enter the convent, and after numerous difficulties finally prevailed. One day as she was meditating on a crucifix, she received a wound on her forehead, as though a thorn from the crown of thorns had pierced her flesh. This stigma remained with her until her death, and it was not only very painful but repulsive to some of her fellow nuns, as the wound festered and developed worms. Saint Rita took all of this in stride. She lightheartedly referred to the worms as her "angels," since they aided in her sanctification, and she spent the last fifteen years of her life in her cell to avoid grossing out the rest of her community. Her incorrupt body (with the wound still visible) may be seen in a glass reliquary in the Basilica of Cascia.

Our impish side wants to recommend angel hair pasta in honor of Rita's stigma critters, but that would be distasteful in more ways than one. So would adding dried yellow mealworms to your pasta, which of all things the European Union sanctioned in 2021 on the grounds that they are edible and gentler on the environment than other animal proteins!

Instead, let us turn to an old story for inspiration. As a child, Saint Rita was found surrounded by white bees without being harmed. This sweet Italian dessert will remind you of God's sweet love and protection for each one of us, especially through Saint Rita's intercession.

Pignolata Honey Balls

4 eggs

1 Tbsp. sugar

¼ tsp. salt

THE SYRUP

¼ cup sugar

¼ cup water

1 orange, zested

2 Tbsps. vegetable oil

2½–2¾ cups all-purpose flour, divided

3–4 cups vegetable oil

1 cup honey

2 Tbsps. sprinkles (optional)

1. Sift ¼ cup of the flour onto a work surface.
2. Using a stand mixer, beat together the eggs, sugar, salt, and oil with the paddle attachment.
3. Replace the paddle attachment with a dough hook. Sift the remainder of the flour, add 2–2¼ cups of it to the mixture, and mix to combine. If the dough is too sticky, add more flour, a little at a time.
4. When the dough has come together, remove it from the bowl, move it to the floured work surface, cover it with a towel, and let it rest for 30 minutes.
5. Cut the dough into 8 long, thick noodles, about ½ inch thick.
6. Cut each dough noodle into smaller pieces, ½ inch thick and ½ inch wide.
7. Form the dough into small balls, covering each with a dusting of flour so that they won't stick to each other.
8. Heat the oil in a sauce pan over medium heat to 350°F.
9. Add about 6 dough balls at a time and fry until they are evenly golden brown.
10. Remove the fried dough balls and place them on a wire rack to drain or on a plate lined with paper towels.
11. Repeat the process until all the balls are fried.
12. Make the syrup by adding sugar, water, and orange zest to a large skillet over high heat and stirring constantly until the sugar dissolves.
13. Whisk in the honey and reduce the heat to medium.
14. Add the fried balls to the syrup and let them soak for a few seconds.
15. Once coated, use tongs or a spoon to carefully remove the fried dough balls from the pan, now covered with syrup, and begin to assemble on a plate, stacking it like a pyramid.
16. Add sprinkles or more orange zest to decorate.
17. Allow to cool before serving.

FOOD FOR THOUGHT

Our personalities can be bitter or sour. Let us pray that we may develop a temperament that allows others to experience the sweetness and consolation of God. Perhaps you can make this sweet treat for someone with whom you're having struggles.

MAY 26
SAINT PHILIP NERI

ven as a layman, Philip of Neri (1515–1595) was a force for the good as he visited the rough quarters of Rome and struck up conversations with people that would change their lives. After being ordained a priest, he founded the Congregation of the Oratory (the Oratorians). Saint Philip could prophesy, read others' hearts, and see heavenly spirits. He also had a wry sense of humor, which he combined with psychologically astute spiritual instruction. When a disciple asked for the saint's permission to wear a hairshirt, Philip said yes but on one condition: he had to wear it on the *outside* of his clothing. "If ever there was a saint who set his face against humbug," Saint John Henry Newman wrote, "it was Saint Philip."[4] And centuries before Saint Josemaría Escrivá's apostolate to sanctify work and the Second Vatican Council's universal call to holiness, there was Saint Philip Neri's "greatest delight and special desire…that men should make themselves saints in their own homes." Sounds like a good patron saint for this book!

Saint Philip was known for his burning love of God—and we mean that literally. Once during prayer, a mystical ball of fire entered his mouth and lodged in his chest, causing his heart to be so aflame with divine fervor that the saint had to rip open his clothes and cool himself on the stone floor. After his death, it was discovered that two of his ribs were dislodged over his heart, which had expanded with the love of God. On different occasions Saint Philip's heart would become so filled with joy and consolation that he would roll on the ground and cry out, "No more, my Lord! No more!"

Saint Philip was abstemious when it came to the pleasures of the table. The little food that he ate he received as alms from others, as a way of practicing detachment from the world. But he was extremely generous when it came to feeding the youth who came to him for spiritual guidance. "The holy old man took great pleasure in seeing them eat and be merry," writes one of his biographers, "and he used to say, 'Eat, my sons, and do not have any scruple about it, for it makes me fat to watch you.'"[6]

The saint also used food as a means of humiliating himself, but sometimes it backfired. Once, when he was invited to dine with a cardinal, Philip brought with him his own bowl of cooked lentils in order to look like a social moron. Far from being offended, the cardinal and his guests eagerly sampled Philip's dish and said that they had not tasted such good pottage in a long time!

We have something better than lentils. This classic dish brings hearty Roman flavors to your dinner table to celebrate a patron of Rome and an apostle of joy. Even though the recipe includes breakfast ingredients, carbonara is perfect any time of the day. In fact, you can serve bacon and eggs for dinner, in the knowledge that Saint Philip would approve of the topsy-turvy choice.

Disciple of Rome's Classic Carbonara
Serves: 4   Cooking time: 30 minutes

1 lb. spaghetti

1 Tbsp. salt

½ lb. guanciale (or substitute pancetta or thick-cut bacon), cut into ¼-inch pieces

1 tsp. olive oil

4 eggs and 2 egg yolks

1 cup grated Pecorino Roman cheese, divided (or substitute parmesan cheese)

2 Tbsps. butter

1 Tbsp. freshly ground black pepper

1. Fill a large pot with water, add salt, and bring it to a boil over high heat. Add pasta and cook it according to the instructions on the package, but shorten the cooking time by 1–2 minutes, until the pasta is cooked al dente.
2. Reserve 2–3 Tbsps. of the pasta starch water, then drain the pasta and put it back in the pot to keep it from cooling too fast.
3. To an unheated frying pan, add olive oil and the guanciale. Turn the heat to medium-high, cook until the guanciale is crispy, and remove and set it aside.
4. Pour all but 1–2 Tbsps. grease out of the pan and discard it.

5. Turn the heat down to medium, allow the pan to cool slightly, and add the butter in small pieces.
6. In a separate bowl, combine the eggs and egg yolks and whisk them together until frothy.
7. Add ½ cup of the Pecorino Romano cheese and ½ Tbsp. of the pepper. Whisk together until the consistency is essentially smooth, though grainy because of the grated cheese.
8. Take the hot pasta out of the pot and put it into the pan you cooked the guanciale in.
9. Immediately pour the egg mixture onto the pasta and stir all the ingredients together.
10. Add the starchy water, the cooked guanciale, and the remaining ½ Tbsp. of the black pepper and mix together.
11. Plate the pasta and top the dish off with the remaining ½ cup of Pecorino Romano cheese.

FOOD FOR THOUGHT

Saint Philip considered cheer to be more authentically Christian than melancholy, and he lived by this conviction: as he used to say, "A joyful heart is more easily made perfect than a downcast one." To be a faithful Catholic, we should be like Saint Philip Neri, who took his faith but not himself seriously. He won many people over simply by his joyful disposition. Think of ways to bring the Good News to others in the spirit of Saint Philip Neri.

MAY 30
SAINT JOAN OF ARC

Saint Joan (1412–1431), the "Maid of Orléans," was a peasant from eastern France who led the French army in several important victories against the English. At the age of thirteen she had a vision of Saints Michael, Catherine of Alexandria, and Margaret of Antioch in which Joan was instructed to drive out the English and bring Charles VII to Reims for his coronation. Voices from above persisted, and she gradually learned that she was being called to lead the French army. She was also guided by these

voices to find an ancient sword buried behind the altar of a chapel.

After successfully completing her military mission, Saint Joan was captured by the Burgundians, betrayed to the English, put on trial for heresy, unjustly condemned, and burned at the stake at the age of nineteen. Twenty-five years later, Pope Calixtus III declared her innocent of the charges. She was canonized in 1920 and made one of the patron saints of France.

In honor of the Maid of Orléans and the great heroine of France, try a French dish such as Creamy Dijon Chicken (August 21), Gratin Dauphinois (August 9), or French Onion Soup (July 19). Then finish up with a French dessert like Éclairs (October 3) or Madeleine Cookies (July 22).

FOOD FOR THOUGHT

Following a vocation is never easy, but when God calls, the only true path to happiness is to answer yes, even if the path involves passing through a fiery gate in order to get to the bliss on the other side.

CHAPTER 6

June Saints

JUNE 4
SAINT FRANCIS CARACCIOLO

Francis Caracciolo (1563–1608), related to Saint Thomas Aquinas on his mother's side, was born in the Kingdom of Naples. After being miraculously cured of a rare skin disease similar to leprosy, he entered the priesthood. Five years later the saint received a letter by accident informing him of the founding of a new congregation of Clerics Regular Minor (the "Adorno Fathers"). He decided to join and ended up a cofounder. Saint Francis became renowned for his love of God and his participation in the lowly duties of the order, such as sweeping floors and washing dishes. On his deathbed at the age of forty-four, he cried out, "Let's go!" The priest by his bed asked, "Where?" "To Heaven, to Heaven!" the saint replied. They were his last words.

Even as a youth, Francis was not much of a gourmand. He loved to feed the poor rather than himself, and you could say that as a priest he would rather be consumed than consume, for he spent hours in adoration of the Blessed Sacrament, occasionally exclaiming, "The zeal of Thy house hath eaten me up!" (Psalm 69:9). And yet the saint is the patron of Italian cooks, as well as of the city of Naples. So let us turn to the great legacy of Neapolitan cuisine.

Naples is the home of the Italian pizza. Surely Saint Francis Caracciolo must have made a few pizzas in his days, especially since pizza was considered humble man's food.

Authentic Neapolitan Pizza
Yields: Eight 10-inch pizzas   Cooking time: 1 hour

2½ cups all-purpose flour

3 tsps. baking powder

1 tsp salt

4–7 oz. cold water

3 Tbsps. olive oil

1 cup tomato sauce

2 cloves garlic, finely minced

1 tsp. salt

1 tsp. red chili pepper flakes

2 cups fresh mozzarella cheese

1 cup fresh basil leaves

1 cup grated parmesan cheese

1. Combine flour, salt and baking powder in a large mixing bowl and whisk together.
2. Combine oil and water in another bowl and mix together.
3. Add half of the water-and-oil mixture to the dry ingredients and use your hands to bring the dough together. Continue to add water a little at a time until the dough is soft but not sticky. Continue to knead until all the flour is incorporated and the dough is soft and can be formed into a ball.
4. Cover the dough with a damp towel and rest for 15 minutes.
5. Dust your work surface with flour.
6. Roll the dough onto the work surface and cut it into 8 equally sized pieces. Set aside until the other ingredients are prepared.
7. Combine the tomato sauce, fresh minced garlic, salt, pepper flakes, and olive oil and stir together.
8. Place a large pizza stone in your oven and preheat it to 450°F. If you don't have a pizza stone, you can substitute a cast-iron skillet or large sheet pan.
9. Prepare the first pizza crust by rolling one of the dough balls into an 8–10-inch pizza shape and placing it on a pizza paddle (also known as a baker's peel—see May 16).
10. Lightly coat the dough with a few spoonfuls of tomato sauce, covering most of the surface of the dough. Sprinkle mozzarella cheese to cover the pizza and sprinkle parmesan cheese on top.
11. Carefully transfer the pizza onto the hot pizza stone (or the surface of the cast-iron skillet or the baking dish) in the oven and cook for 10–15 minutes, or until the cheese is melted and the dough turns golden brown.
12. Remove the pizza from the oven, rip some basil leaves, and sprinkle them over the pizza while it's still hot. Add a little drizzle of olive oil and chili pepper flakes, slice, and serve.
13. Repeat the process to make the other pizzas.

JUNE

FOOD FOR THOUGHT

Humble foods made with artisanal excellence become gourmet foods. The same transformation happens with the saints. Humble faith fortified by attentiveness in prayer, kindness, and charity elevates a poor soul to an image of the true, the good, and the beautiful. Let us be grateful for how humble, poor, and faithful people (perhaps our parents, grandparents, or friends) have an almost artisanal way of sharing and expressing their faith.

JUNE 6
SAINT NORBERT

Norbert of Xanten (1080–1134) was a cleric at the court of the archbishop of Cologne who had succumbed to worldliness when a near-death experience in a storm prompted him to change his ways. He sold his goods and eventually founded a religious community of canons regular called the Order of Premonstratensians, better known as the Norbertines. Later Saint Norbert was appointed archbishop of Magdeburg.

When it comes to matters of ingestion, Saint Norbert is most famous for consuming something not on the menu. Once when he was celebrating Mass, he noticed a venomous spider in the chalice; rather than spill one drop of Christ's Precious Blood, he drank the entire contents in the chalice, spider and all, and was miraculously preserved from harm. Consequently, one of Saint Norbert's symbols in Christian art is a spider.

Don't worry. Although people in some parts of the world (Cambodia, for example) like snacking on fried spiders, we are not about to recommend arachnophagy (the fancy word for spider eating). Instead, enrich your palate and your soul with Stamppot. This German sausage-and-potato dish is a great example of the simple but satisfying flavors of Saint Norbert's earthly homeland.

Stamppot

Serves: 4–5   **Cooking time: 1 hour**

4 large russet potatoes, peeled and cut into 1-inch pieces

2 Tbsps. butter

½ cup milk

2 Tbsps. and 2 tsps. kosher salt, divided

2 tsps. black pepper

1 medium-sized onion, peeled and finely chopped

2 cloves garlic, minced

1 tsp. white vinegar

1 lb. pork sausages, cut into thin medallions

2 Tbsps. olive oil

2 scallions, thinly sliced

1. Peel the potatoes, cut them into 1-inch squares, put them into a large pot filled with cold water, and add 2 Tbsps. of the kosher salt. Heat over medium-high heat. When water comes to a boil, reduce to medium-low heat and cook for another 10–15 minutes, or until the potatoes are fork-tender.
2. Reserve 1 cup of the starchy water and drain the rest.
3. Add the butter, milk, pepper, and 2 tsps. of the salt.
4. Use a potato masher to crush the potatoes, leaving them a little chunky or else mashing them more finely, to achieve your preferred consistency. Set aside.
5. Heat the olive oil in a separate skillet over medium heat. When the oil is hot, add the sausage slices and cook 2–3 minutes on each side, or until each side is well caramelized.
6. Turn off the heat, add the vinegar and onions, and allow them to cook with the residual heat.
7. Put a scoop of potatoes in a bowl, top off with a few slices of the sausage and onions, and garnish with fresh scallions and a little drizzle of olive oil.

JUNE

FOOD FOR THOUGHT

If Saint Norbert could eat a fresh spider out of love for Christ, and if Cambodians can actually enjoy eating fried spiders, then surely it should not be difficult to obey the words of Our Lord in Luke 10:8: "And into what city soever you enter, and they receive you, eat such things as are set before you."

JUNE 10 *(NOVEMBER 16)*
SAINT MARGARET OF SCOTLAND

argaret (1045–1093) was a great-niece of Saint Edward the Confessor and an English princess. After her land had been overrun by invaders, she fled to the court of King Malcolm III of Scotland, who soon fell in love with her. Saint Margaret bore him eight children and was an exemplary wife and mother. She had a civilizing effect on her rough husband—who is accurately portrayed by Shakespeare as the man who killed the infamous MacBeth—and what she did for him, she did for the country. She embroidered priests' vestments herself, and it is said that she is the one who introduced tartans to Scotland in an effort to cheer the place up.

The idea of eating stuffed sheep stomach may be as challenging as it is daunting, for acquiring the ingredients and preparing them properly can be difficult. Still, the essential ingredients are organ meat and aromatic herbs and spices—no different from hash or a country-style pâté. Our Holy Haggis Hash includes no sheep intestines, but it remains true to the concept of haggis, a favorite of Margaret's adopted country.

Holy Haggis Hash
Serves: 4–6   Cooking time: 1½ hours

½ lb. chicken livers	1 tsp. salt
1 lb. ground lamb	1 tsp. allspice
½ lb. beef liver	1 tsp. dried thyme
½ Tbsp. butter	½ tsp. ground cinnamon
1 onion, minced	1 cup beef or chicken stock
1 tsp. black pepper	½ cup uncooked oatmeal
½ tsp. ground coriander	2 Tbsps. parsley, minced

1. Preheat oven to 350°F.
2. In a large oven-safe pot, melt butter over medium heat. Add the onions and sauté until slightly caramelized.
3. Clean the chicken and beef livers, cut them into small pieces, and add them to the pot along with the ground lamb.
4. Season with salt, pepper, coriander, allspice, thyme, and cinnamon.
5. Stir together until all the meat is fully cooked, about 15 minutes.
6. Add the oats and stir together to mix.
7. Add the stock and stir together.
8. Cover the pot, put it into the oven, and cook for 20 minutes.
9. Carefully remove the lid and cook for another 10–15 minutes, until the oats soak up all the liquid but the meat is still moist and tender.
10. Plate and sprinkle with parsley. Serve with a side of mashed potatoes.

FOOD FOR THOUGHT

You have to have a tough stomach to become a saint. What foods can you not stomach, and why not? Saint Margaret had to deal with dishes not to her taste, but with her tears and her efforts this pearl of great price (Margaret means "pearl," by the way) turned the gritty sand of her new home into a refined gem.

JUNE 11
SAINT BARNABAS

If you ever need to make a little money, bet a friend to identify the fourteen *saints* with the title of apostle honored with a liturgical feast (and no epithets, please, such as apostle of Ireland, et cetera). The answer is the eleven original apostles, Judas's replacement (Saint Matthias), Saint Paul, and today's saint.

Barnabas was a Levite from the island of Cyprus who converted before Saint Paul and who introduced the newly converted Paul to Saint Peter in Jerusalem. He accompanied Paul on his first missionary journey, but when Paul embarked on his second mission, Barnabas returned to Cyprus and was martyred.

Barnabas is also credited with being one of the first bishops of Milan. In 1538 the Clerics Regular of Saint Paul took possession of the old Monastery of Saint Barnabas by the city wall of Milan and hence became known as the Barnabites.

If encouragement had a color, what would it be? For this saint, known as the Son of Encouragement, we would say it is the color of the sun as it's rising or setting on a clear day. That bright orange and yellow, which shows a brightness that offers warmth and comfort, happens to be the color of Risotto alla Milanese.

Risotto alla Milanese
Serves: 4   **Cooking time: 1 hour**

2 cups arborio rice

4 Tbsps. unsalted butter, divided

1 Tbsp. olive oil

½ cup shallots, finely chopped

2 tsps. fresh garlic, finely minced

2 tsps. saffron

1 cup white wine

1–1½ quarts chicken broth, heated

¼ cup grated parmesan cheese

2–3 Tbsps. parsley, finely chopped

1–2 tsps. salt

1. In a Dutch oven or large cast-iron skillet, melt the oil and 2 Tbsps. of the butter over medium heat.
2. Add the shallots and garlic and stir for about 1 minute, or until the shallots become translucent.
3. Add the arborio rice, stirring until the grains become translucent, approximately 3 minutes.
4. Deglaze the Dutch oven or pan by adding the white wine and saffron, and mix all the ingredients together, cooking for about 2–3 minutes.
5. When the wine is almost evaporated, reduce the heat to medium-low and ladle in the heated chicken broth, a ladle at a time, until the rice is covered by half an inch of liquid.
6. Add 1 tsp. of the salt and a few more ladles of hot broth. Taste test and add more salt if necessary.
7. Cook and stir continuously for 15–20 minutes, adding a ladle of hot broth every time the liquid almost evaporates, until almost all the broth is used and the rice is cooked—soft to taste, not grainy or hard, but also not mushy.
8. At the end of the cooking process, add 2–3 Tbsps. of the parmesan cheese and the remaining 2 Tbsps. of butter and stir all the ingredients together.
9. Garnish with a sprinkle of parmesan cheese and freshly minced parsley and serve.

JUNE

FOOD FOR THOUGHT

The word encouragement comes from the word *cor*, which means "heart." Encouraging people helps put their heart back into life, while discouraging people causes them to lose heart. Consider who fills your heart with strength and goodness, thank them, and do the same for others who seem to have lost their heart along life's way.

JUNE 13
SAINT ANTHONY OF PADUA

Saint Anthony of Padua (1195–1231) is also known as Saint Anthony of Lisbon since his life began in the latter city and ended in the former one. A Doctor of the Church and a priest of the Franciscan order, Anthony preached with such power that after Pope Gregory IX heard him, the pontiff called him *Arca Testamenti*—a living repository of Scripture. Saint Anthony is often portrayed with the infant Jesus—a singular tribute to a male saint other than Saint Joseph and the prophet Simeon. According to his biography, the Divine Child once came to Saint Anthony and showered him with kisses until he responded in kind. And Saint Anthony is the well known patron saint of lost objects because he raised so many lamentations after his precious copy of the Bible had been stolen that the exasperated devil told the thief to return it.

Anthony is also the patron saint of faith in the Blessed Sacrament because of food—donkey food. When a man refused to listen to arguments about the Real Presence of Jesus in the Eucharist, Anthony asked him if he would believe if he saw his own mule adore the Blessed Sacrament. The man accepted the challenge but heightened the stakes: he starved his mule for three days and had Anthony and the Eucharist stand opposite a pile of hay. On the day of the test, the hungry mule came in, ignored the hay, approached Anthony, and bent its front legs in adoration before the Eucharist. Seeing this, the astonished man knelt down as well.

And there is another food associated with the saint. Like other Franciscans, this Doctor of the Church was a champion of the poor; on his feast day, "Saint Anthony's bread" is distributed to the needy (though there is no special recipe attached to it). Anthony is also a patron of harvests and against starvation because he miraculously restored a crop after it was trampled by a crowd that had come to hear him preach.

For reasons that are not perfectly clear, it became the tradition in some parts of Europe to serve liver on Saint Anthony's Day. Here is another opportunity (in addition to Saint Margaret's Day—see June 10) to up your annual consumption of offal. Liver is quite good, but if the prospect makes some of your guests lose their appetite, seek the intercession of Saint Anthony to help them find their courage.

Faithful Fegato (Liver) alla San Antonio
Serves: 4   **Cooking time: 2½ hours**

1½ lbs. calf's liver, sliced into 4 pieces

2 cups buttermilk

2 tsps. dried oregano

1 tsp. salt

1 tsp. black pepper

¼ cup flour

4 Tbsps. butter, divided

1 lemon, half cut into slices or wedges and the other half juiced

1 Tbsp. finely minced parsley, divided

1. Mix the buttermilk and oregano together in a large bowl.
2. Add the liver slices and allow to them marinate for a minimum of 2 hours.
3. Remove the liver and pat it dry with a paper towel. Discard the paper towel and buttermilk mixture.
4. Season the liver with the salt and pepper, dredge it in the flour, and shake off the excess flour.
5. In a large pan over medium-high heat, melt 2 Tbsps. of the butter.
6. Cook the liver slices for 2–3 minutes on each side, remove them from the pan, and set aside.
7. To the same pan, add 1 tsp. of the parsley, the lemon juice, and the remaining 2 Tbsps. of butter.
8. To serve, add a serving of the butter-parsley-lemon sauce to a plate, put a slice of the liver on top of the sauce, and garnish with more parsley and a slice or wedge of lemon.

FOOD FOR THOUGHT

The more we have, the more we have to lose. Saint Anthony not only helps us find things that we've lost but helps us to give some of our things away in order to find out that maybe we don't need all of the things that clutter our lives and our attention. Give something away and see how you may find more peace in your generosity and the spirit of simplicity.

JUNE 14 *(JANUARY 2)*
SAINT BASIL THE GREAT

Born in Caesarea, Cappadocia, Basil the Great (ca. 329–379) came from a remarkable family. His grandfather was a martyr, and he also had four siblings recognized as saints: Gregory of Nyssa, Macrina the Younger, Naucratius, and Peter of Sebaste. He was also a lifelong friend of Saint Gregory of Nazianzus, who along with Basil and Saint John Chrysostom are honored in the Eastern churches as the Three Holy Hierarchs.

As a monk, Saint Basil wrote the *Rule of St. Basil*, which the monasteries of the East still follow. And as bishop of Caesarea, despite severe health problems, he stood firm against both the Arian heresy and imperial bullying. When a prefect of the emperor, an Arian sympathizer, threatened to tear out Basil's liver if he did not comply, Basil smiled and said, "Good. My liver's been giving me trouble for years." When the astonished prefect, who was accustomed to Arian bootlickers, said that no one had ever talked to him like that before, Basil replied, "Perhaps you've never talked to a *Christian* bishop before."

Basil and his monks lived an ascetical vegetarian life. "Our daintiest meal," he wrote to Saint Gregory of Nazianzus, was herbs and "vegetables with coarsest bread, and vapid wine."

Vapid wine doesn't sound too good, but how about Turkey Basil Cutlets? Basil lived in what is now modern-day Turkey, and he shares a name with an herb. It's a perfect combination that makes a hearty meal to celebrate his name and his contributions to the Catholic faith.

Turkey Basil Cutlets

Serves: 4 **Cooking time: 45 minutes**

4 turkey cutlets, fileted and slightly pounded thin

2 cloves garlic, minced

8–10 fresh basil leaves, cut chiffonade or in thin strips

2 Tbsps. olive oil

2 Tbsps. butter, divided

1 cup flour, divided

½ cup white wine

1 cup chicken broth

2½ tsps. salt, divided

2 tsps. black pepper

2 cups large-pearled couscous

2 cups water

1. Preheat oven to 400°F.
2. Lightly pound turkey cutlets to about ¼-inch thickness.
3. Season with salt and pepper and dredge in all but 2 tsps. of the flour. Discard the excess flour from the dredging and set the cutlets aside.
4. In a large skillet, melt the olive oil and 1 tsp. of the butter over medium heat.
5. Panfry the turkey cutlets for 2–3 minutes on each side, until golden brown.
6. Remove turkey from the pan and set aside.
7. To the same pan, add the remaining butter and 2 tsps. of flour and whisk together.
8. Add the white wine and whisk together until flour comes together.
9. Add the chicken broth and whisk together.
10. Add the fresh basil and mix.
11. Add the turkey cutlets back into the pan in the oven to cook for 10 minutes.
12. Boil the water, add the remaining ½ tsp. salt, stir in the couscous, remove from the heat, allow to rest for 10 minutes, and fluff with a fork.
13. Put a serving of the couscous on each plate, add a turkey cutlet, and top with a healthy spoonful of the basil sauce.

FOOD FOR THOUGHT

While basil is an herb often used to brighten up savory foods, it can also give depth to sweet desserts. The next time you use whipped cream, instead of topping it off with mint leaves, consider using finely shredded leaves of fresh basil. It's diverse, adaptable, and useful, just like our saint's personality.

JUNE 18 *(JUNE 9)*
SAINT EPHREM

Saint Ephrem the Syrian (306–373) was a deacon, the greatest of the Syriac Church Fathers, and a Doctor of the Church. Also known as Saint Ephrem of Edessa, he wrote numerous hymns, poems, sermons, and biblical commentaries so popular that for centuries other authors wrote under his name.

Ephrem's magnificent hymns, of which over four hundred still exist, earned him the sobriquet "Harp of the Holy Spirit." Many of them were written to help his flock understand orthodox Christianity and reject its heretical impostors, and some of them are among the first in history to attest to the Christian belief in the total purity of the Blessed Virgin Mary, a belief undergirding the doctrine of the Immaculate Conception.

This savory and fragrant chicken dish celebrates some of the ingredients and spices of Saint Ephrem's earthly homeland.

Syrian Chicken with Couscous
Serves: 4   **Cooking time: 1½ hours**

4 chicken thighs, bone-in and skin on

2 Tbsps. olive oil

1 tsp. cumin powder

2 tsps. ground cinnamon

1 tsp. salt

1 tsp. black pepper

2 Tbsps. fresh ground ginger

4 cloves garlic, minced

1 yellow onion, thinly sliced

2 tsps. chili pepper flakes

14–16 oz. chopped tomatoes (canned or fresh)

2 cups chicken broth

2 tsps. saffron

105

2 cups large-pearled couscous

3–4 sprigs of fresh thyme or 2 tsps. of dried thyme

¼ cup dried cranberries or currants

1 lemon, zested and juiced

½ cup yogurt

¼ cup fresh mint, roughly chopped

¼ cup fresh cilantro leaves, roughly chopped

1. Preheat oven to 350°F.
2. Wash and dry chicken thighs and put them in a large bowl.
3. Season with cumin, cinnamon, salt, and black pepper. Mix well and let sit to marinate for 30 minutes.
4. In a large oven-safe pan (or Dutch oven), heat the olive oil over high heat.
5. Carefully sear the chicken skin-side down until golden brown or dark bronzed, approximately 3–5 minutes.
6. Turn the chicken, cook for another 3–5 minutes, remove from the pan, and set aside.
7. Turn the pan down to medium heat and scoop out or drain away half of the remaining oil.
8. Add the onion, garlic, ginger, and chili pepper flakes, and sauté until the onion is translucent.
9. Add the couscous, crushed tomato, chicken broth, saffron, thyme, and currants or dried cranberries and stir together.
10. Nestle the chicken, skin-side up, into the broth and couscous.
11. Cover the pan with a lid and bake in the oven for 25–30 minutes.
12. Carefully remove the pan from the oven, drizzle the lemon juice and yogurt into the softened couscous, and gently stir.
13. Garnish the chicken with lemon zest, mint, and cilantro leaves.

FOOD FOR THOUGHT

"Harp of the Holy Spirit"—what a nickname! May we all be so in harmony with the promptings of the Holy Spirit, the Lord and Giver of Life. And to paraphrase from a prayer by Pope Pius XII, may the Holy Spirit prevent us from the misfortune of resisting His inspirations.

JUNE 24
SAINT JOHN THE BAPTIST

Saint John the Baptist has the distinction of being the only other person besides Our Lady and Our Lord whose earthly birthday is a Church feast (his heavenly birthday, or martyrdom, is observed on August 29). This no doubt has something to do with the Baptist's miraculous conception, his unique role as the "Precursor of the Lord," and, most of all, his uncommon holiness. According to an ancient tradition, Saint John was cleansed of original sin while still in the womb when his mother Saint Elizabeth heard the voice of the Blessed Virgin Mary (Luke 1:44).

Johnsmas, as this feast was once called, fittingly occurs shortly after the longest day of summer. Just as the days after the birthday of Christ, the Light of the world, begin to lengthen, the days after the birthday of John, who famously declared that Jesus "must increase and I must decrease" (John 3:30), begin to shorten.

There are several ethnic customs associated with this feast, but the most famous is a large country bonfire the night before (June 23). It was once common in parts of Europe to see bonfires dotting the hillside on this night, and even today fireworks are lit in some Catholic countries.

It is appropriate to celebrate John's memory with a "wild man" fire. Saint John is famous for his diet of locusts and wild honey (see Matthew 3:4). Did the precursor of the Lord really eat bugs? (Some etymologists tell us that the word in question means a kind of bean; others declare that it was a cake of some type made from a desert plant.)

Happily, the great Catholic tradition offers a variety of more palatable options. In Sweden the fare for the day is salmon and new potatoes; in Italy, Cozze alla Toscana; in Mexico, empanadas, chicken tamales, and stuffed peppers. But we are going to land on Finland's tradition of pancakes enjoyed around a bonfire on Saint John's Eve. To paraphrase Ron Swanson in *Parks and Rec*, only fools think that breakfast is only for breakfast.

Saint John's Finnish Flapjacks
Yields: 6–8 pancakes   Cooking time: 30 minutes

2 eggs, beaten

1 tsp. salt

4 Tbsps. sugar, divided

2 cups milk

1½ cups of all-purpose flour, sifted

1 Tbsp. melted butter

1 cup raspberries

2 Tbsps. lemon juice

2 Tbsps. fresh basil, cut chiffonade

1. To a large bowl, add the eggs, salt, milk, 2 Tbsps. of the sugar, and the flour. Whisk together until the batter is smooth.
2. Lightly brush a nonstick skillet over medium heat with melted butter.
3. Use a small ladle to scoop out 2–3 oz. of the batter into the skillet to make a pancake. Repeat.
4. Cook pancakes for 2–3 minutes, or until bubbles form in the batter, and then carefully flip and cook for another 2–3 minutes.
5. Set pancakes aside and prepare the raspberry drizzle: To a sauté pan, add the raspberries, lemon juice, and the remaining 2 Tbsps. sugar and cook over medium heat. Use a potato masher and break up the raspberries until they are liquified with just a few remaining raspberry chunks.
6. Serve pancakes with a drizzle of the raspberry mixture and garnish with basil.

Use the raspberry mixture for the topping on Saint John's Eve. If you serve the pancakes on the feast day itself, substitute one of these other toppings. Spread some cream cheese on the pancakes and top off with either:

- Smoked salmon, chopped hard-boiled eggs, and capers
- A drizzle of honey
- Or the locust bean, also known as the carob, which has a caramel flavor that substitutes for chocolate. If you can't find locust or carob bean, top off the pancake with chocolate chips.

FOOD FOR THOUGHT

John the Baptist said that he must decrease while Jesus must increase. What a great creed to live by! How liberating it is to get our egos out of the way and let the Person of Jesus Christ take center stage. Jesus needs to be more a part of our speech, our thoughts, and our actions, starting now. Perhaps this will require us doing less talking and more listening, more complimenting than criticizing, and being more generous to others rather than wanting to be the center of attention. Saint John the Baptist, pray for us, for this is harder than eating bugs.

JUNE 26
SAINT JOSEMARÍA ESCRIVÁ

During the Spanish Civil War, Josemaría Escrivá de Balaguer (1902–1975) often had to hide from Republican troops who were under orders to kill priests. On one occasion militiamen apprehended a man whom they thought was Josemaría and hanged him outside the house of Josemaría's mother. But Father Josemaría survived, and so too did Opus Dei, the organization he had founded in 1928. Latin for the "Work of God," Opus Dei is a prelature of laypersons and clergy dedicated to the universal call to holiness and the sanctification of work. "The Work," as it is often called, is currently in sixty-six countries with over sixty thousand members from eighty different nationalities.

Saint Josemaría Escrivá was renowned for his fidelity to the magisterium and his obedience to the Church, but that does not mean he lacked a lighter side. Among his many charming qualities was his great fondness for donkeys. He liked the idea of the donkey as a faithful pack animal and as the beast of burden that carried Christ into Jerusalem. The humble monsignor even called himself a "mangy donkey" frequently, and he used the image of a donkey turning a waterwheel to teach how one can achieve holiness in the fulfillment of one's ordinary duties.

Don't worry: we won't be asking you to eat donkey tonight. Instead, we honor Josemaría's lighter side with a Spanish treat. This marzipan cookie recipe is uniquely sweet, delicious, and a perfect way to get everyone involved in the work of making them.

The Founder's Panellets
Yields: 20 cookies   Cooking time: 1½ hours

3 eggs, divided

1 lemon, zested

1½ tightly packed cups of brown sugar

3½ oz. Yukon gold potatoes, cooked, peeled, and mashed

18 oz. almond flour

1 cup pine nuts, toasted

1 cup walnuts, toasted and crushed

1. In a large mixing bowl combine one of the eggs, the lemon zest, and the brown sugar and mix until fully combined.
2. Add the mashed potato and mix until fully incorporated.
3. Add the almond flour and mix with your hands. Let the dough fully form, but be careful not to overwork it.
4. Roll out the dough, shape it into a large disk, cover it with plastic wrap, and refrigerate for at least 1 hour (and up to 48 hours).
5. Preheat the oven to 425°F.
6. Prepare the panellets by cutting the disk of dough into 1-inch pieces and rolling it into balls or logs.
7. Whisk 1 egg with 1 tsp. of water.
8. Spread the pine nuts and walnuts on a plate.
9. Dunk the dough ball in the egg wash and then roll it in the plate of nuts, gently pressing them gently into the dough. Place each covered dough ball onto a baking dish lined with parchment paper. Repeat until all the dough is rolled and covered.
10. Beat the remaining egg and brush each ball with the beaten egg.
11. Place the cookies on a baking sheet and bake for 10 minutes, or until golden brown.
12. Serve the cookies warm. (Or they will keep in a sealed container at room temperature for a week.)

JUNE 29
SAINTS PETER AND PAUL

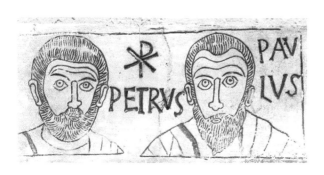

Technically, June 29 is the feast of the two great apostles of Rome, Peter and Paul. But it is the traditional practice to focus on Saint Peter today and Saint Paul tomorrow. No point in double-fisting it when you can stretch the party out over two days, is there?

Zeus faber is a tasty species of fish with a distinctive yellow-ringed black mark about the size of a U.S. quarter on each of its two flat sides. According to an old legend, this is the fish that Saint Peter caught when Christ told him, "Go to the sea, and cast in a hook; and that fish which shall first come up, take: and when thou hast opened its mouth, thou shalt find a stater [a silver coin]" (Matthew 17:26). To commemorate the honor bestowed on it, the legend continues, the fish henceforth bears on its sides the mark of a coin (other versions of the story say the black marks are Saint Peter's fingerprints). Inspired by this legend, the Spanish call the fish San Pedro and the French Saint-Pierre, but in English it is known as John Dory. That may seem to have little in common with the name that Christ gave his chief apostle, but the name may be a variation of one of Saint Peter's titles, the *Janitor* or Doorkeeper of Heaven. Indeed, in Italian the fish is called a *janitore*. Appropriately, the John Dory is a favorite traditional dish on the feast of Saint Peter, June 29.

But since John Dory is, alas, not commercially available in the United States, let us turn to tilapia, which also vies for the honor of being the fish that Saint Peter retrieved from the Sea of Galilee. Saint Peter's Fish, as it is also called, has become the most important fish species around the world, grown and locally consumed in more than one hundred countries.

We recommend a fried fish that's cooked whole in hot oil. While it's easy to make, we recommend that you cook it outside so that your house doesn't smell. An outdoor fish fry is also a nice nod to when the Risen Lord cooked fish on the beach for Saint Peter and six other disciples (John 21:1–10).

Saint Peter's Fried Fish

Serves: 4   **Cooking time: 20 minutes**

4 tilapia, gutted and scaled but kept whole

8 tsps. salt

4 tsps. black pepper

2 tsps. fresh rosemary leaves, finely minced

4–5 cups of oil for frying

1 lemon, cut into wedges

1. Make sure the fish is cleaned and scaled, but left whole with the head still on.
2. Score the fish by cutting 2–3 slits on both sides of each fish, cutting through the flesh to slightly expose the fish bone.
3. Season both sides and inside the cavity of the fish with the salt and pepper.
4. Spread the rosemary throughout the cavity.
5. Heat the oil to 350–375°F in a deep frying pan large enough to hold a whole fish.
6. Carefully place the entire fish in the hot oil and make sure it is completely submerged.
7. Cover the pan partially, leaving room to let out some steam.
8. Cook the fish for 8–10 minutes, or until it is golden brown and the frying noise is reduced.
9. Carefully remove the fish, allowing excess oil to drain, and place the fish on a baking dish with a wire rack on top of it. This will allow more excess oil to drain and will rest the fish.
10. Top with wedges of lemon and serve with potatoes or rice.

FOOD FOR THOUGHT

Eating a whole fish may be a bit dramatic for people who aren't used to their food staring back at them. But perhaps this is an opportunity to look at life's challenges—including the challenging people in our lives—and stare directly into their eyes, not with anger but with compassion and a hungry determination to make things better. Come on, you can do it: Saint Peter did.

JUNE

CHAPTER 7

July Saints

JULY 1
SAINT JUNÍPERO SERRA

The Franciscan friar Fr. Junípero Serra (1713–1784) was a highly regarded professor of philosophy in Spain, but he joined the missionary college of San Fernando in Mexico and volunteered for mission work among the Native Americans. He went to great lengths to call his Indian congregation to repentance during his sermons, pounding his breast with a stone, scourging himself, and applying a lit torch to his bare chest. He also learned their language and translated the catechism for them. Serra was appointed superior of a group of fifteen Franciscans that founded the twenty-one California missions. He traveled on foot despite a chronic and painful leg injury and bravely resisted the imperial encroachment of the government. Saint Serra passed away on August 28, but his feast is observed on July 1, the date that he first set foot in what is now San Diego.

Saint Junípero Serra is catching a lot of flak these days on the theory that he was an oppressive colonizer, but the truth is that he was more a part of the solution than the problem. His plan for the native population was Christian, humane, and self-governing. It was the Mexican government's secularist schemes that quashed his vision and led to the depredation of the Indian peoples.

When a saint shares a name with food, we have no choice but to take the hint. Juniper berries are edible (see May 4 and October 6), but they are put to their best use in making gin. Our recipe takes gin and eggs and combines them with avocado, a native fruit of Mexico that was introduced to California in the nineteenth century. The Spanish, incidentally, named this healthy fruit after the Holy Spirit, the Paraclete or Advocate, and it was obviously the Holy Spirit that made Junípero Serra a saint.

Gin-Infused Egg-and-Avocado Toast
Serves: 2   Cooking time: 20 minutes

4 slices of bread, to toast	2 Tbsps. butter
¼ cup cream cheese	2 tsps. salt, divided
2 Tbsps. sour cream	1 tsp. black pepper, divided
1 Tbsp. gin	1 avocado, thinly sliced and divided by 4
4 eggs, beaten	1 tsp. chives, finely minced

1. In a mixing bowl, combine cream cheese, sour cream, gin, 1 tsp. of the salt, and ½ tsp of the black pepper and whisk until smooth.
2. Toast your bread in a toaster oven to your preference.
3. Crack the eggs into another bowl and whisk together, seasoning with remaining salt and pepper.
4. Melt the butter in a nonstick pan over medium heat.
5. In the butter, cook the eggs to a soft scramble, whisking them gently until they begin to stiffen up. Remove from the heat immediately. Continue to whisk, allowing the residual heat of the pan to cook the eggs thoroughly. If the eggs are still too wet for your liking, return them to a low heat and continue to whisk until they are cooked to your liking.
6. Place a fourth of the cream cheese mixture on a piece of toast and spread it evenly.
7. Add a fourth of the avocado slices on top of the cream cheese mixture.
8. Place a quarter of the scrambled eggs on top of the avocado.
9. Repeat the process to create four avocado toasts.
10. Sprinkle with chives and serve immediately.

JULY

FOOD FOR THOUGHT

Being a missionary is hard work. You encounter new people, new languages, and new customs, all the while trying to share your passion and faith in Jesus with people who may not want to hear something new. This week, consider how you're called to be a missionary or how you're called to welcome a missionary. And pray for Saint Junípero Serra's California, which needs our prayers (Mike says this as a native of the Golden State).

JULY 3/DECEMBER 21
SAINT THOMAS

In the new (Novus Ordo) calendar, the feast of Saint Thomas the Apostle is celebrated on July 3, when his remains were transferred from India to Syria, while the old rite keeps his feast on December 21. Even if you already celebrated Saint Thomas's feast in December, in the spirit of doubting Thomas you have to ask yourself: Are you *sure* you celebrated it? How do you know that it wasn't just a dream? Wasn't it the year before that you are remembering, not last year? And did you really celebrate it properly? Better to celebrate it again, just in case. (See December 21 for Saint Thomas's Kletzenbrot.)

JULY 6
SAINT MARIA GORETTI

Saint Maria Goretti (1890–1902) is the young girl who chose martyrdom over yielding to the sexual advances of a man whose lusts had been aggravated by pornography. After his conviction and incarceration, Maria's murderer remained unrepentant. Years later in prison, however, he had a dream of Maria gathering lilies and handing them to him. The man felt the peace of forgiveness, and his heart was forever changed. It has been claimed that he and Maria's mother, among over 250,000 people, attended Maria's canonization ceremony on June 24, 1950.

Addressing that immense multitude, Pope the Venerable Pius XII delivered a touching homily. "Why does this story move you even to tears?" he asked the crowd. "Why has Maria Goretti so quickly conquered your hearts, and taken first place in your affections?" The pope continued:

The reason is because there is still in this world, apparently sunk and immersed in the worship of pleasure, not only a meager little band of chosen souls who thirst

JULY

for heaven and its pure air—but a crowd, nay, an immense multitude on whom the supernatural fragrance of Christian purity exercises an irresistible and reassuring fascination. During the past fifty years, coupled with what was often a weak reaction on the part of decent people, there has been a conspiracy of evil practices, propagating themselves in books and illustrations, in theaters and radio programs, in styles and clubs and on the beaches, trying to work their way into the hearts of the family and society, and doing their worst damage among the youth, even among those of the tenderest years in whom the possession of virtue is a natural inheritance.

That was in 1950. Imagine what the supreme pontiff would have to say today! So let us unabashedly feast to that old-fashioned and adorable virtue of purity.

The different recipes for this famous Italian dessert are almost as controversial as the death of this young saint. We believe that Saint Maria would have approached dessert-making as she approached life itself: rather than buying costly ingredients like ladyfingers and mascarpone cheese, she woud have humbly used what she had. This version will give you just as much flavor without the expense or the fuss.

Goretti Tiramisu

Serves: 4–6   Cooking time: 1 hour (plus 1 hour refrigeration time)

1 box of vanilla wafer cookies

1–2 cups strong coffee

2 cups whipped cream

1 lb. cream cheese

¼ cup condensed milk

¼ cup evaporated milk

1 cup cocoa powder

1. Prepare the filling by combining the whipped cream, cream cheese, condensed milk, and evaporated milk and mix together to a smooth but thick consistency.
2. In a baking dish, layer the vanilla wafers until the bottom of the dish is covered.
3. Brush a little of the coffee onto the vanilla wafers, being careful not to get them so wet that they crumble. Pour the cream cheese mixture over the cookies evenly, one ladle at a time, until the mixture is about ¼ inch thick in the dish.
4. Layer the remaining vanilla wafers evenly on top of the cream cheese mixture.
5. Brush on more coffee.
6. Add the remaining cream cheese filling on top of the cookies.
7. Dust with cocoa powder.
8. Refrigerate for at least 1 hour before serving.

FOOD FOR THOUGHT

Purity of heart needs no adornment in order to be beautiful, but it does not reject all external embellishment either. The prince married Cinderella for her virtue and goodness, but the dress, carriage, and glass slippers didn't hurt. Similarly, you might want to dress up our humble tiramisu by presenting it in fancy martini glasses, the glass slippers of our age.

JULY 8 *(JULY 4 AND JULY 5 IN THE U.S.)*
SAINT ELIZABETH OF PORTUGAL

Elizabeth (also known as Isabel or Isabella in Spanish and Portuguese) (1271–1336) was named after her great-aunt Saint Elizabeth of Hungary. Even as a girl Elizabeth said the entire Divine Office, went to High Mass at least once a day, fasted and did penance, and avoided frivolous amusements. She was married young to a dissolute king who kept a corrupt court. Elizabeth maintained her virtue and went to extraordinary lengths to help the poor. Her goodness inspired jealousy, and she was falsely accused by a page of infidelity with another page. The enraged king sent the accused page to a limeburner to be thrown into his furnace. On the way, however, the good page stopped for Mass. Impatient over the lack of any news, the king sent the wicked page to see what had happened, and the limeburner threw *him* into the furnace. The astonished king interpreted these events as a divine confirmation of Elizabeth's innocence.

Elizabeth is sometimes called "the Peacemaker." She once reconciled her son and husband when the son, tired of his father's preferences for his illegitimate children, rebelled. Elizabeth rode in between the two opposing armies and made peace before the battle was joined.

Portugal's food and beverage scene is impressive, but it is especially famous for port wine and diverse culinary creations that include cod. We provide here a fail-proof recipe that combines simplicity and refinement, a perfect description of our saint of the day.

In Cod We Trust

Serves: 4   **Cooking time: 30 minutes**

4 4–6-oz. cod filets, patted dry with a paper towel

¼ cup mayonnaise

2 Tbsps. port wine

2 tsps. salt, divided

2 tsps. black pepper, divided

1 tsp. garlic powder

1 tsp. paprika

4 cups frozen spinach, thawed and drained of excess water

2 cloves garlic, minced

2 tsps. olive oil

4 lemon wedges

1. Preheat oven to 400°F.
2. In a bowl, mix together the mayonnaise, 1 tsp. of the salt, 1 tsp. of the black pepper, the garlic powder, paprika, and port wine.
3. Put the spinach in an oven-safe baking dish and season it with the olive oil, the remaining 1 tsp. of salt, and the garlic. Mix together and spread out in 4 equal but separate sections.
4. Place a cod filet on top of each of the spinach portions.
5. Using a spoon, spread a quarter of the mayonnaise mixture over each of the four pieces of fish, covering each filet and allowing some of the mixture to drip onto the spinach.
6. Put the dish in the oven and bake for 15–18 minutes.
7. Serve the fish with the spinach and a lemon wedge.

JULY

FOOD FOR THOUGHT

Elizabeth of Portugal was known for her charity to the poor. Take a look around your home and ask yourself if there is something that you can give to the less fortunate. If there is nothing material that you can give away at this time, then perhaps you can "give away" the fear of encountering people in poverty. The less that we are afraid to get to know them, the more that we can love and help them.

JULY 19 *(SEPTEMBER 27)*
SAINT VINCENT DE PAUL

Saint Vincent de Paul (1581–1660) has become a household name because of the numerous Catholic charities named after him. Born in Gascony, France, Vincent had an eventful life. After he was ordained a priest, he was captured by Barbary pirates, taken to North Africa, and auctioned off to the highest bidder. Vincent remained a slave for two years until he escaped; some say that he converted his master. Back in France, Father Vincent was eager to relieve all forms of distress: chiefly the moral and material poverty of the peasantry, but also the terrible conditions of galley slaves, convicts forced to row in galley-ships. He founded the Congregation of the Priests of the Mission (the Vincentians) and, with Saint Louise de Marillac, the Daughters of Charity. Saint Vincent's example inspired a renewal of spirituality in the priests of France during the seventeenth century.

French onion soup is a classic, and its layers of flavor and diverse cooking techniques perfectly represent the simple but profound Saint Vincent de Paul. Once considered peasant food, onion soup is now celebrated as great cuisine when done well. In Willa Cather's novel *Death Comes for the Archbishop*, Fr. Vaillant prepares a dark onion soup with croutons for his friend Fr. Jean Marie Latour on the barren frontiers of New Mexico. "When one thinks of it," Fr. Latour remarks gratefully, "a soup like this is not the work of one man. It is the result of a constantly refined tradition. There are nearly a thousand years of history in this soup."[1]

So true. Our version draws out deep flavors from simple ingredients as it basks in the glow of a constantly refined tradition.

Onion Soup for the Soul
Serves: 4   Cooking time: 1 hour

2 medium white onions, thinly sliced (about 4 cups)

½ cup butter

2–3 cloves of garlic, finely chopped

2–3 bay leaves

2–3 sprigs of fresh thyme

2 tsps. salt

2 tsps. black pepper

1 cup red wine

2 tsps. Worcestershire sauce

2 Tbsps. flour

2 quarts beef broth

8 ¼-inch-thick slices of baguette, toasted

2 cups Gruyere cheese, grated

2 Tbsps. parsley, finely chopped

1. In a large soup pot, melt the butter over medium heat and add the onions, bay leaves, and sprigs of thyme. Cook for 10–15 minutes, stirring occasionally to avoid burning the onions.
2. When the onions are soft and slightly browned, remove the bay leaves and the sprigs of thyme and discard them.
3. Add the red wine and cook for about 5 minutes, stirring occasionally, until the harshness of the alcohol is cooked out and the liquid is almost evaporated.
4. Preheat the oven to low broil.
5. Add the flour to the soup pot, mix it in, and cook approximately another 5 minutes, long enough to create a paste but not to burn the flour.
6. Add the beef broth, one ladleful at a time, whisking to prevent lumps of flour from forming. When all of the flour has been incorporated, add the remaining broth.
7. Add the Worcestershire sauce and continue to whisk.
8. Cook until the liquid begins to boil and thicken.
9. Remove from the heat.
10. Place 4 oven-safe bowls on a baking sheet.
11. Use tongs to divide the onions equally among the bowls.
12. Ladle the broth equally into the bowls, leaving at least 1 inch of space at the top of each bowl.
13. Add 2 slices of toasted baguette to each bowl.
14. Spread the shredded Gruyere cheese over the bread and onto the broth, allowing some of the cheese to rise above the lip of each bowl.
15. Put the sheet pan of soup bowls in the oven under the broiler and cook for 3–5 minutes, or until the cheese is melted, slightly browned, and bubbling.
16. Carefully remove the sheet pan from the oven.
17. Sprinkle each bowl of soup with chopped parsley.
18. Serve the soup with a warning about the very hot bowl.

JULY

FOOD FOR THOUGHT

Soup for the soul is all about comfort food for those who need a little warmth. Think about someone who needs a little consolation or encouragement and bring them a cup of this onion soup; or, if that is not possible, send them the recipe with a kind note.

JULY 22
SAINT MARY MAGDALENE

We know that Mary Magdalene was a follower of Jesus, that she had seven demons cast out of her, that she was at the foot of the cross, and that she was the first person to see the risen Lord and report the resurrection to the apostles (for this reason, she is called "the Apostle to the Apostles"). And we suspect that she was wealthy, since she is listed among the female disciples who supported Jesus's ministry "out of their resources."

We also have reason to believe that she is the same Mary who is the sister of Martha and Lazarus of Bethany and that she is the "sinful woman" who washed Christ's feet with her tears, dried them with her hair, and anointed them with a bottle of oil (Luke 7:37–50). At least, that is the traditional Western interpretation of these passages. The identification of Mary Magdalene as the weeping woman at Jesus's feet (as well as her weeping at the tomb on Easter Sunday morning) fired the imagination of Christian artists: the medieval portraits of her shedding tears were so numerous that they led to the term "maudlin" (a British pronunciation of "Magdalene") for something that is mawkish. "Maudlin" has even been defined as being overly sentimental because of drunkenness: "to drink maudlin" is an obsolete phrase for reaching the stage of inebriation where one becomes tearfully emotional.

Thankfully, very few people eat maudlin, and so we can recommend two delicious foods for today. There is no official link between this patron saint of penitents and madeleine cookies, which are said to have been invented by a woman of that name in the seventeenth or eighteenth century in Lorraine, France. Still, many Catholic families like to honor Mary Magdalene with these dainty sponge cakes, and we are not going to stand in their way. Madeleines are shaped like a shell and dipped into melted chocolate. Their lemony buttery flavors are delicate and delicious, making madeleines perfect for serving at teatime or as a late-night snack. As we will see with the feast of Saint James on July 25, the scallop shell represents pilgrimage, and so we can let these cookies remind us of Mary's pilgrimaging with Jesus during His earthly ministry and her pilgrimaging to spread the Gospel after His resurrection. For according to a medieval legend, Saint Mary went to Marseille, France, converted the governor of that city, and spent the last thirty years of her life as a penitent in a nearby cave (for more of this story, see July 29).

Madeleine Cookies
Yields: 20–25 cookies   Cooking time: 1½ hours

2 eggs

¼ tsp. vanilla extract

¼ tsp. almond extract

¾ cup all-purpose flour, plus ½ cup for the baking pans

½ tsp. lemon zest

1 cup confectioner's sugar

¼ tsp. baking powder

½ cup butter, melted and then cooled to room temperature

½ cup chocolate chips

1 Tbsp. milk

1 Tbsp. sugar

nonstick cooking spray

1. Preheat oven to 375°F.

1. Prepare a madeleine mold by applying some nonstick cooking spray and flour, or you can substitute a greased and floured baking sheet. In either case, be sure to shake off the excess flour.

2. In a large mixing bowl combine the eggs, vanilla and almond extracts, and lemon zest and mix for 3–5 minutes, or until the eggs are properly whipped.

3. Add the confectioner's sugar ¼ cup at a time, until the batter is thick but silky.

4. Sift the flour and baking powder together.

5. Add the flour and baking powder to the liquid ingredients gradually, ¼ cup at a time, and gently fold all the ingredients together until all the flour is incorporated.

6. Add the melted and cooled butter and continue to fold all ingredients together.

7. Spoon the batter into the madeleine molds until they're about ½–¾ full. If you are using a baking sheet, drop one Tbsp. of batter at a time on the baking sheet, allowing each spoonful of batter to take its own form, and spreading the cookies 1 inch apart.

8. Bake for about 10–12 minutes, or until the edges are golden and the batter springs back if you touch it with your finger.

9. Allow the cookies to cool for about 5 minutes.

10. While they're cooling, combine the chocolate chips, milk, and sugar in a small saucepan, cook over medium heat until the chocolate is melted, and then transfer the mixture to a shallow bowl.

11. Decorate the cookies by dipping 1 side or half of each cookie in the chocolate. You can also just drizzle the chocolate over the cookie, making any design you want.

12. Put the cookies on a baking rack, allow the chocolate to cool and harden, and serve.

Here's a bonus recipe for Saint Mary Magdalene's Day. For what was Mary Magdalene penitent? The traditional answer is that she was a prostitute. Although there is no clear evidence to

JULY

support this claim, she may well have lived a "salty" life while those seven demons were possessing her. This traditional pasta is a classic with a very particular backstory from the back alleys of one of Italy's great seaport towns. "Puttanesca" means "lady of the night" and is attributed to the prostitutes of Naples, Italy. Some speculate that it was a quick meal cooked up by the ladies between clients, others that its distinctive aroma mirrored that of a Neapolitan house of ill repute. Either way, it is a delicious sauce that can be converted, like Mary Magdalene, to the service of the true, the good, and the beautiful.

Puttanesca Pasta

Serves: 4–6   **Cooking time: 30 minutes**

1 lb. spaghetti	2 cloves garlic, thinly sliced	1 Tbsp. capers
28–30 oz. chopped tomatoes (if canned, drain away and discard the liquid or use it in another dish)	1 shallot, finely minced	1–2 tsps. salt
	2–3 anchovy filets	1 tsp. black pepper
	¼ cup red wine	1 tsp. red pepper flakes
3 Tbsps. olive oil, divided	¼ cup pitted brined green olives, thinly sliced	2 Tbsps. fresh parsley, finely minced

1. In a large pot, boil water and cook spaghetti for 2–3 minutes less than the cooking directions on the package.
2. While the pasta is cooking, heat 2 Tbsps. of the olive oil in a large skillet over medium-low heat.
3. Add the anchovy filets, using a wooden spoon to break them up until they almost disappear into the oil.
4. Add the shallots, garlic, and red pepper flakes and cook for about 1–2 minutes.
5. Add the chopped tomatoes and red wine and cook for about 5 minutes, or until the juices start to boil and the tomato begins to break down.
6. Add the chopped olives and capers.
7. Add salt and pepper to taste.
8. Continue to cook until ingredients are fully incorporated and juices simmer.
9. When the pasta is cooked, reserve ¼ of the starchy water, use a colander to drain the rest from the spaghetti and then tongs to transfer the spaghetti immediately to the skillet of sauce.
10. Add the ¼ cup of pasta water to the sauce, stir, and cook for another 2–3 minutes.
11. Drizzle the remaining 1 Tbsp. of olive oil over the pasta, garnish with chopped parsley, and serve.

JULY

FOOD FOR THOUGHT

If, as we think, Mary Magdalene is Mary of Bethany, then she is the one who "took her place at the Lord's feet and listened to His words" (Luke 10:39). Our Lord commended her for this and said, "Only one thing is necessary; and Mary has chosen for herself the best part of all, that which shall never be taken away from her" (10:42). Let us pray to Saint Mary Magdalene that we may all make such a wise choice.

And if as a parent you have difficulty answering questions about the birds and the bees, then discusing Saint Mary Magdalene's past will create real *agita*. Before talking to your kids about the world's oldest profession, it might be good to talk to God about it first. And do pray for those who live in difficult situations and for one reason or another end up on the streets.

JULY 24
SAINT SHARBEL MAKHLUF

Charbel or Sharbel is the religious name that Youssef Makhluf (1828–1898), a shepherd who had lost his father at the age of three, took when he entered the Monastery of Saint Maron in Annaya, near Beirut. After being ordained a priest, Saint Sharbel was "ruthless on himself," practicing great asceticism and spending the last twenty-three years of his life as a hermit. Months after he died, a mysterious light radiated from his tomb, and it was discovered that his body, still secreting sweat and blood, was completely incorrupt. Saint Sharbel's body was still incorrupt and flexible the last time it was examined by doctors in 1950.

Saint Sharbel's holiness, Pope Paul VI explained in 1965, helps us "understand, in a world so often fascinated by wealth and comfort, the irreplaceable value of poverty,

JULY

of penance, and of asceticism in liberating the soul in its ascent to God."[2] And Saint Sharbel, a Maronite Catholic, also reminds us who practice the Roman Rite that there are twenty-three Eastern Churches, each with its own liturgical traditions, in full communion with the bishop of Rome. The Maronite Church, which had its beginnings in the mountains of Lebanon, has a beautiful history of fidelity to the Holy See; in fact, it is the only Eastern Church never to have been in schism. So on this day, when we celebrate one of her great sons, let us enjoy a feast from the culinary traditions of Lebanon. This chickpea dipping favorite requires only a few ingredients and is great for gatherings large and small.

Holy Hummus
Serves: 4–6 (as an appetizer)   Preparation time: 20 minutes

1 can of chickpeas, drained and rinsed, divided

1 large lemon, zested and juiced (yielding ¼ cup of juice)

¼ cup tahini

1 clove garlic, minced

3 Tbsps. olive oil, divided

½ tsp. cumin

½ tsp. turmeric

1–2 tsps. salt

2–3 Tbsps. water

2–3 tsps. paprika

2–3 Tbsps. fresh cilantro leaves

1. Reserve 2 Tbsps. of the chickpeas and set aside.
2. In a food processor, combine the rest of the chickpeas, the lemon juice, tahini, garlic, cumin, turmeric, and 2 Tbsps. of the olive oil.
3. Pulse and then blend all ingredients together until the mixture becomes creamy, adding 1 Tbsp. of water at a time to make it looser.
4. Taste the mixture and then add salt according to taste.
5. Spoon the hummus to a large plate, use a spoon to hollow out a well in the center, and add the 2 Tbsp. of whole chickpeas to the center of the plate.
6. Sift some paprika and lemon zest on the hummus, drizzle with olive oil, and garnish with cilantro leaves.
7. Serve with warm pita chips.

JULY

FOOD FOR THOUGHT

What makes this dish fun is the unique designs you can make with the creamy hummus, the chickpeas, and the warm pita chips. Go ahead and be creative with your plating, playing with the textures by using different types of dipping chips, including potato chips, nachos, or fancy crackers. And while you're having fun, give thanks to God for the salutary diversity of liturgies and traditions in the Church Catholic, the universal Church. In an age when "diversity" is often misused as a concept, it is good to remember that there is more than one way to get things right. The Holy Spirit is versatile.

JULY 25
SAINT JAMES THE GREATER

Saint James (d. 42 or 43) was the brother of Saint John the Apostle. Our Lord nicknamed the two of them "Sons of Thunder." James is also given the epithet "the Greater" to distinguish him from "James the Lesser" (or the Younger), another apostle, who was Our Lord's cousin. Together with Saints Peter and John, James the Greater was one of the three apostles given the special privilege of witnessing the Transfiguration of Jesus on Mount Tabor and His Agony in the Garden. Saint James was beheaded in Jerusalem on the orders of Herod Agrippa.

Saint James's feast day is most famously tied to Santiago de Compostela in Spain ("Santiago" is a Galician development of the vulgar Latin *Sanctu Jacobu*). According to legend, Saint James preached the Gospel on the Iberian Peninsula for a while before returning to the Holy Land. After he was martyred, his body was taken to Jaffa, where a marvelous stone ship transported it back to Spain. James's disciples asked a deceitful pagan queen for a place to bury the body, and they buried it at the current site of Compostela after foiling a number of her traps. The body was rediscovered in the ninth century when a star led the local bishop to its location. Hence the name Compostela, which is believed to be a corruption of *campus stellae*, or field of the star.

Whatever the truth behind these tales, one thing is certain: Santiago de Compostela was an enormously significant pilgrimage site by the Middle Ages, third only in popularity to Rome and the Holy Land. To this day, the pilgrimage to Santiago, called El Camino or The Way, is piously made by many of the faithful.

The primary symbol of the Camino de Santiago is a scallop shell: in fact, the scientific name of this shellfish is *Pecten jacobaeus*, James's scallop (and if we're going nerdy, we might as well add that the French is *Coquille Saint-Jacques* and the German is *Jakobsmuscheln*, or James's mussels). Scallops are therefore the obvious choice for tonight, and our recipe is particularly delicious (and you can save the shells and have the kids paint Santiago crosses on them).

Other mollusks get to share in the glory of the scallop on this day. There is an old English proverb: "He who eats oysters on Saint James's Day shall not lack for money." So if you are looking for a financial windfall, you know what to do.

But if seafood is not your thing, pull out the leftover madeleines, with their scallop shape, from Saint Mary Magdalene's Day (July 22). A couple of legends about the cookie are connected to the Camino. In one version, a woman named Madeleine brought the recipe back from her pilgrimage to Compostela; in another, a chef named Madeleine offered these treats to pilgrims passing through Lorraine.

Santiago Scallops
Serves: 4   **Cooking time: 30 minutes**

20 fresh medium-sized scallops
¼ cup butter
2 Tbsps. olive oil
2 tsps. salt
2 tsps. black pepper

2 cloves garlic, kept whole
2–3 sprigs of fresh thyme
1 lemon, zested and juiced
2 Tbsps. fresh parsley, minced

1. Heat olive oil in a large skillet over high heat.
2. Use a paper towel to gently dry the scallops.
3. Season them with the salt and pepper.
4. Place the scallops individually around the skillet, being careful not to overcrowd the pan.

5. After 2 minutes, the scallops should be caramelized on the bottom side. Gently turn them over.
6. Immediately add the cloves of garlic, the sprigs of thyme, and the butter and melt it until it becomes frothy.
7. Lower the heat to medium.
8. Use a spoon to baste the scallops with the juice in the pan as you cook them for 2–3 more minutes.
9. Sprinkle the lemon zest and parsley over the scallops and add the lemon juice to the pan and baste for another minute.
10. Serve the scallops with crusty bread.

FOOD FOR THOUGHT

Physical pilgrimages like the one to Santiago de Compostela are important because they remind us of our more basic status as pilgrims passing through this world on our way (God willing) to our heavenly home. Did you know that the word "parish" is from a Greek term for a colony temporarily dwelling in a foreign land? Even our "home church" is not our true home.

Consider going on a pilgrimage to a sacred destination: there are options both foreign and domestic. (Shameless plug: Father Leo and Mike occasionally lead pilgrimages through an organization called Cruises by Select.) As the Spanish say to Compostela pilgrims, *¡Buen Camino!*

JULY

JULY 26
SAINT ANNE

Like many devotions, the cult of Saint Anne developed in the East and came to the West with the Crusaders returning from the Holy Land. According to the story, Anne and her husband Joachim were a childless elderly couple who prayed to God for offspring and were rewarded with a daughter whom they named Miriam (the Blessed Virgin Mary). Saint Anne went on to become an extremely popular saint. She is the patroness of numerous places and peoples, as well as of grandmothers, housewives, pregnant women, horseback

riders, carpenters, broom-makers, lace-makers, seamstresses, and miners (to name a few). She is also invoked against poverty and sterility.

And, because of a rumor that Saint Anne had three husbands in her lifetime, she is also invoked by spinsters and maidens to find them a mate. After all, if Anne could marry successfully three times, why can't she find just one guy for me? Hence Anne was implored with little ditties such as this:

I beg you, holy mother Anne,
Send me a good and loving man.

JULY

The vigil of Saint Anne's Day (Saint Anne's Eve) was a great occasion for matchmaking and debutante balls: both Johann Strausses (senior and junior) composed "Anne Polkas" for these festivities. Following an old saying that "all Annes are beautiful," these events would be called a "festival of all Annes," that is, a festival of all beautiful ladies. Fireworks would light the summer sky and the sound of laughter, music, and dancing would fill the air.

Saints Anne and Joachim are often depicted wearing red and green in Christian art. These colors of divine love are beautifully displayed by this delicious fresh fruit strudel. Plus, as we will see with the feast of the Assumption (August 15), the strawberry is a symbol of their beloved daughter.

Kiwi-and-Strawberry Puff Pastry
Yields: 8 pastries   Cooking time: 30 minutes

puff pastry, cut into 8 2-x-2-inch squares
1 Tbsp. butter, melted
1 cup cream cheese
2 Tbsps. sugar
1 tsp. lemon extract

8 strawberries, stems removed and cut into halves
2 kiwis, peeled and cut into quarters
4 Tbsps. confectioner's sugar

1. Preheat oven to 375°F.
2. Brush the puff pastry with the melted butter and put it into the oven for 15 minutes.
3. In a mixing bowl combine the cream cheese, sugar, and lemon extract. Mix together until you achieve a smooth, creamy consistency.
4. Divide the cream cheese mixture and spread an equal portion on each of the puffed pastry squares.
5. Put one strawberry and one kiwi fruit quarter on top of each puffed pastry square. Design it any way you want.
6. Sift the confectioner's sugar over all the puff pastries and serve.

FOOD FOR THOUGHT

Regardless of whether you are a single person looking for a spouse or a married person wishing the best possible match for your single friends and family members, let us all toast to Saint Anne today with the invocation, "We beg you, holy mother Anne, send our Christian maidens a good and loving man."

And pay a little extra attention to your grandparents. Give them a call and let them know that they are a cherished part of your life. If you're unable to reach out to your own grandparents, consider spiritually adopting some senior citizens in your parish or neighborhood. Pray for them, be more patient with them, and maybe even take them on an outing to keep them young at heart.

JULY

JULY 29
SAINT MARTHA

What an honor to have been Martha, Mary Magdalene, or Lazarus, the three siblings in Bethany whom Jesus loved to visit when he was in Judea. On one of these occasions, Martha was hustling to make her Guest comfortable while her sister Mary sat at the Lord's feet, absorbing every word. When Martha asked Jesus to make her sister help her, He replied, "Martha, Martha, thou art careful and art troubled about many things: but one thing is necessary. Mary hath chosen the best part, which shall not be taken away from her" (Luke 10:41–42). So in Christian tradition Martha and Mary came to be seen

as embodiments of the active life and the contemplative life, respectively. The active life is by no means bad, but the contemplative life, which everyone is called to have at least some share in, is closer to the bliss of the Beatific Vision.

Of course, being active has its merits too. According to legend, Martha, Mary Magdalene, and Lazarus were put in a rudderless ship and sent out to sea to die, but God guided their boat to the south coast of France. At the time, a river dragon was terrorizing the locals; one of the monster's more peculiar habits was that when it was being chased it defecated on its pursuers an ordure half an acre wide that was like glass and made whatever it touched burn like fire. The townsfolk begged Martha to intervene, which she did: she found the dragon and stopped it from eating a man by sprinkling holy water on it and showing it the cross. The dragon then became docile, allowing Saint Martha to leash it with her girdle and lead it back to the people, who then ganged up on it and stabbed it to death (not exactly the happy ending of Saint Francis and the wolf of Gubbio!). The dragon's name was Tarasconus, and ever since the town in France has been called Tarascon. Since 1474, Tarascon has had an annual festival celebrating Martha's defeat of the dragon.

The city of Marseille gets into the act with a special cookie called a *navette*, or "little boat" (in honor of the craft that brought these saints to French shores). Served cold, these hard cookies are traditionally dunked in coffee, tea, or wine before being consumed. That's right—wine. We don't include a recipe for *navettes* because we are still snacking on madeleines (see July 22).

Since stabbed dragon isn't as common as it used to be in the meat section of your local supermarket, we suggest Chicken Tarragon. "Tarragon," the common word for a yummy plant called *Artemisia dracunculus*, is etymologically related to "dragon," and it even kind of looks like a variation of "Tarascon." This delicious chicken recipe pays homage to the grace of God working in and through Saint Martha's defeat of the dragons in her life.

Chicken Tarragon
Serves: 4   **Cooking time: 1 hour**

2 lbs. boneless chicken breasts

4 Tbsps. fresh tarragon leaves, roughly chopped

3–4 scallions, minced

1 shallot, minced

2 garlic cloves, minced

½ cup white wine

1 cup chicken stock

¼ cup heavy cream

3 Tbsps. butter, divided, plus 1 Tbsp. melted butter

1 tsp. olive oil

2 Tbsps. and 2 tsps. flour, divided

1 tsp. salt

1 tsp. white pepper

1–2 sheets of puff pastry (depending on the size of the baking dish

1. Preheat oven to 350°F.
2. Measure the puff pastry to fit the top part of the pan and set aside.
3. Cube the chicken breasts into ½-inch pieces, season them with salt, pepper, and 2 Tbsps. of the flour, and mix together so that all pieces are lightly coated with the flour.
4. In a large cast-iron skillet or oven-safe pan over medium, heat the olive oil and 1 tsp. of the butter.
5. Place the chicken in the pan and allow it to cook for about 2 minutes, until 2 sides of the chicken cubes are golden brown.
6. Add the tarragon, shallots, and garlic and sauté for approximately 1 minute, or until the shallots become translucent.
7. Remove the chicken, garlic, and tarragon from the pan and set aside.
8. Deglaze the pan: add the white wine and scrape any browned bits from the bottom.
9. Add the remaining butter and flour to the pan and mix until you form a paste.
10. Add the chicken stock, a little at a time.
11. Return the chicken, tarragon, garlic, and shallots to the pan and stir until the mixture begins to thicken slightly.
12. Place the pre-cut puff pastry on top of the chicken mixture to make a crust and brush it with the melted butter.
13. Cook in the oven for about 20–25 minutes, or until the puff pastry is golden brown.
14. Take the pan out of the oven, allow the dish to rest for about 5 minutes, and serve.

JULY

FOOD FOR THOUGHT

When she asked Jesus to tell Mary to help her, Martha was gently reminded by Our Lord that Mary had chosen the better part because she was hanging on His every word. But what about all the things that still needed to be done? Perhaps Martha should have asked Jesus to help her in the kitchen. Would He have done so? In our opinion, yes, for that's what Jesus does: He helps us in all our needs. Florence Berger makes a similar point in her book *Cooking for Christ*. "If I am to carry Christ home with me from the altar," she writes, "I am afraid He will have to come to the kitchen because much of my time is spent there."[3] So the next time you need help, ask Jesus before asking anyone else. He will give you His grace or send someone your way.

JULY 31
SAINT IGNATIUS OF LOYOLA

Íñigo López de Loyola (1491–1556) was born in the castle of Loyola above Azpeitia, Spain, located in Basque country. He is described as being "of a somewhat fiery and warlike nature," which is a nice way of saying that he was a poster boy for Latino machismo, coupled with powerful family connections to get him out of trouble for gambling, quarreling, and swordplay (oh, and he also had an eye for the ladies). Not surprisingly, Ignatius became a military officer. After a battle in which he was wounded by a cannon ball, his leg did not heal properly and had to be broken and reset (without anesthesia). The leg healed this time, but with a bony protrusion below the knee. Ignatius found this unacceptable, as it made it impossible to wear the tight-fitting boots and hose of a courtier, so he ordered the doctors to *saw off* the offending knob (again without anesthesia). Who knew that the wages of vanity could be so high?

During his long recuperation Ignatius wanted to read romance novels, but since the family castle had none he had to settle for a book on the life of Christ and a book on the saints. The effect on him was dramatic. Saint Ignatius abandoned his worldly ways and founded the Society of Jesus. Better known as the Jesuits, the order became renowned for its notable educators, missionaries, and scientists.

Saint Ignatius of Loyola is known to have enjoyed sweet treats as a child in the Basque country of Spain. This delicious Basque Burnt Cheesecake is a perfect nod to the sweetness that eventually came from Saint Ignatius's conversion. By the time he died, acquaintances could not believe that the meek and gentle soul they knew had once been a proud and fierce man who, for instance, had almost killed a Muslim for saying something offensive about the Blessed Virgin Mary.

Basque Burnt Cheesecake
Serves: 6–8   **Cooking time: 2 hours**

2 Tbsps. unsalted butter to grease the baking pan

1½ lbs. cream cheese, softened to room temperature

6 cups sugar

2 eggs

1 cup heavy whipping cream

1 tsp. salt

1 tsp. vanilla extract

⅓ cup all-purpose flour

¼ cup confectioner's sugar

fresh fruit as garnish (optional)

1. Preheat oven to 400°F.
2. Butter a 10-inch springform pan, line it with parchment paper to at least 2 inches above the sides of the pan, and place the pan on a baking sheet.
3. Combine the cream cheese and sugar in a stand mixer and use the paddle attachment to beat for 2–3 minutes, or until the sugar has dissolved.
4. Add the eggs one at a time, allowing the mixture to come together before adding the next egg. Make sure to scrape down the sides of the bowl.
5. Carefully add the sifted flour to the cream cheese mixture a little at a time, allowing the paddle to mix the ingredients together until the batter becomes silky and has no lumps.
6. Pour the batter into the prepared springform pan and cook on the middle rack of the oven for about 60–75 minutes, until the cake is a deeply golden-brown color but its center is still very loose and jiggly.
7. Allow cake to cool for about 20 minutes before releasing the springform and peeling away the parchment paper.
8. Cut into slices and serve with a sprinkling of confectioner's sugar (and fresh fruit).

JULY

FOOD FOR THOUGHT

The founder of the Jesuits experienced a conversion as a result of reading the lives of the saints. Meditating on the saints is a good and holy practice for all the faithful. *Dining with the Saints* is, of course, a good start, but it is only the tip of the iceberg. Consider getting a devotional that gives a reflection on a saint every day.

CHAPTER 8

August Saints

AUGUST 1
LAMMAS DAY

I n the universal Church calendar before 1960, today was the feast of Saint Peter in Chains. In the post–Vatican II calendar, it is the feast of Saint Alphonsus Liguori. But in the British Isles during the Middle Ages and Renaissance, the first of August was better known as "Loaf Mass Day," or Lammas Day for short.

Lammas Day was a wheat harvest festival in which a loaf of bread made from the recent crop was brought to church and blessed. Lammas Day was a time of merriment: the town of Ballycastle in Northern Ireland, for example, has been celebrating Ould Lammas Fair for the past four hundred years. Lammas was a well-known feature of life in times past. In *Romeo and Juliet* we learn that Juliet's fourteenth birthday is on "Lammas-eve at night" (I.iii.19). And it was also used to designate property: "Lammas lands" were the fields used in common for winter grazing, while "Lammas wheat" was winter wheat, presumably planted in early August.

Among the Scottish and the Irish, bannocks were popular on this day. A type of round unleavened oatcake baked on a hot griddle, bannocks once had nine knobs that symbolized gift offerings to the nine creatures that could harm the field and flock, including the fox, the eagle, and the crow. After the introduction of Christianity, the knobs were replaced by an X on one side and a O on the other, symbols of the crucifixion and resurrection of Jesus Christ.

In Scotland, the Lammas bannock was called "bonnach lunastain." The following recipe is known as a quarter bannock because it was prepared on one of the four quarter days of the year, when rents were due, Lammas Day being one of them in Scotland and Ireland.

Bread is as diverse as the different grains or seeds that can be used to make up the dough. This oat-dough bread, heated in a pan rather than an oven, has a unique texture. It's a distinctive bread not usually found in grocery stores, which you can certainly consider a blessing.

Quarter Bannock Bread

1 cup finely ground oatmeal (or use ground barley as a substitute)

2 Tbsps. flour or 2 more Tbsps. ground oatmeal, for dusting

⅛ tsp. baking soda

⅛ tsp. salt

1 tsp. melted shortening (or butter)

1 Tbsp. sugar, divided

4–6 Tbsps. hot water

1 Tbsp. butter, divided

1. In a mixing bowl, mix together the oatmeal (or barley), baking soda, salt, and melted shortening (or butter).
2. Add the hot water, 1 Tbsp. at a time.
3. Use your hands to mix and knead the ingredients until a dough is formed, incorporating all the ground oats. Allow the dough to rest for about 30 minutes.
4. Dust your work surface with the flour or more ground oats, separate the dough, and roll the pieces into small balls about 2 inches thick.
5. With a rolling pin or your hands, flatten the balls of dough into round disks about ⅛ inch thick.
6. Melt the butter in a pan over medium-high heat and sprinkle it with a little sugar.
7. Lower the heat to medium-low, place each disk of dough in the pan, and cover with a lid.
8. Cook for about 8–10 minutes on one side and 5–7 minutes on the other side.
9. Serve hot and top off with your preferred toppings, sweet or savory.

FOOD FOR THOUGHT

People in biblical times saw bread as "life." Ask yourself what gives you life and ask God's blessing upon it all, in the same way you would bless bread.

AUGUST 4 *(AUGUST 8)*
SAINT DOMINIC

Saint Dominic (1170–1221) was born in Caleruega, Spain, and from an early age exhibited a passion for helping others. When the land was struck by famine, Dominic fed the hungry by giving away his money and selling his clothes, his furniture, and even his

AUGUST

precious manuscripts. He also tried, on two occasions, to sell himself into slavery in order to liberate Christians held captive by the Moors. Dominic would go on to found the Order of Preachers, or Dominicans, one of the great reforming agents of the medieval Church and a durable cradle of great theologians and saints. Dominic himself was an effective preacher who combated the destructive, body-hating Albigensian heresy through intelligent persuasion and who promoted Marian devotion and the use of the rosary: some even say that Our Lady gave him the first rosary.

Saint Dominic is said to have planted the first orange tree in Italy. This sweet orange flan dessert is a nod to Saint Dominic's home country of Spain. Flan can carry unique flavors, from fruity to sweet and even a little tart, while the caramel sauce gives it extra decadence. Enjoying it is the perfect proof that you are not a body-hating Albigensian.

Flan de Naranja
Serves: 4   **Cooking time: 1 hour**

THE CARAMEL SAUCE

⅓ cup of sugar

2 Tbsps. water

½ tsp. orange juice

2 tsps. orange zest

1. Preheat oven to 350°F.
2. Add the sugar, water, and orange juice to a saucepan and cook over medium heat. Do not stir. After 5–7 minutes, the sugar will melt and become an auburn or copper color. Whisk ingredients together until all the sugar is melted and you have a loose caramel sauce.
3. Carefully pour the caramel sauce into 4 separate ramekins and set aside.

THE CUSTARD

4 large eggs, beaten   1½ cups of orange juice, pulp-free

⅓ cup sugar

1. Mix the eggs and sugar in a bowl until the sugar is dissolved and the mixture has a creamy yellow color and soft texture.
2. Slowly add the orange juice, a little at a time, and whisk together until all ingredients are fully incorporated.
3. Divide the egg mixture between the four ramekins, pouring it on top of the caramel sauce.

THE FLAN

1. Place the ramekins in a casserole dish. Pour cold water into the casserole dish to half the height of the ramekins. Be careful not to allow any water to drip into the egg mixture.
2. Carefully put the casserole dish with ramekins into the oven and cook for 45 minutes.
3. Remove the casserole dish from the oven, take the ramekins out, and allow the flan to cool for 20–30 minutes at room temperature.
4. Cover the ramekins and place them in the refrigerator for 20 minutes.
5. When the flan is cooled, use a paring knife to cut around the inside of each ramekin, separating the flan from the ramekin. You should be able to jiggle the flan now.
6. Place a plate over each ramekin and quickly flip the dish, releasing the flan from the ramekin.
7. Sprinkle a little orange zest on top of each flan and serve!

FOOD FOR THOUGHT

Regale your guests tonight with a joke. A catechumen was trying to gain a better understanding of Catholic religious orders, and so he asked his Catholic friend about the difference between the Dominicans and the Jesuits. His friend told him that the Dominicans are an order founded by Saint Dominic in the thirteenth century to fight the Albigensian heresy, and that the Jesuits are an order founded by Saint Ignatius in the sixteenth century to fight the Protestant heresy. The catechumen then wanted to know which order was better. "Well," his friend replied, "let me put it to you this way. When was the last time you met an Albigensian?"

AUGUST

AUGUST 9 *(AUGUST 4)*
SAINT JOHN MARY VIANNEY

Jean-Marie Vianney (1786–1859) almost did not become a priest. His Latin scores were terribly low, and he had to dodge a couple of drafts into Napoleon's armies. But it's a good thing he prevailed. Once this unassuming man became the pastor (or curé) of Ars, he not only transformed the tiny French village of 253 people but enriched the entire Church. The "Curé d'Ars" was an indefatigable priest, spending up to sixteen hours a day in the confessional and having the gift of reading people's hearts. The devil was not pleased with the saint's success and plagued him for what may possibly be the longest period of diabolical infestation in Church history. For decades, Satan kept the saint awake at night with terrifying noises, once even setting his bed on fire. Saint John Mary took it all in stride. The devil spent so much time at the rectory that the curé once quipped, "We're practically friends."

Saint Jean-Marie Vianney was known to practice very strict dietary fasts for the salvation of souls, sometimes eating no more than a bite of a boiled potato each day. While not as sacrificial as a plain boiled potato, this rich French dish celebrates the richness of God's grace working in and through Saint Jean-Marie Vianney.

Gratin Dauphinois
Serves 4–6 people (as a side dish)   Cooking time: 90 minutes

2 lbs. baking potatoes, peeled and cut crosswise into ¼-inch slices

5 cups whole milk

2 cloves garlic, minced

1½ cups heavy cream

1 ½ cups creme fraiche (or substitute sour cream)

2 tsps. salt

1 tsp. black pepper

½ tsp ground nutmeg

2 Tbsps. unsalted butter

1 cup shredded Gruyere cheese, divided

2 Tbsps. fresh parsley, chopped

1. Preheat oven to 350°F.
2. To a large pot, add the potatoes, milk, and garlic and bring to a light simmer over medium heat. Cook approximately 15–20 minutes, until the potatoes are fork-tender but have not lost their shape. Do not break up or mash them.
3. Remove the potatoes using a slotted spoon. Reserve 2 Tbsps. of the milk and pour the rest out and discard it.
4. In the same pot, combine the heavy cream, creme fraiche (or sour cream), salt, pepper, and nutmeg and bring to a light boil, then immediately turn off the heat.
5. Add half of the cheese and mix together until the cheese is melted into the sauce.
6. Assemble the potatoes: Grease an oven-safe baking dish with the butter. Put a little of the cream sauce in the bottom of the baking dish and add a layer of potato slices. Spoon more of the cream sauce on top of the potatoes. Repeat the process until all of the potatoes and cream sauce are used.
7. Use the rest of the cheese to top the dish.
8. Put the baking dish on top of a rimmed baking sheet, place the baking sheet in the oven, and cook for 50–60 minutes.
9. When all of the cream is absorbed into the potatoes and the cheese is bubbly and golden brown, remove the dish and allow to rest about 10 minutes before serving.
10. Garnish with fresh parsley and serve as a side dish.

FOOD FOR THOUGHT

Saint John Mary Vianney was a man of a few words except when he talked to God. He was also known as a great confessor, which requires the discipline of listening to how God is working in the life of the penitent. Consider doing more listening than talking this week, and allow your actions to speak louder than your words about your faith. And go to confession!

AUGUST

AUGUST 10
SAINT LAWRENCE

Lawrence of Rome (c. 225–258) was born in Spain and became the archdeacon of Rome. In August 258, the emperor Valerian commanded that all Catholic clergy be executed. When Lawrence was arrested, he asked for three days to assemble the Church's wealth. The prefect of Rome, eager for lucre, agreed. Lawrence proceeded to give away as much money as he could to the poor and on the third day appeared before the prefect with a delegation of the poor, the crippled, and the blind. "Behold the true treasures of the Church," Lawrence told the stunned prefect. Enraged, the prefect ordered him to be slowly roasted alive on a gridiron, but even here the fearless deacon got the last laugh. After a long period of suffering, Saint Lawrence declared, "You can turn me over; I am done on this side." Not to be outdone in black humor, the Church has made Saint Lawrence the patron saint of comedians, cooks, and grillers.

On this feast day, nuns in Rome would give out bread and ham (*panis et perna*), a custom that explains the name of Panisperna Street, which runs by one of Saint Lawrence's four churches in the Eternal City. You can imitate this custom with a good cold-meat deli sandwich. Understandably, there is a tradition of not eating grilled meats on Saint Lawrence's Day. Lasagna is the traditional fare in Florence, while in Spain it is gazpacho and *bizcocho de San Lorenzo* (a chestnut biscuit, the name of which means "twice-cooked"!). Whatever the fare, it should be suitable for a patron saint of cooks but not so fancy that it favors the rich over the poor.

Gazpacho is a cold Spanish soup that is quite refreshing on a hot summer's day. Our Gazpacho alla Lorenzo honors Lawrence's ancestry and avoids any macabre reminders of his martyrdom. Plus, it's really good.

Gazpacho alla Lorenzo

Serves: 4–6   **Cooking time: 30 minutes (plus 1–2 hours of refrigeration)**

4–5 overripe tomatoes, chopped to yield 2 cups

1 cucumber, chopped to yield 1 cup

2 cloves garlic

¼ cup extra virgin olive oil, plus extra for garnish

½ cup red wine vinegar

½ cup day-old bread, cut into cubes

1 bell pepper, seeded and chopped

½ red onion, diced to yield ¼ cup

¼ cup fresh parsley leaves, minced and divided

1 cup ice

¼ cup sour cream

2 Tbsps. of water

1. In a blender, combine the tomatoes, cucumbers, garlic, olive oil, red wine vinegar, bread, bell pepper, red onion, and 1–2 Tbsps. of the fresh parsley. Blend until smooth.
2. Pour the soup into your serving bowl or glass and add your ice. Stir together and place in the refrigerator for 1–2 hours, or until the ice is completely melted.
3. Remove from the refrigerator and stir.
4. Combine the sour cream and water and stir together to create a smooth "cream" that you can drizzle on top of the individual servings of soup, along with a little drizzle of olive oil. Garnish with the remaining fresh parsley and serve.

FOOD FOR THOUGHT

Think of what you consider valuable. If it is simply expensive things, you may have to fight the temptation of being materialistic. If you think that valuable things are connected to memories and the faith, then you are on your way to holiness.

AUGUST 12 *(AUGUST 11)*
SAINT CLARE

Chiara Offreduccio (1194–1253), better known as Saint Clare of Assisi, was eighteen years old when she heard Saint Francis of Assisi preach and left her father's home, renouncing his plans for her to marry. With the help of Saint Francis, she founded the Order of Saint Clare (also known as the Clarisses or Poor Clares) and wrote their rule of life, the first woman in Church history to do so.

AUGUST

Saint Clare has had a nominal impact on the world, literally: several locations in North America are named after her. She is also the patron saint of television because once, when she was too ill to attend Mass, she saw and heard the Mass illuminated on the wall of her room. Is it any coincidence that Mother Angelica, founder of EWTN, was a Poor Clare? Probably, to be honest. In any event, Pope Pius XII made our saint the patroness of television in 1958.

To honor the saint, the Santa Clara convent in Mexico has given us Tortitas de Santa Clara, Santa Clara cookies. This popular Mexican treat is like a shortbread made with a pumpkin-seed glaze.

Clare is also a patron saint of good weather, a patronage that may come from the fact that her name means "clear." Filipino Catholics bribe the saint with eggs wrapped in colorful cellophane paper so they'll have clear skies on their wedding days and other important occasions. Why eggs? Perhaps because the egg whites are called *claras* in Spanish. But pious legend has it that Saint Clare received many eggs from the faithful at her monasteries as thanksgiving offerings for her powerful intercession.

Putting all of this together, enjoy our egg-rich Saint Clare's Italian Potato Frittata.

Saint Clare's Italian Potato Frittata
Serves: 4   **Cooking time: 40 minutes**

1 large potato, boiled, cooled, and cubed	2 Tbsps. butter
1 clove garlic	1 Tbsp. olive oil
1 small onion	½ tsp. salt
½ cup scallions, chopped	½ tsp. pepper
6–8 eggs, beaten	1–2 Tbsps. herbs, finely minced, for garnish
¼ cup grated parmesan cheese, divided	

1. Preheat oven to 400°F.
2. Whisk together the eggs, salt, pepper, and 2 Tbsps. of the parmesan cheese.
3. Heat the olive oil in an oven-safe pan on medium heat.
4. Sauté the onion, garlic, scallions, and potato cubes until fragrant.
5. Turn the heat up to high.
6. Add the butter and melt, making sure to grease the sides of the pan.
7. When the butter is fully melted and spread out over the entire inside of the pan, add the egg mixture.
8. Continue to cook the eggs over high heat until you see them pull away from the sides of the pan.
9. Lightly cover the pan with aluminum foil and place in the oven for about 10–12 minutes, or until the center of the eggs is firm and not jiggly.
10. Remove the pan from the oven, carefully put a large flat plate or a baking sheet over the pan, and carefully but quickly flip the pan, transferring the frittata onto the plate or baking sheet.
11. Garnish with a little more parmesan cheese and a sprinkle of herbs and serve.

FOOD FOR THOUGHT

The next time you watch TV, ask for Saint Clare's prayers that we watch only good things that help us see Jesus.

AUGUST 15
THE FEAST OF THE ASSUMPTION OF THE BLESSED VIRGIN MARY

The infallible dogma that Mary the Mother of God was "assumed," or taken up into Heaven body and soul, was not solemnly defined until 1950 by Pope Pius XII, but the belief itself stretches back to the earliest centuries of Christianity and has been celebrated liturgically since the sixth century. Among Catholic and Orthodox Christians, the only real debate has been whether the Blessed Virgin Mary died and was then assumed into Heaven or whether she was taken up to Heaven alive like Elijah. Pius XII circumvented this controversy by simply stating that the Blessed Virgin Mary, "having

AUGUST

completed the course of her earthly life, was assumed body and soul into heavenly glory."

Traditionally, the Assumption is one of the greatest feasts of the year, accompanied by grand processions and festivities. One custom is particularly interesting: the blessing of herbs and fruits, for which there is a detailed ceremony in the traditional Roman Ritual. In Germany and Poland, the feast was called "Our Lady's Herb Day." The city of Würzburg in Bavaria was once a favorite center of these blessings, which gave it its name in the twelfth century (*Würz*: spice herb). The old Roman Ritual provides a rich series of blessing of herbs and fruits on Assumption Day which read like a medieval insurance policy: lest anything be left unsaid, it prays specifically for protection against snakes (both venomous and nonvenomous), witchcraft and sorcery, and more.

There are so many herbs and fruits from which to choose! How about something with strawberries? In medieval art the strawberry is a symbol of, among other things, Mary's fruitful virginity because the plant bears both flowers and fruits at the same time. This simple but delicious dessert combines the freshness of strawberries with the sweetness of natural honey and the brightness of lemon juice and zest to create a dessert that celebrates the purity of flavors—and the flavors of purity.

Macerated Strawberries with Whipped Cream
Serves: 4   **Cooking time: 30 minutes**

2 lbs. fresh strawberries, washed, cored, and cut into ½-inch pieces

2 lemons, zested and juiced

1 cup local honey

5–6 leaves fresh mint, ripped into small pieces, plus more for garnish

2 cups heavy whipping cream

¼ cup sugar

1. Combine the strawberries, lemon zest, lemon juice, local honey, and fresh mint in a bowl and gently stir together.
2. Refrigerate for about 30 minutes.
3. In a cold bowl, combine whipping cream and sugar and whisk them together until you have created a sweetened whipped cream with soft peaks.
4. To plate, place a small dollop of whipped cream at the base of your serving dish, top with fresh strawberries, and cover with more whipped cream. Garnish with a fresh mint leaf.

FOOD FOR THOUGHT

Pure flavors are difficult to find these days because in our processed age we cover up everything with extra chemicals and artificial additives. Make a resolution to keep your cooking simple and pure, and you will discover a world of greater flavor and health. You will also have another clue into the spiritual life: keep it simple, (aspiring) saint!

AUGUST 16
SAINT ROCH

Roch (also known as Rocco, Roque, or Rock) is traditionally thought to have been born in Montpellier, France, around 1295 and to have died around 1327. En route to Rome on a pilgrimage, he encountered victims of a plague and helped them, sometimes even curing them with the sign of the cross. Eventually Saint Roch contracted the disease himself and fled to the wilderness, but he was healed by a dog that brought him bread and licked his wounds. There is a legend that upon Roch's death God promised that anyone who "calleth meekly" to Saint Roch will not be hurt by any pestilence. Accordingly, Roch is often invoked against the plague.

AUGUST

Saint Roch was a poor man in the things of this world, but he was rich in many other ways. Although we do not know why this creamy dessert is known as "Saint Roch's Fingers," we can say that every saint is like the hands and feet of Jesus, doing the Lord's will. When Roch's fingers ministered to plague victims or made the sign of the cross over them, they were like the fingers of an artist bringing the beauty of holiness and healing into the world.

Saint Roch's Fingers
Serves: 4 (dessert)   Cooking time: 1 hour

1 cup whole milk

2 egg yolks

2 Tbsps. sugar

½ tsp. salt

1 Tbsp. brandy

16 ladyfingers

1. Boil the milk on high heat for approximately 1 minute, until it scalds.
2. In a separate bowl, combine the egg yolks and sugar and whip together until the mixture has a creamy yellow consistency.
3. Add 1–2 Tbsps. of the hot milk to the egg mixture and whisk immediately. Continue adding a little bit of milk at a time and keep whisking the eggs to avoid cooking the egg mixture. Repeat this process until all the milk is fully incorporated into the egg mixture.
4. Transfer the egg mixture to a small saucepan and cook over medium to low heat, continuing to whisk until the sauce thickens. Do not allow the mixture to come to a boil.
5. When the sauce is thickened and the milk is almost evaporated, transfer it to another bowl and place into the refrigerator for 30–40 minutes to make the mixture firmer.
6. While the egg mixture is in the refrigerator, break the ladyfingers in half.
7. To assemble the dessert: Place 1–2 Tbsps. of the egg mixture in 4 ramekins or small bowls. Align the 8 ladyfinger halves in each ramekin so that they are standing upright around the sides of the bowl in the creamy egg mixture. Pour the remaining egg mixture into the ramekins, refrigerate for 20–30 minutes, and serve.

AUGUST

FOOD FOR THOUGHT
As you enjoy Saint Roch's Fingers, don't forget the faithful dog that nursed him back to health. Thank God for man's best friend!

AUGUST 17
SAINT HYACINTH

Saint Hyacinth (1185–1257) was a Polish priest who saw Saint Dominic perform a miracle and became a Dominican friar. He was one of the first Dominicans to study in Rome and was sent, along with a number of his confrères, to establish the Dominican order in Poland. On their way to their destination of Kraków they established a number of monasteries, each time leaving behind one friar as the superior. Saint Hyacinth is credited with spreading the faith throughout several other areas of northern Europe, including Prussia, Lithuania, Denmark, Sweden, Norway, and Russia, on which account he is called "the Apostle of the North."

Dumplings are pieces of dough stuffed with your favorite fillings, then boiled, steamed, or fried. Dumplings are universal, but they enjoy a pride of place in Poland, where they are known as pierogis. An old-fashioned Polish exclamation, the equivalent of our "Holy smoke!," is *Święty Jacek z pierogami!* (SHFYENT-ee YAH-tzek s pyair-o-GAH-mee!)—"Saint Hyacinth and his pierogi!"

Our simple dumpling dough recipe can be used to encase any type of stuffing. You choose. Just make sure the dumplings are properly sealed and not overstuffed.

Pious Perogies
Serves: 4   **Cooking time: 30 minutes**

2 large eggs, beaten, at room temperature

½ tsp. salt

⅓ cup warm water

2 cups all-purpose flour, or more as needed

3 Tbsps. butter

1. Add the eggs, flour, and salt to a large bowl and mix all together, adding ⅓ cup warm water a little at a time and continuing to knead until the dough is smooth and slightly elastic.
2. Form the dough into a tight ball and let it rest at room temperature for half an hour.

AUGUST

3. Prepare your preferred filling. Here you can be creative and combine cooked minced meats, vegetables, or even cream cheese and diced fruit.

4. Make the dumplings: Divide the dough into smaller pieces and make balls 2–3 inches in diameter. Flatten the balls with a rolling pin to make circular disks about 4 inches in diameter. Place a dollop (approximately 1 Tbsp.) of your chosen pierogi filling in the center of each circle.

5. Fold the pierogi dough over in half to cover the filling and make a half-moon-shaped dumpling.

6. Using a fork, crimp or press the edge of the pierogi to seal it.

7. Cook the perogies: Bring water to a boil in a large pot over high heat and melt the butter in a large skillet or frying pan over medium-high heat. Drop the perogies into the water and boil them until they begin to float. Remove them from the water and place them in the hot butter for approximately 1–2 minutes, until they start to turn yellow. Turn them over to cook for another 1–2 minutes on the other side.

FOOD FOR THOUGHT

Practice makes perfect, especially when it comes to something as traditional as making pierogis. A staple in many Polish families, dumpling-making is a disciplined craft that involves common ingredients, trial, error, and perseverance. Think of it as yet another helpful metaphor for the spiritual life.

AUGUST 18
SAINT HELENA

elen or Helena (ca. 250–330) was the consort of Emperor Constantius and the mother of Constantine, the Roman emperor who ended the imperial persecution of Christianity and supported the Church with favorable laws and donations of land and buildings. Constantine is a complex historical figure whose motives and character are not always clear, at least in the eyes of the Latin Church. But the same is not true of his unambiguously holy mother. Helen was an old woman when she journeyed to the Holy Land and, with considerable energy and discernment, successfully completely the arduous task of finding the True Cross and building churches.

Germany honors Constantine's holy mother with *Helenschnitten mit Marzipan*, Helen cookies with marzipan, but we honor her with something from the Holy Land she knew so well.

Jerusalem Falafel
Yields: 15–20 falafels   Cooking time: 1½ hours

2 cups chickpeas, drained and dried

½ cup onion, minced

2 cloves garlic, minced

1 Tbsp. flat-leaf parsley, finely minced

2 Tbsps. cilantro leaves, finely chopped

½ tsp. cayenne pepper

½ tsp. ground cumin

½ tsp. ground coriander

½ tsp. ground cardamom

½ tsp. baking powder

1 tsp. salt

1½ Tbsps. all-purpose flour or chickpea flour

oil for frying

2 Tbsps. sesame seeds

1. Add the chickpeas, onions, garlic, parsley, cilantro leaves, cayenne pepper, cumin, coriander, cardamom, baking powder, and salt to a food processor. Pulse until ingredients are thoroughly combined but almost grainy, not mushy.
2. Pour into a large bowl and stir in 3 Tbsps. water, a little at a time, to soften the mixture.
3. Add the flour and mix it in with a wooden spoon or your hands until it is fully incorporated.
4. Refrigerate for at least 1 hour.
5. In a deep pot or Dutch oven, pour oil until it is 4 inches deep and heat it over medium-high heat to 350°F.
6. Meanwhile, use a melon baller or a large spoon to gather a 1–1½–Tbsp. portion of the mixture and use your hands to form it into an oblong patty. Repeat until you have formed all the dough into 15–20 patties.
7. Sprinkle some sesame seeds and gently press them into the falafel patties.
8. When oil is hot, carefully fry 4–5 patties at a time, being careful to avoid overcrowding the pot.
9. Cook the falafels for 3–5 minutes, turning over the patties occasionally until they are golden brown.
10. Remove the patties from the hot oil and place them on a wire rack or paper towel to drain the excess oil.

AUGUST

AUGUST 21 *(AUGUST 12)*
SAINT JANE FRANCES DE CHANTAL

When Baroness Jane Frances Frémiot (1572–1641) was widowed at the age of twenty-eight, she remained a widow in order to devote herself to the education of her children. But after meeting Saint Francis de Sales, and under his spiritual direction, she gradually realized that her vocation was to become a religious and to found the Visitation Order. Not all of her children had the same insight: in order to enter the convent, Saint Jane had to step over her sobbing fifteen-year-old son, who had thrown himself to the ground in front of the doorway. Saint Jane left the boy and her house "with tears spilling down her cheeks."

Our saint has a special connection to the city of Dijon (her hometown and the place where she met Saint Francis de Sales), so tonight let us cast aside our tears and enjoy a local delicacy in her honor. Our recipe only sounds fancy. It uses basic cooking techniques and ingredients and is something that Saint Jane, who took the simple things of life and made them beautiful, would appreciate.

....

Creamy Dijon Chicken
Serves: 4   **Cooking time: 30 minutes**

2 lbs. boneless, skinless chicken breasts, cut into 4 slices ½–1 inch thick

1 tsp. salt

½ tsp. white pepper

2 Tbsps. extra virgin olive oil

1 Tbsp. butter

AUGUST

2 shallots, peeled and thinly sliced, yielding 1 cup

1 cup flour, for dredging

½ cup dry white wine

½ cup chicken broth

4 Tbsps. Dijon mustard (smooth or whole grain or a combination of both)

1 tsp. fresh thyme leaves

½ cup heavy whipping cream

1. Wash the chicken slices, dry them with paper towels, and discard the paper towels.
2. Season with salt and white pepper.
3. Dredge with the flour, discard the excess flour, and set aside the chicken.
4. In a large skillet, heat the olive oil over medium heat.
5. Add the chicken and cook for 2–3 minutes on both sides, or until slightly golden brown. Remove from the pan and set aside.
6. Add the butter to the same skillet and melt it.
7. Add the shallots and cook, stirring occasionally, and let simmer approximately 2 minutes, or until they become translucent.
8. Add the white wine to deglaze the pan, scraping the browned bits off the bottom of the pan and cooking until the wine is almost completely evaporated.
9. Add the chicken broth and cook until it begins to bubble.
10. Add the Dijon mustard and cream and stir until the sauce begins to thicken and bubble.
11. Reduce heat to low, return chicken to the pan, cover it, and let it simmer for approximately 12 minutes.

FOOD FOR THOUGHT

Every year that Mike reads his wife and children the story of how Saint Jane Frances de Chantal stepped over her sobbing son, they all debate whether she was being cold-hearted and negligent in her first vocation as a mother or whether her son was a passive-aggressive mama's boy who needed to grow up and let his mom follow her divine calling. Interestingly, every member of Mike's family varies in his or her opinion from year to year (he should have kept a log!). One thing is clear: the way we react to stories often depends on where we are in our life's journey. As an old medieval adage puts it: whatever is received is received according to the mode of the receiver. Let's try to make our "mode of receiving" more in line with the Holy Spirit's.

AUGUST

AUGUST 23
SAINT PHILIP BENIZI

Saint Philip (1233–1285) was the superior of the Servite Order. Once, when his monks ran out of food, he prayed to the Blessed Mother. No sooner had he finished when there was a knock at the door. The monks opened the door and to their surprise found ten big baskets of bread. On another occasion, Philip was sent by the pope to preach in the town of Forlì, a hotbed of anti-papal sentiment. The humble mendicant was violently attacked by an eighteen-year-old whippersnapper named Peregrine Laziosi, but after seeing how meek Philip was, Peregrine repented and joined the Servites, eventually becoming a saint himself and the patron saint of cancer (see May 1).

Tonight, give yourself a break and order out, for surely Saint Philip Benizi is the perfect unofficial patron saint of speedy food delivery.

AUGUST 25
SAINT LOUIS

The Crusader king Saint Louis IX of France (1214–1270) was brought up right by his mother Queen Blanche, who once said to him, "I love you, my dear son, as much as a mother can love her child, but I would rather see you dead at my feet than ever have you commit a mortal sin." Louis took these words to heart. As an adult he asked a friend if he would rather contract leprosy or commit a mortal sin. Without hesitation the friend chose sin. The king replied, "This is a wild, foolish answer. When a man dies, all his sicknesses end, but mortal sin is a terrible disease which does not end with death. If you love me, I beg you to choose any suffering rather than give in to mortal sin!" To make sure that he himself would never do so, Saint Louis prayed for several hours and attended two Masses every day.

Saint Louis ruled his kingdom justly and fought corruption in the administration of royal justice, setting up a court that would eventually become the French parliament. He participated in two Crusades, the second of which took his life through illness. He is the only canonized king of France, and according to the estimable Bossuet he "was the holiest and most just king who ever wore the crown."

Saint Louis was a grave and responsible monarch, but he knew the importance of occasionally keeping it light. When the religious and clerics at Saint Louis IX's table wanted to delve into serious matters, he replied: "It is not now the time to quote texts, but to divert ourselves with some cheerful conceits; let every man say what he desires, but innocently."[1] The saintly king was also a model of charity, often having poor people at his table or going to their homes to feed them himself. And we have already seen his charity at table towards Saint Thomas Aquinas, who was having a serious conversation in his own mind (see March 7).

What we have in store for tonight is a feast fit for a king. Louis may not have been from Burgundy, but as the king of France, he knew the finest his country had to offer. This meal celebrates some of France's finest flavors while hopefully creating a table for family and friends called to the heavenly banquet.

Beef Bourguignon
Serves: 4   **Cooking time: 2½ hours**

3–4 lbs. of chuck roast or other stewing beef, cut into 2-x-2-inch cubes

2½ tsps. of salt, divided

1 tsp. black pepper, divided

4 slices of thick-cut bacon, cut into ¼-inch pieces

1 medium-sized onion, finely chopped

1 large carrot, peeled and cut into ½-inch cubes

2 cloves garlic, minced

1 Tbsp. tomato paste

2 Tbsps. all-purpose flour

2 cups Burgundy red wine

1 cup beef broth

2 bay leaves

1 tsp. sugar

1 Tbsp. olive oil

2 cups pearl onions, peeled and halved

2–4 Tbsps. flat-leaf parsley, finely chopped

1. Season the beef with 2 tsps. of the salt and ¾ tsp. of the pepper and set aside for 30 minutes.
2. In a large Dutch oven or heavy-bottomed pot with a lid, cook the bacon over medium heat until crisp. Transfer crispy bacon, using a slotted spoon, to a plate lined with paper towels, but leave the bacon fat in the pot.
3. Preheat the oven to 350°F.
4. Heat the pot on high until the oil begins to smoke slightly. Carefully place the beef in the pot and sear until brown on all sides of the beef. Do this in small batches to avoid overcrowding the pot. When browned, set the beef aside.
5. Reduce heat to medium and add the onions and carrots for about 2–4 minutes, or until the onions become translucent.
6. Add the tomato paste and garlic, stir together, and cook for about 1 minute or until the paste begins to brown, stirring occasionally.
7. Add the flour and mix together.
8. Add the burgundy wine, one cup at a time, mixing together and scraping up all the browned bits from the bottom of the pot.
9. After adding all the wine, add the broth, sugar, bay leaves, and olive oil and mix ingredients all together.
10. Return the bacon and the beef to the pot and cover.
11. Cook in the oven for a total of 1½ hours, but turn the beef at the halfway cooking point.
12. Carefully remove the pot from the oven and return it to the stove.
13. Remove the cover and cook over medium-high heat.
14. Remove the bay leaves with tongs, being careful not to break up the beef, which will be very tender.
15. Add the pearl onions.
16. Taste test and add more salt and pepper if needed.
17. Cook for another 15 minutes to help thicken the sauce and cook the pearl onions.
18. Sprinkle with fresh parsley and serve.

FOOD FOR THOUGHT

A dish like this takes a long time to prepare, but it's worth the wait. In your own meditation or prayer journal, think about your prayers that God seems still not to have deigned to answer. Ask for the gift of trust in the Lord and tell yourself that when God answers your prayers, it will definitely be worth the wait.

AUGUST 28
SAINT AUGUSTINE OF HIPPO

Saint Augustine (354–430) is famous for converting to the Catholic faith after a lascivious life involving two consecutive mistresses and an illegitimate son. He went on to become the bishop of Hippo Regius in what today is Algeria, a devastating opponent of the schisms and heresies of his day, and the most influential and important of the Church Fathers (which is saying a lot: there wasn't a dud among them). His autobiography, the *Confessions*, is a spiritual masterpiece: it was the second-most-read book in Western Christendom (next to the Holy Bible) until the sixteenth century. We understand that the Hackett edition, translated by F. J. Sheed, is particularly good.

Saint Augustine can come across as a bit of a prude when it comes to physical pleasure. In his *Confessions* he frets,

This You taught me, that I should learn to take my food as a kind of medicine. But while I am passing from the pain of hunger to the satisfaction of sufficiency, in that very passage the snare of concupiscence lies in wait for me. For the passage is itself a pleasure, yet there is no other way to achieve sufficiency than that which necessity forces us to travel. And while we eat and drink for the sake of health, yet a perilous enjoyment runs at the heels of health and often enough tries to run ahead of it: so that what I say I am doing and really desire to do for my health's sake, I do in fact for the sake of the enjoyment. For there happens not to be the same measure for both: what suffices for health is too little for enjoyment; so that often it is not at all clear whether it is the necessary care of my body calling for more nourishment, or the deceiving indulgence of greed wanting to be served. Because of this uncertainty my wretched soul is glad, and uses it as a cover and an excuse, rejoicing that it does not clearly appear what is sufficient for the needs of health, so that under the cloak of health it may shelter the business of pleasure. Day after day I fight against these temptations, and I call upon Thy right hand and to Thee refer my perplexities, for I have no clear guidance upon this matter.[2]

Fair enough, dear saint. We should indeed be wary of eating as a guise for gluttonous enjoyment. And because of the power of sin, we must always be on guard against self-delusion and self-rationalization. But do you not also essentially say that every fragrance and food is an echo of the love of God?[3] Did God not give us the sweetness of honey in order to prepare us for the sweetness of spiritual joy? Ah, but we think that you knew that, and were trying to edge us along the right path in a stern but winsome way.

This is our conviction: that our North African Chicken Couscous, which honors Augustine's earthly homeland, is delicious enough to remind those at table of the love of God, but not so overpowering that it will make them forget their eternal destination. (It is, after all, chicken and not Kobe beef, wink, wink.) And our one-pot wonder takes the drama and fuss out of the kitchen while producing an authentic local dish that hits all the savory flavors and some of the sweet. It's comfort food that is easy to prepare (especially if you have chicken leftovers), and it will help you remember Saint Augustine's upbringing and his theology, which changed the world for the better. These flavors also help us remember how he, both in his marvelous life and in his marvelous writings, was a combination of savory, spicy, sweet, and above all consoling and comforting to souls.

AUGUST

North African Chicken Couscous
Serves: 4 **Cooking time: 30 minutes**

3–4 cups of water to boil the couscous

1½ cups of uncooked couscous

½ cup golden raisins

½ cup frozen orange juice concentrate

½ cup lemon juice

2 Tbsps. olive oil

2 tsps. ground cumin

1 tsp. ground coriander

1 tsp. ground cinnamon

1 tsp. salt

½ tsp. black pepper

3 cups of cooked chicken, shredded

1 red bell pepper, diced

1 cup cucumbers, diced

fresh cilantro leaves for garnish

1. In a large pot over medium-high heat, bring the water to a boil and add the couscous. Cook for 10 minutes or until the couscous is softened.
2. Reserve one cup of the starchy water and drain and discard the rest.
3. Add all of the remaining ingredients except the cilantro to the pot and stir together.
4. Cook, stirring occasionally and making sure to scrape the bottom of the pot, for 10 minutes, or until the ingredients are fully warmed and the consistency of the mixture is like a very chunky fried rice.
5. If the ingredients begin to stick to the bottom of the pot, add a little starchy water, stir the mixture, and scrape the bottom of the pot.
6. Serve with a garnish of cilantro leaves.

FOOD FOR THOUGHT

Saint Augustine was known for praying to be given the grace of purity, only "not yet." While he wanted God's fullness, he was not completely willing to give up his sinful habits. In your own prayers, identify what sins or vices you are holding onto and ask God's grace to help you to let go and let God eradicate them…now!

AUGUST

AUGUST 30 *(AUGUST 23)*
SAINT ROSE OF LIMA

Rose of Lima (1586–1617), born in the capital of Peru, was named Isabella, but she was called Rose because a servant saw her face as an infant transformed by a mystical rose. As she matured, Rose's beauty became a problem, attracting the unwanted attention of male admirers. Her solution was simple: she rubbed her face with peppers until it was swollen and unsightly. Rose took a vow of chastity as a Third Order Dominican, practiced extreme asceticism, and helped the poor and sick before dying at the age of thirty-one. She is the first canonized saint born in the Western Hemisphere and the patroness of South America.

Rose had Incan blood in her veins from her mother's side and is the patron saint of Peru and the Americas' indigenous peoples. Peru's cuisine is a remarkable fusion of South American and even Asian flavors. Today, fusion dishes such as "ceviche" sound like high society, but we must remember that this kind of cooking was originally for simple people who didn't have much. In the Peruvian summers, dishes like this would give ordinary folks great flavors and nutrition without a lot of cooking fuss.

Peruvian Ceviche
Serves: 4   **Cooking time: 20–30 minutes**

2 lbs. mahi mahi filets (or substitute another white fish)

3–4 lemons, juiced, yielding at least ½ cup of juice

6–8 limes, juiced, yielding at least ½ cup of juice

1 shallot, finely minced

2–3 habanero peppers, deseeded and minced

½ cup of cilantro leaves

1 tsp. grated (fresh) ginger

1 Tbsp. soy sauce

pinch of salt

dash of chili sauce (optional)

4 cups ice

AUGUST

1. Cut the fish filets into equal 1-inch cubes and refrigerate.
2. Put the ice in a large bowl and place a smaller bowl on top of the ice.
3. To the top bowl, add the lemon juice, lime juice, shallots, habanero peppers, ginger, and soy sauce and mix all together.
4. Add the fish and carefully fold it into the juices, making sure that all of it is equally coated.
5. Refrigerate for about 30 minutes, stirring the fish around after 15 minutes: when the acid in the citrus juices has "cooked" the fish, the fish will turn opaque and tender, as if it has been cooked by heat. (But it must remain chilled during this process.)
6. Discard the bowl of ice and scoop out equal amounts of fish and juice into 4 individual bowls or serving cups.
7. Put a dash of salt on top of the fish, add a few dashes of chili sauce (optional), garnish with cilantro, and serve with taro or fried plantain chips.

FOOD FOR THOUGHT

The story of Rose rubbing her cheeks with peppers hits us like a punch in the face. In an age that idolatrizes beauty, it sounds strange to make oneself less attractive, especially for the sake of keeping *other* people from committing the sin of lust. And yet, doesn't our own age employ techniques that mar beauty? When he worked in prison ministry, Mike met female inmates who shared with him that they got tattoos on their neck and face to tell the world to stay away from them; after more sober reflection, they regretted their decision. Let us reflect on why we make ourselves beautiful and why we make ourselves ugly. There could be spiritual dangers to both options.

CHAPTER 9

September Saints

SEPTEMBER

SEPTEMBER 2 *(AUGUST 16)*
SAINT STEPHEN OF HUNGARY

When Vajk, duke of Hungary (967–1038), was baptized at the age of ten by Saint Adalbert, he was renamed Stephen. Later crowned by the pope, Stephen became Hungary's first king. He was a devout Catholic who introduced many of his people to the faith, established bishoprics, founded monasteries, and greatly enhanced the welfare of the country. Saint Stephen was devoted to Mary the Mother of God, and he dedicated Hungary to Our Lady of the Assumption. Fittingly, he died on August 15, the feast of the Assumption. In 1696, Pope Innocent XI assigned his feast on September 2, the day on which Emperor Leopold won back Buda, the ancient capital of the Kingdom of Hungary, from the Turks. In Hungary, on the other hand, his feast is kept on August 20, the day that his relics were transferred. In the new 1969 Roman calendar, his feast falls on August 16.

The Hungarian classic beef stew known as "goulash" (pronounced GOY-ash) takes the fruits of the harvest and puts them in a dish that is as diverse as the regions of the old Austro-Hungarian Empire. There are different styles of goulash, but they all have the power to bring the family together for a shared meal. Our recipe for this one-pot wonder is an intimidation-free version of the classic recipe.

Hungarian Goulash
Serves: 4–6   **Cooking time: 1½–2 hours**

4 Tbsps. lard (or substitute butter, tallow, or bacon grease)

2 large onions, chopped

¼ cup Hungarian sweet paprika

1½ lbs. stewing beef, cut into ½-inch cubes

5 cloves garlic, minced

2 red bell peppers, deseeded and cut into ½-inch pieces

2 tomatoes, diced

2 carrots, peeled and diced into ½-inch pieces

2 medium-sized potatoes, peeled and cut into ½-inch cubes

5 cups beef broth

1 bay leaf

2 tsps. salt

1 tsp. black pepper

½ tsp. crushed caraway seeds (or substitute fennel seeds)

optional: sour cream for the end of the cooking process

1. Melt the lard (or butter, tallow, or bacon grease) in a large soup pot or Dutch oven on medium-high heat.
2. Add the onions and sauté until translucent, approximately 5 minutes, stirring occasionally.
3. Add the beef and cook until it starts to brown, approximately 7–10 minutes, stirring occasionally.
4. Add the bell peppers, tomatoes, and garlic and cook until the peppers become tender, approximately 5 minutes, stirring occasionally.
5. Lower the heat and add the paprika, salt, pepper, and caraway seeds (or fennel seeds) and stir until fragrant, approximately 2–3 minutes.
6. Add the beef broth and the bay leaf, turn the heat to high, and bring to a boil.
7. Reduce the heat to medium and add the potatoes, carrots, and salt and pepper to taste.
8. Cover the pot and simmer for another 40 minutes.
9. Test to make sure the beef is nice and tender and add more salt or pepper according to your preference. Remove and discard the bay leaf.
10. Serve in individual bowls with crusty bread.
11. Optional: add 1 Tbsp. of sour cream to each serving.

FOOD FOR THOUGHT

When a king is humble and rules according to the mercy and justice of Jesus Christ, he becomes more than a king: he becomes a true father, a parent of his people. Consider how parents have a responsibility to "rule" their family not as authoritarians but as servants, in the same way Saint Stephen served the people of Hungary.

SEPTEMBER 3 *(AUGUST 21)*
SAINT PIUS X

The future Pope Pius X (1835–1914) was born Joseph Sarto in Riese, Italy, the son of the town mailman. The family's humble circumstances did not stop little Giuseppe from being generous to a fault. His sisters had to hide his laundry because when "Beppi," as he was called, came across a poor person, he would literally give him the shirt off his back! Joseph grew up to be a fine parish priest, bishop, patriarch of Venice, and pope.

As supreme pontiff, Pius X worked to restore the liturgy to its proper place in people's hearts. He promoted Gregorian chant, frequent reception of Holy Communion, and active participation in the Mass (a concept much misunderstood these days, but that's not his fault). Saint Pius X also declared war on the heresy of Modernism, which is the infatuation with all things modern to the detriment of the ancient and unchanging faith.

Saint Pius X's hometown of Treviso is famous for its unique radicchio, a bitter leaf, purple in color, that has similar properties to chicory and endive. It's included in many Italian dishes as a main flavor profile and not simply a garnish. This roasted radicchio salad recipe is healthy, hearty, and delicious. It's a great way to remember a saint who helped to keep the Church in good health.

Roasted Radicchio di Treviso with Ricotta Cream
Serves: 4   **Cooking time: 30 minutes**

1 head radicchio, cut into quarters

3 Tbsps. extra virgin olive oil, divided

1 Tbsp. kosher salt, divided

1 lemon, zested and juiced

1 cup ricotta cheese

1 clove garlic, finely minced

1 Tbsp. fresh herbs (mint, basil, or parsley), minced

1. Place the radicchio quarters in a large bowl, drizzle with olive oil, and season with 1 tsp. of the kosher salt. Set aside for about 10 minutes to marinate and draw out some of the bitterness.
2. In a separate bowl, combine the ricotta cheese, lemon juice, lemon zest, 1 Tbsp. of the olive oil, and 1 tsp. of the salt. Mix all together and set aside.
3. To a frying pan over medium-high heat, add the olive oil. When the oil begins to smoke, lower the heat to medium, add the radicchio, and cook until it begins to char and wilt, using tongs to stir occasionally and break the leaves apart so that all of them cook.
4. Add the garlic and sauté for another 2–3 minutes, or until the oil is fragrant and the radicchio is wilted but not flimsy or mushy.
5. To plate, add a dollop of the ricotta sauce to a plate and smear it in any design, add the radicchio on top, and finish with a pinch of the remaining kosher salt and a sprinkle of herbs.

FOOD FOR THOUGHT

Physical health can serve as a metaphor for spiritual health. Health begins with eating healthy foods, like this radicchio salad for the body, but it also includes digesting the spiritual teachings of great saints. Think about what you need in order to be healthier in body, mind, and spirit.

SEPTEMBER 5
SAINT TERESA OF CALCUTTA

A good litmus test of a person's basic decency is whether he or she smiles at the sight of a little child—or at a photograph of Mother Teresa (1910–1997). It is difficult not to be moved by Blessed Teresa of Calcutta's signature radiant smile, her incredible story of helping India's most helpless poor and sick, and her successful founding of the Missionaries of Charity, which today has over 4,500 sisters in 133 countries who run orphanages, schools, missions, shelters, AIDS hospices, and charity centers.

Mother Teresa was born Anjezë Gonxhe ("Agnes Rosebud") Bojaxhiu to Albanian parents in what was at the time the Ottoman Empire. She first joined the Loreto Sisters and took the name Teresa after Saint Thérèse of Lisieux (she chose the Spanish spelling because another nun had already taken "Thérèse"). Later, she answered a call from God to serve the "poorest of the poor" and to start her own order. Some of Mother Teresa's letters were published posthumously, revealing her spiritual struggles, in which she experienced a great "silence and emptiness." Some critics tooted this as a "crisis of faith," but anyone who is familiar with Saint Ignatius of Loyola or Teresa of Ávila's writings on spiritual dryness or Saint John of the Cross's "dark night of the soul" knows that such trials have been part of the process of sanctification in the lives of many great saints.

Our recipe for the day is inspired by a famous dish from Mother Teresa's native Albania along with a hint of India, the country where she served the poorest of the poor and fed them with more than just bodily sustenance.

Fërgëse alla Teresa of Calcutta
Serves: 4   **Cooking time: 1 hour**

5 red bell peppers	2 Tbsps. Greek yogurt
2 Tbsps. olive oil for roasting the peppers	2 Tbsps. fresh basil, chopped
1 medium-sized onion, diced	1 tsp. salt
2 tomatoes, chopped	1 tsp. black pepper
1½ cups feta cheese	1 tsp. curry powder
2 Tbsps. butter	2 Tbsps. fresh parsley, minced
2 tsps. all-purpose flour	

1. Preheat the oven to broil. Rub the peppers with a little olive oil and place them on a baking dish. Roast the peppers by placing the baking dish on the lower rack of the oven and cooking them until they are blackened. Turn the peppers occasionally to char them on all sides. Remove them from the oven, put them in a bowl, cover it with plastic wrap, and let them rest for about 20 minutes.
2. Turn the oven from broil to bake and lower the temperature to 350°F.
3. When the peppers are cool, peel off the burned skin, remove the seeds, and cut them into thin strips.

4. In a Dutch oven or a heavy-bottomed pot over medium-high heat, heat the olive oil and sauté the onions until translucent, approximately 5 minutes.

5. Add the chopped tomatoes and bell peppers and allow the juices to simmer, approximately 5 minutes, stirring occasionally.

6. Make a roux: In a separate small saucepan, melt the butter over medium heat, add the flour, and stir with a whisk until the mixture forms a paste. Add the yogurt and feta and continue stirring to create a thick sauce.

7. Add the roux to the vegetable mixture and stir all together.

8. Add the curry and mix together.

9. Transfer to a baking dish and cook for 30 minutes.

10. Carefully remove from the oven and garnish with minced fresh parsley.

FOOD FOR THOUGHT

Mother Teresa was known for saying, "Do small things with great love." Consider some small act of kindness for five people today, and do them with love and prayerful devotion. You may discover that even the smallest acts of kindness can be difficult, but they are made easier with even the smallest of prayers.

SEPTEMBER 12
FEAST OF THE HOLY NAME OF MARY

If you are wondering why there is a feast honoring the name of the Mother of God, consider a story about Saint Francis. When the saint compelled the devil to admit what he was afraid of, he mentioned three things: the Holy Name of Jesus, the brown scapular, and the Holy Name of Mary.

The first Feast of the Holy Name of Mary took place in 1513 on September 15, the octave day of her nativity (as faithful Jews, Saints Joachim and Anne would have named their daughter Mary eight days after her birth). Over time, however, the feast moved around to various dates, eventually landing on September 12, thanks in large part to the Battle of Vienna in 1683. The battle pitted a beleaguered city, at the time the eastern outpost of Western Christendom, against a much larger and superior army from the Ottoman Empire led by the formidable strategist Kara Mustafa. If Vienna had fallen, the Turks would have quite possibly taken the rest of Western Europe. However, the king of Poland, John Sobieski, staged a spectacular counterattack with a coalition of troops from various Catholic countries, thus essentially ending Ottoman aggression in the region and saving Europe from Muslim conquest.

Both croissants and cappuccinos are said to come from the Battle of Vienna. According to one legend, the Turks had tried to tunnel under the city's walls in the early morning. A baker heard them and notified the Viennese troops, who staged a counterattack of their own. After the battle, the baker was rewarded with a patent to produce a bread commemorating the victory over the Turks, whose flag bore a crescent, the symbol of Islam. The result: the croissant, which is French for crescent.

As for the cappuccino, Blessed Marco d'Aviano was a Capuchin monk, a powerful preacher of repentance, and a priest whose blessings miraculously cured many sick and infirm. According to Pope Saint John Paul II, d'Aviano was also instrumental in promoting unity among the Catholic powers seeking to defend themselves from Ottoman aggression in the seventeenth century. On the eve of the Battle of Vienna, d'Aviano rallied Catholic and Protestant troops, boosting their morale and helping them gain victory the following day. But d'Aviano is better remembered for what happened afterwards. According to legend, he found sacks of coffee beans that the Turkish forces had left behind in their haste. D'Aviano brewed himself a cup, but finding it too bitter for his taste he added milk and honey, thus turning the coffee brown. The grateful Viennese dubbed the drink, "little Capuchin," or cappuccino, in honor of d'Aviano, whose Capuchin habit was the same color.

Marco d'Aviano was beatified by Pope John Paul II on April 27, 2003, the penultimate step to canonization. As one journalist quipped, however, d'Aviano is "already a saint in the eyes of many."

Guess what you are having for breakfast this morning! Baking a croissant is difficult, even with Saint Jude's help (patron of impossible cases). Feel free to patronize your local baker instead. On the other hand, making a unique cappuccino, infused with local honey, is not only doable but a delicious way to remember the name of Mary, our sweet spiritual Mother.

Honey-Infused Cappuccino

Serves: 1   **Cooking time: 5 minutes**

2 shots espresso   1 tsp. honey

2 Tbsps. cream

1. Make your espresso as you would normally prepare it and it put into a regular-sized coffee cup or mug.
2. Heat the cream in a small saucepan over low heat and, when it begins to steam, use a frother to create foam.
3. Add the honey to the warm and frothy cream.
4. Pour the honeyed cream directly into the espresso and stir.

FOOD FOR THOUGHT

On this holy day celebrating the power of Mary's holy name, let us remember the power of her perpetual help. Say a Hail Mary in thanksgiving to God for giving us an intercessor such as Our Lady.

SEPTEMBER 17
SAINT HILDEGARD

Known as the "Sibyl of the Rhine" for her poetic prophecies, Saint Hildegard of Bingen (1098–1179) was born to a noble German family and entered the cloister of Disibodenberg before founding her own convents at Rupertsberg and Bingen. Her reputation for prophecy and holiness spread (against her will), and soon Hildegard was corresponding with kings and popes. Hildegard composed several dozen hymns, in addition to writing over three hundred letters and fifteen books on subjects ranging from theology to natural science. Most of Hildegard's works are still available today, and one hundred albums feature her musical compositions. In

2012, Pope Benedict XVI declared Saint Hildegard a Doctor of the Church, the fourth woman in history to receive that honor.

Hildegard had a keen interest in medicine and healing and was ahead of her time as an herbalist. As such, she knew how to make healthy food digestible and delicious. Her Cookies of Joy, she claimed, "remove hate from the heart" and "give one a joyful spirit." Who are we to gainsay a Doctor of the Church?

Here is our slight tweaking of Hildegard's classic cookie. You can use regular flour for this recipe, but the original ingredient of spelt flour is better.

Saint Hildegard's Cookies of Joy, Hildegardplätzchen
Yields: 10–12 cookies   **Cooking time: 30 minutes**

¾ cup soft butter at room temperature

1 cup brown sugar

1 egg, beaten

1 tsp. baking powder

1 pinch salt

1½ cups spelt flour (or substitute all-purpose flour)

1 tsp. ground cinnamon

½ tsp. ground nutmeg

½ tsp. ground ginger

½ tsp. ground cloves

1. Preheat oven to 350°F and grease and flour a baking dish.
2. Add the softened room-temperature butter, brown sugar, and egg to a large bowl and mix together until creamy.
3. Sift the flour, baking powder, cinnamon, pinch of salt, nutmeg, ginger, and cloves together and add to the moist ingredients.
4. Form dough balls about 1½ inches in diameter, place them on the prepared baking dish, and carefully flatten each ball into a small cookie about ⅛ inch thick.
5. Bake for 12–15 minutes, or until just golden brown.
6. Remove, cool on a rack for 5–10 minutes, and serve.

FOOD FOR THOUGHT

As a learned naturalist and a woman of deep devotion, Saint Hildegard knew that faith requires a combination of inspiration and education, a balance of head and heart. A heart-driven faith sometimes shies away from the theological side of things, while the overly educated believer may forget that faith involves emotion, the visceral awareness of and response to divine and human realities. Consider which type of believer you are, and ask God for a better balance through Saint Hildegard's intercession and example.

SEPTEMBER 19
SAINT JANUARIUS

Little is known of the life of this fourth-century martyr and bishop of Benevento (d. 305), but much is known about his posthumous career. According to the Roman martyrology, after Saint Januarius was beheaded, his body was brought to Naples "and there honourably interred in the church, where his holy blood is kept unto this day in a phial of glass, which being set near his head becomes liquid and bubbles up as though it were fresh." The head and the dried blood are brought together several times a year (including on today's feast), egged on by a group of poor women known as the *zie di San Gennaro* (aunts of Saint Januarius) who "make themselves specially conspicuous by the fervour, and sometimes, when the miracle is delayed, by the extravagance, of their supplications." When even the saint's melodramatic aunts cannot convince him to effect the desired miracle, impending disaster is predicted. In 1941, when the dry red powder in the phial failed to liquefy, Mount Vesuvius erupted. Another time, when liquefaction did not occur and Vesuvius began to rumble, twenty thousand pilgrims processed up the volcano with Saint Januarius's skull. Their prayers were heard, and the lava ceased flowing.

This skewered sword fish is a fine example of the seafood flavors of Naples, where San Gennaro shepherded his people. And the red chili pepper oil reminds us of the blood that was shed for his faith that usually liquefies on his feast day.

SEPTEMBER

San Gennaro Pesce Spada Spiedini
Serves: 4   **Cooking time: 40 minutes**

2 lbs. filets of swordfish

2 Peppadew peppers, deseeded and minced

2 serrano chilis, deseeded and minced

2 tsps. salt, divided

1 tsp. garlic powder

2 Tbsps. olive oil, divided

1 tsp. dried oregano

1 lemon, zested and juiced

4 wooden skewers

1. Soak 4 skewers in water.
2. Cut the swordfish into 1-inch cubes and place in a bowl.
3. Season the fish with the garlic powder, 1 tsp. of the salt, 1 Tbsp. of the olive oil, and the lemon zest.
4. Make the chili oil: In a separate bowl, combine the Peppadew peppers, serrano chilis, oregano, lemon juice, and the remaining 1 tsp. salt and 1 Tbsp. olive oil. Mix together and set aside.
5. Divide the fish cubes into four equal parts, impale a quarter of the cubes on the first skewer, packing the cubes tightly together, and repeat for the other three skewers.
6. Heat a grill pan over high heat and lightly brush it with olive oil.
7. When the grill pan begins to smoke, lower the heat to medium, place the skewers of fish onto the pan, leaving some space between the skewers, and cook for 2 minutes on each side.
8. After all sides of the fish show some grill marks, remove the skewers from the pan and set them on a plate.
9. Spoon the chili oil directly onto the skewers of fish and serve immediately.

FOOD FOR THOUGHT

Many people think of Christian martyrdom as a thing of the distant past, but there were more Christians killed for their faith in the twentieth century (more than one million, in fact) than in all previous centuries combined. In the contemporary Western world, we do not usually live under the threat of martyrdom, but we do experience a type of soft martyrdom when people try to "cancel" us for our beliefs. Tonight, pray for protection with the intercession of this popular saint whose blood is still fresh (at least on this day) and for the people who belittle us because of our faith. Maybe you can even win them over with a delicious meal.

SEPTEMBER 20
SAINT EUSTACE AND COMPANIONS

According to legend, Saint Eustace (or Eustachius) and his wife and sons were roasted alive in a bronze bull for refusing to sacrifice to the gods in the second century AD. Eustace went on to become one of the Fourteen Holy Helpers, invoked against family discord.

Eustace is also associated with the same legend surrounding Saint Hubert, namely, that he converted to Christianity while hunting when he saw a miraculous cross between a stag's antlers. Understandably, Eustace is now a patron saint of hunters.

In the piazza of San Eustachio in Rome, you may find a local restaurant that serves an amazing pasta dish flavored with pistachio nuts. Not only is it surprisingly delicious, but its name, "Eustachio Pistachio Pasta," is a delight to utter. It certainly beats a pot roast in Eustace's honor, given the details of his martyrdom.

Eustachio Pistachio Pasta
Serves: 4–6　　　　**Cooking time: 30 minutes**

1 lb. penne pasta

½ cup pistachio nuts, shells removed and roughly chopped

1 Italian sausage

1 clove garlic, minced

1 shallot, minced

¼ cup white wine

½ cup parmesan cheese, grated

½ cup heavy whipping cream

2 Tbsps. fresh herbs (parsley, basil, oregano, thyme, or a combination), minced

1. Cook pasta according to the instructions on the package, but reduce the cooking time by 1–2 minutes, until the penne is cooked al dente.

2. While pasta is cooking, remove and discard the casing from the sausage and cook the sausage in a large sauté pan over medium heat. Use wooden spoons to break up the sausage into smaller pieces.

3. When the sausage is almost completely browned, add the garlic and shallots and cook together for about 2 minutes.
4. Add the white wine to deglaze the pan, making sure to scrape the browned bits from the bottom, and cook for 1–2 minutes.
5. Add the pistachios, cheese, and whipping cream and allow the sauce to come to a light simmer.
6. When the pasta is cooked, reserve a cup of the starchy water, drain and discard the rest of the water, add the pasta immediately to the pan of sauce, and stir together.
7. Add ¼ cup of the parmesan cheese and mix all together.
8. If the sauce is too thick, add a little of the reserved pasta water, a little at a time, and mix until you achieve the desired consistency.
9. Serve the pasta with another sprinkle of parmesan cheese and a garnish of the herbs.

FOOD FOR THOUGHT

Saint Eustace saw a miraculous cross between a buck's antlers that led to his conversion. Feel free to use venison sausage in this recipe instead of pork. Either way, share this meal with your hunting or military friends. They'll be impressed by how pistachio nuts can be part of a real meal and not just something to snack on while drinking beer.

SEPTEMBER 23
SAINT PIO OF PIETRELCINA

The Capuchin priest Francesco Forgione (1887–1968) is better known to the world as Padre Pio. As a boy he was already eager for the ascetical life (his mother had to stop him from sleeping on the floor with a stone pillow), and he was already having mystical visions: he had two-way conversations with Jesus, the Blessed Virgin, and his guardian angel, and he was surprised to learn that not everyone else did too.

The first priest to receive the stigmata (Saint Francis of Assisi was a deacon), Padre Pio was renowned even in his lifetime for his bilocation and miracles, his spiritual suffering, his

physical battles with the devil and other demons, and his reading of people's hearts. Once, a young Polish priest visited the holy man and went to him for confession. Afterwards Padre Pio told the cleric that he would one day ascend to "the highest post in the Church, though further confirmation is needed." The young priest was Karol Wojtyła, the future Pope Saint John Paul II. Padre Pio continues to astound today: forty years after his death, his body remains mostly incorrupt.

Saint Padre Pio was known to love broccoli rabe. This recipe is healthy, comforting, and even a little spicy. We feel that it captures the personality of this adorable and formidable saint, who was known for speaking to the heart of people who came to him for confession, even if he sometimes had to put the heat on some of his penitents.

Rapini (Italian Broccoli Rabe)
Serves: 4 (as a side dish)   **Cooking time: 10 minutes**

1 lb. of broccoli rabe, washed and the stems trimmed

2 cloves garlic, minced

1 Tbsp. olive oil

1 tsp. chili pepper flakes

½ lemon, juiced and zested

2 tsps. aged balsamic vinegar

2 Tbsps. parmesan cheese, grated

1. Wash the broccoli rabe and use a peeler and paring knife to shave off and trim some of the bottom stems to make it more tender.
2. In a large sauté pan over medium-high, heat the olive oil until it begins to smoke and then lower the heat to medium.
3. Add the broccoli and cook for 1–2 minutes on each side.
4. When all sides have been sautéed, add the chili pepper flakes, 2 Tbsps. of water, and the lemon zest and juice, cover the pan, and cook for about 3–5 minutes.
5. Plate the broccoli rabe and pour the juice from the pan over it.
6. Drizzle with the balsamic vinegar and sprinkle with the parmesan cheese.
7. Serve with crusty bread to make a nice meal or a delicious side dish.

SEPTEMBER

FOOD FOR THOUGHT

Padre Pio was attacked not only by demons but by his own Church. In 1923, envious enemies succeeded in preventing him from teaching teenagers on the grounds that he was "a noxious Socrates"(!), and for several *years* the Vatican banned him from celebrating Mass publicly or even giving spiritual direction. That's the same Vatican, incidentally, that later canonized him.

Whenever you experience rejection at the hands of your spiritual brethren (or superiors) for simply trying to live out the faith, remember that you are not alone: in fact, you are in very good company, starting with Jesus and stretching all the way up to Padre Pio and beyond. Respond to persecution, then, like Jesus and Padre Pio, by enduring the injustice patiently and praying, "Father, forgive them, for they know not what they do."

SEPTEMBER 27 *(SEPTEMBER 26)*
SAINTS COSMAS AND DAMIAN

These brothers, possibly twins, hailed from Arabia and became physicians famous for their miraculous skills. Their exploit that has attracted the most attention from later generations of artists is when they reputedly grafted the leg of a recently deceased Ethiopian onto a European whose leg had to be amputated.

Around AD 287, Cosmas and Damian were tortured for the faith and beheaded. In the Eastern churches, these martyrs are among a group of saints called "Unmercenary Physicians," physician-saints who accepted no payment but worked purely for love for God and neighbor. In the Latin Church, Cosmas and Damian are mentioned in the Litany of the Saints and the Canon of the Mass (Eucharistic Prayer I in the new Roman Rite).

These caring doctors knew that herbs and spices have great healing properties. The Arabian-inspired recipe below includes a spice rub that will help wake up your tastebuds and maybe even your faith.

Chicken Kabsa

Serves: 4 **Cooking time: 40 minutes**

THE SPICE RUB

½ tsp. ground cardamom

½ tsp. white pepper

¼ tsp. saffron

½ tsp. ground cinnamon

½ tsp. ground allspice

1 lime, zested and juiced

2 tsps. of salt

½ tsp. cayenne pepper

½ tsp. paprika

2 Tbsps. olive oil

1 tsp. garlic powder

1. In a bowl, combine the cardamom, white pepper, saffron, cinnamon, allspice, lime zest and juice, cayenne pepper, garlic powder, paprika, and olive oil and mix to form a paste.

THE GLAZE

½ cup orange juice

2 Tbsps. honey

2 Tbsps. olive oil

1. Combine the orange juice, olive oil, and honey in a small bowl and mix together.

THE CHICKEN

4 chicken leg quarters

1. Score the chicken quarters, cutting 3–4 slits on the meaty side of each leg.
2. Coat every side of all 4 chicken legs with the spice rub, applying it as evenly as possible, and then allow the chicken to marinate at least 2 hours.
3. Heat your outdoor grill or a grill pan to medium-high heat and brush it with a light coating of olive oil.
4. Place your chicken on the grill or pan, bone-side down, exposing the part of the chicken that was scored.
5. Brush the chicken with the glaze.
6. Cook the chicken on the grill for 10–15 minutes, brushing on more of the glaze every 2–4 minutes and cooking until the skin is crispy brown and the internal temperature is 160°F.
7. Remove the chicken from the grill and rest for 5 minutes before serving with your favorite side dishes.

SEPTEMBER

FOOD FOR THOUGHT

Saints Cosmas and Damian were Arab strangers in a foreign, Roman land. Allow your taste buds to go outside their comfort zone and be open to different spices and ingredients. Think of yourself as a culinary pilgrim, seeking for foods that satisfy and inspire as you travel toward your heavenly destination.

SEPTEMBER 28
SAINT LORENZO RUIZ

Saint Lorenzo Ruiz de Manila (1594–1637) lived up to his name. Like his namesake Saint Lawrence (August 10), this martyr for the Church endured incredible tortures for the faith. A Chinese-Filipino from Binondo, Manila, with a wife, two sons, and a daughter, Lorenzo had to leave his native land when he was falsely accused of killing a Spaniard. He and several Catholic priests sailed to Japan. Alas, the Tokugawa shogunate was persecuting Christians out of a fear that the faith was a Trojan horse for Spanish invasion. After two years of imprisonment, Lorenzo was subjected to the Japanese torture of *tsuruchi* (made famous by Shusaku Endo's 1966 *Silence*), in which the victim was hung upside down over a pit; one hand was left free so that the person could signal their desire to apostasize. But Lorenzo, like Lawrence, did not. We relay his last words in the "Food for Thought" section. Appropriately, Saint Lorenzo Ruiz is considered the protomartyr of the Philippines.

To honor Saint Lorenzo Ruiz's Chinese-Filipino ancestry, enjoy some Pancit Canton. This noodle dish is a fusion of Chinese and Filipino flavors and a signature dish in Binondo, Saint Lorenzo Ruiz's earthly homeland. There is a Filipino tradition of eating long noodles on major feast days to ensure a long life. Although Italy is known for its pasta, noodles originally come from Asia. This dish is a fusion of ingredients from the Philippines and China, creating a delicious savory noodle without any sauce.

Pancit Canton
Serves: 4   **Cooking time: 1 hour**

1 package of Pancit Canton noodles

1 Tbsp. canola or vegetable oil

1 boneless, skinless chicken breast, cut into small strips

8–12 shrimp, cleaned, deveined, and shelled

2 links of sausage, cut diagonally

1 large carrot, julienned

2 stalks of celery, thinly cut on the bias

½ white onion, sliced thinly

1 Tbsp. fresh ginger, grated

2 cloves garlic, minced

½ cabbage, sliced thinly, yielding 2 cups

2 Tbsps. soy sauce

2 Tbsps. oyster sauce

2 tsps. sesame seed oil

1 cup chicken broth

1 tsp. salt, to taste

2 hardboiled eggs, cut into wedges

2 Tbsps. celery leaves

1. Soak the noodles in hot water until tender, then drain and set aside for approximately 10 minutes.
2. To a large pan or wok, add 1 Tbsp. of cooking oil and heat over medium heat.
3. Add the chicken and sauté for 3–5 minutes.
4. Add the shrimp and cook another 3–5 minutes.
5. Remove the chicken and shrimp and set aside.
6. To the same pan or wok, add the carrots, celery, onion, ginger, and garlic and sauté approximately 3 minutes, until the carrots are softened and the onions become translucent.
7. Return the chicken and shrimp to the pan.
8. Add the soy sauce, oyster sauce, sesame seed oil, and chicken broth and stir until the mixture begins to boil.
9. Reduce the heat to medium-low, add the noodles and the cabbage, and cook until the noodles are warmed through and all the ingredients are fully incorporated.
10. Taste and add salt as needed.
11. Top with hard-boiled egg wedges and celery leaves and serve.

SEPTEMBER

FOOD FOR THOUGHT

According to Latin missionary accounts, Saint Lorenzo's last words were: "I am a Catholic, and with a quick and ready spirit I accept death for God. Had I a thousand lives, I would offer them all to Him." Dear God, give us and ours the quick and ready spirit of Saint Lorenzo!

While it may be a superstition for Filipinos to eat noodles on feast days as a way to prolong their lives, Saint Lorenzo Ruiz teaches us the way to eternal life by teaching the faith and living it fully, even if it means dying as a martyr. Ask yourself what you think will help you and your family live longer and fuller lives, and then ask God to find His course for you and the ones you love.

SEPTEMBER 29
SAINT MICHAEL

In the (post–Vatican II) ordinary form of the Roman Rite, today is the combined feast of the archangels Michael, Gabriel, and Raphael; in the (1962) traditional calendar, each archangel has his own feast day. From the Middle Ages to the nineteenth century, the feast of Saint Michael, or "Michaelmas" (pronounced MICK-el-mus), was celebrated as a major holy day. Michaelmas fairs, parades, plays, and similar events were held in honor of the great archangel who cast Satan into hell. Michael is further honored as the guardian angel of the Church Militant, the "banner bearer" who conducts souls to Purgatory and Heaven, and the *praepositus* or "governor" of Heaven (in contrast to Lucifer, who is the "ruler" of Hell).

Michaelmas was also known as "Devil's Spit Day." According to an Irish-English legend, when Lucifer was cast out of Heaven he is said to have fallen on a blackberry bush and angrily spit on it. Consequently, one can eat blackberries on but not after Michaelmas Day, September 29 (or, in those parts of England that unofficially held on to the Julian calendar, Old Michaelmas Day, October 11).

There are several culinary traditions surrounding Michaelmas. One is to make waffles baked in a gaufrette iron. For a pancake alternative, see March 25. In Scotland, the treat of the day was Saint Michael's Bannock, or Struan Micheil. This large scone-like cake is traditionally "made from cereals grown on the family's land during the year, representing the fruits of the fields, and is cooked on a lamb skin, representing the fruit of the flocks." When the eldest daughter of the family made the bannock she prayed: "Progeny and prosperity of family, Mystery of Michael, Protection of the Trinity." You can honor this tradition by borrowing the bannock recipe for Lammas Day (see August 1).

Scottish women would harvest carrots on this day with a three-pronged mattock, digging triangular holes. (No doubt they did so in honor of the Holy Trinity, whom Saint Michael serves so well, but the mattock can also symbolize a trident in the hands of the archangel.)

And the main course was roasted goose. On "Goose Day" (as Michaelmas is also called), farmers held "goose fairs" and brought their geese to market. A Michaelmas goose was an appropriate way to celebrate the end of the harvest in Ireland and England, especially when the bird in question was a "stubble goose," an adult that had grown plump on the stubble of the wheat fields. A large-winged creature makes a fitting tribute to an angel, and a nice fat goose auspiciously evokes the financial hopes of the quarter days. Hence the old superstition:

> Eat a goose on Michaelmas Day,
> Want not for money all the year.

Michaelmas geese were popular in Ireland and England and have recently experienced a minor comeback in Great Britain. But if roasting a goose is too much trouble (even with the promise of money!), how about a delicious duck? Duck was also a popular option for Michaelmas in medieval times. And when it comes to duck recipes, ours is a surefire, easy, and delicious way to get the duck crispy yet juicy, savory yet sweet, and quickly prepared for a hungry family. A well-feathered duck evokes the tradition of Saint Michael's leaving a feather from his angelic wings as a relic for people who have a devotion to him. The orange zest gives the duck a deep citrus flavor, while the orange juice helps to flavor the gravy. The brightly colored carrots, which pay homage to the old Scottish tradition, are reminiscent of Michael's pointed spear, ablaze with the fire of God's justice.

Roasted Duck with Oranges and Carrot
Serves: 4–6   **Cooking time: 2 hours 45 minutes**

1 duck, approximately 5 lbs., cleaned and at room temperature

2 large oranges, zested and juiced

2 cloves garlic, finely minced

2 tsps. salt, divided

2 tsps. black pepper

2 tsps. paprika

1 bouquet garni (tied up bunch of fresh herbs: 1 sprig of rosemary, 4–5 sprigs of thyme, 3–4 sage leaves, 4–5 sprigs of parsley)

2 Tbsps. butter

1 cup chicken broth

4–6 carrots, peeled but kept whole

2 tsps. flour

1 cup arugula

1. Preheat oven to 375°F.
2. In a small bowl, combine the orange zest, garlic, salt (reserving a pinch for the gravy), pepper, and paprika, mix together, and rub the mixture all over the duck, inside and out. If any is left over, put it in the cavity of the duck.
3. Place the duck legs upward on a roasting rack inside a roasting pan, insert the bouquet garni into the cavity of the duck, and put the roasting pan in the oven.
4. While the duck is roasting, put the butter and chicken broth in a small saucepan over medium-high heat and bring to a boil.
5. Use this broth to baste the duck after it has cooked for 45 minutes.
6. After 1 hour and 30 minutes, carefully remove the duck from the oven and place the carrots in the roasting pan underneath the duck so that the melted duck fat will confit the carrots.
7. Return the roasting pan and cook for approximately 30 minutes more, until the duck is dark golden brown with crispy skin and an internal temperature of 160°F.
8. Remove the roasting rack from the roasting pan and set aside to allow the duck to rest.
9. Remove the carrots, place them in a sauté pan over medium-high heat, cook for 2–3 minutes until they begin to caramelize, and set aside.
10. Make gravy: Carefully remove about 2 Tbsps. of the duck fat from the bottom of the roasting pan and place it in a small saucepan over medium heat. Add the flour, whisk together to make a paste, and cook for 1–2 minutes. Add about ½ cup of the basting broth, a little at a time, to the saucepan, whisking constantly to incorporate the broth into the flour paste. Add the orange juice and whisk together to make a gravy. Add a pinch of salt to taste.
11. Remove the bouquet garni from the cavity of the duck and discard.
12. Serve the duck over a bed of arugula with the carrot spears arranged around the bird.

186

FOOD FOR THOUGHT

During dinner raise a glass and say, "May Saint Michael the Archangel defend us in the day of battle."

CHAPTER 10

October Saints

OCTOBER 2
GUARDIAN ANGELS

very individual has his own guardian angel, and it is also believed that many groups do as well, such as families, churches, dioceses, and nations. Our guardian angels protect us from harm and from the wiles of the devil, and so we owe them a vote of thanks, or at least a toast. And since according to Saint Thomas Aquinas they will remain with us as companions in Heaven, we might as well get used to them.

Our recipe can be made in any type of baking dish. But if you use cupcake pans, you can have more than one piece without feeling too guilty for that extra bite. And besides, when we think of guardian angels, we think of their presence as hidden and small—you know, like a cupcake.

Angel Food Cupcakes
Yields: 8 cupcakes   Cooking time: 1 hour

THE CUPCAKES
¾ cup sugar, divided
4 Tbsps. cake flour
4 Tbsps. all-purpose flour
⅛ tsp. salt

¾ cup egg whites, at room temperature (about 5–6 large egg whites)
¾ tsp. cream of tartar
¾ tsp. vanilla extract

1. Preheat oven to 325°F and prepare a cupcake pan with cupcake liners.
2. Sift the flour, salt, and 6 Tsps. of the sugar together through a fine mesh sieve and set aside.
3. Combine the egg whites, cream of tartar, vanilla extract, and 1 Tbsp. of warm water in a stand mixer on low speed until the mixture becomes foamy.
4. Increase the speed to medium and continue whipping, adding the remaining sugar 1 Tbsp. at a time and waiting 5–10 seconds between additions to allow time for the sugar to be incorporated.
5. Once all the sugar is incorporated, increase the speed to medium-high and whip the mixture until it forms soft peaks.
6. Turn off the mixer and, using a rubber spatula, gently fold the sifted flour mixture into the egg white mixture, a couple of Tbsps. at a time, slowly and gently so as to avoid deflating the egg whites.
7. Spoon the batter into the cupcake liners, filling them three-quarters full.

8. Bake the cupcakes until lightly browned, about 18–20 minutes.
9. Remove cupcakes from the oven and from the cupcake pan and then allow them to cool completely on a wire rack. (The cupcakes will fall a bit as they cool.)

THE WHIPPED CREAM FROSTING

1½ cups heavy whipping cream, cold   1½ tsps. vanilla extract
¾ cup confectioner's sugar

1. Whip together the cream, sugar, and vanilla with the whisk attachment of a stand mixer on medium-high speed. Use this speed to avoid under- or overwhipping the frosting.
2. Stop whipping as soon as the mixture becomes smooth and billowy. (If you whip the ingredients for too long, your frosting will curdle or take on a grainy texture.) Medium peaks should form when you lift up the whisk attachment.
3. Pipe or spread the frosting onto the cupcakes and top with your desired decoration.

FOOD FOR THOUGHT

Thank your guardian angel tonight for the near misses in your life and ask him to keep up the good work. Then, ask your guardian angel to help you become a saint. Should God invite you to Heaven, you won't grow wings and become an angel because you have the dignity of being an embodied creature, a marvelous mix of spirit and matter. But you will get to meet your best friend with wings and thank him for the role he played in your life on earth.

OCTOBER 3 *(OCTOBER 1)*
SAINT THÉRÈSE OF LISIEUX

There were three distinct periods to the brief, twenty-four-year life of one of the most popular saints of the twentieth century. During the first stage, from her birth until the death of her mother when she was only four and a half, Thérèse was a happy, albeit high-strung, child of Saints Louis and Zélie Martin, one of five daughters who would all become nuns.

During the second phase, Thérèse was a sensitive student who sought solitude to escape from school bullies, had a nervous illness that ended when a statue of the Blessed Virgin miraculously smiled at her, and suffered from scrupulosity. This phase ended abruptly on Christmas 1886, when she overheard her kind but exhausted father express exasperation at indulging her childish holiday wishes. In an instant, Thérèse was granted the joy of forgetting herself to make others happy, and she left behind forever the imperfections of childhood.

The third and final phase of Thérèse's life began with her early attempts to enter the Carmelite order when she was fourteen. Excluded because of her age, the determined teenager begged the aged Pope Leo XIII during an audience for admittance into the order. Thérèse then refused to leave his feet and had to be carried out of the room by Swiss Guards!

When Thérèse entered the convent the following year, she was a model novice, strictly obeying the rules and seeking out "the company of those nuns whose temperaments she found hardest to bear." But after six years of religious life, Thérèse was frustrated that she was still far from her goal of becoming a saint. It was then that she came upon two passages from the Old Testament that struck her with particular force: "Whosoever is a little one, let him come to me" (Proverbs 9:4) and "You shall be carried at the breasts, and upon the knees they shall caress you. As one whom the mother caresseth, so will I comfort you" (Isaiah 66:12–13).

Like Saint Paul, Thérèse learned to glory in her weaknesses, which "guaranteed" God's merciful aid. Thérèse's smallness was to be her shortcut or "little way" to Heaven, a way that consists of total trust in Jesus's love and mercy and of offering little daily sacrifices by doing "the least of actions for love." Her celebration of smallness even enriched her understanding of the Eucharist. "I cannot fear a God who for me has made Himself so small!" she wrote.

Chocolate eclairs are not particularly small, nor will they make you small in the waist, but the Little Flower, as she is popularly known, was fond of them. Made with tradition, finesse, and technique, these fancy chocolate donuts suited this young saint perfectly, as she not only loved eating these delicious sweet and creamy treats but also valued the hard but humble work required to produce this pastry delicacy. She worked just as hard on her faith, and it produced something that has spiritually fed people around the world—from scholars to simple believers. Her writings are as satisfying to the saint in the making as eclairs are to a child.

Chocolate Eclairs
Yields: 10–12 eclairs   Cooking time: 2½ hours

THE PASTRIES

½ cup unsalted butter

¼ tsp. salt

1 cup all-purpose flour

4 large eggs, at room temperature

1. Preheat oven to 420°F and line 2 rimmed baking sheets with parchment paper.
2. In a saucepan over medium heat, combine the butter, salt, and 1 cup of water and bring to a boil.
3. When the butter is completely melted, add all the flour at one time and continue to cook, constantly stirring, for approximately 2–3 minutes, until the water evaporates and a dough is formed.
4. Beat the dough in a stand mixer with the paddle attachment and add one egg at a time, making sure each egg is fully incorporated into the dough before adding another egg.
5. Transfer the dough to a pastry bag with a ⅝-inch star tip.
6. Pipe about 4 inches of the dough onto the parchment paper. Repeat until you have used all of the dough.
7. Bake for 10–12 minutes at 420°F, then reduce heat to 370°F. Bake for 18–20 minutes more, until the eclairs are crispy on top but seemingly hollow in the center when lightly tapped.
8. Cool the pastries on a cooling rack for about 30 minutes before filling them with cream.

THE CREAM FILLING

2½ cups whole milk

½ cup granulated sugar

the yolks from 6 large eggs

⅓ cup cornstarch

2 tsps. vanilla extract

1 cup water

1. Warm the milk in a saucepan on medium heat until small bubbles appear.
2. In a separate, heat-resistant bowl, whisk together the sugar, egg yolks, cornstarch, and salt until all the ingredients are fully incorporated in the mixture.

OCTOBER

3. Temper the eggs by adding a few tablespoons of hot milk while whisking vigorously to avoid scrambling the eggs.
4. Pour the rest of the milk in a thin stream into the eggs, continuously whisking.
5. Pour the egg mixture into the saucepan and continue whisking until it reaches a pudding consistency.
6. Remove the saucepan from the stove, cool it in an ice bath, and place a layer of plastic wrap directly on the top of the cream to prevent a skin from forming. Set aside.

THE CHOCOLATE GLAZE

½ cup semisweet chocolate chips   ½ cup heavy whipping cream

1 Tbsp. sugar

1. In a saucepan over medium-high heat, warm the cream until it begins to steam and form small bubbles.
2. Put the chocolate chips in a heat-resistant bowl and pour the cream over them, allowing it to warm the chocolate for about 1 minute, before whisking.
3. Add the sugar and continue to whisk the glaze until it is smooth and silky.

THE ECLAIRS

1. Attach the ³⁄₁₆-inch tip to a piping bag and fill the bag with the cream filling.
2. Poke about 4 holes in one side of each of the eclair pastries.
3. Fill each hole with the cream, using about 1 Tbsp. of cream total for each éclair.
4. Use a spoon to spread the chocolate glaze over the side of the eclairs with the holes.
5. Refrigerate the eclairs for 20–30 minutes to allow them to set before serving.

FOOD FOR THOUGHT

Thérèse sought obscurity and performed discreet acts of charity, yet her posthumously published autobiography, *The Story of a Soul*, made her a household name in the Catholic world. Pius X called her "the greatest saint of modern times." Pius XI canonized her only twenty-eight years after her death and made her the "star of his pontificate." Pius XII named her a co-patroness of France, along with her heroine, Joan of Arc. And in 1997, John Paul II named her a Doctor of the Church, the third woman to receive that honor and the youngest Doctor of all.

Tonight, think about how you can practice small acts of charity, starting with your loved ones. Charity begins at home!

OCTOBER 4
SAINT FRANCIS OF ASSISI

Saint Francis (ca. 1181–1226) was born Giovanni di Pietro di Bernardone, but his father nicknamed him Francesco or "Frenchy," perhaps because of his love of fine culture. This great saint, who dramatically converted to a life of radical poverty after hearing the Gospel passage "Take neither gold nor silver," was exceedingly humble. Even though he was the founder of the Franciscan Order, he refused to be ordained a priest, remaining a deacon throughout his life.

Saint Francis must have been quite a compelling dinner conversationalist. On one memorable occasion, after repeatedly denying the request of his good friend Saint Clare to sup together, he relented at the urging of his disciples. Francis had the table set on the bare ground, which was his custom. The two saints sat down along with several of their companions. As the first course was being served, Francis began speaking of God so sweetly and profoundly that the entire group went into a rapture. Meanwhile, it appeared to the residents of Assisi that Francis's church (Saint Mary of the Angels) and the entire forest around it were on fire. Grabbing their buckets and whatnot, they raced to where the group was dining, only to find them safe and sound, rapt in contemplation. "Then they knew for sure that it had been a heavenly and not material fire that God had miraculously shown them to symbolize the fire of divine love that was burning in the souls of those holy friars and nuns."[1] Happy and relieved, they withdrew.

The ecstasy of Francis and his companions lasted a long time, and when it was over, all were so refreshed by spiritual food that none of them had had a bite of their actual meal.

Saint Francis of Assisi is famous for his tenderheartedness towards animals. He sometimes released animals from traps and fish from nets. And in the famous incident of the wolf of Gubbio, Francis brokered a truce between a ravenous wolf and the town of Gubbio: the wolf would no longer eat the townsfolk and their livestock (something it had been doing with gusto), and the townsfolk in turn would feed the wolf. When the wolf eventually died, the entire town mourned, for the wolf had reminded them of Saint Francis.[2]

But the Poor Man of God, as he is sometimes called, was no vegetarian. Although he abstained from meat in general as part of a penitential life, Francis would eat meat and meat products when

195

they were offered to him or if he was ill. And when Christmas fell on a Friday one year, Brother Morico asked the saint if they could eat meat. "Thou sinnest, brother, in calling the day on which a Child has been born to us 'Friday,'" Francis replied. "I would that the very walls should eat flesh on such a day, or if they cannot, that they should at any rate be greased outside!"[3]

Instead of greasing your walls with lard or tallow tonight, honor the saint and his friendship with Gubbio and its wolf with a savory and light, creamy dish that faithfully combines the flavors of the region.

Umbrian-Style Pollo & Salsiccia Arrosto: Pan-Roasted Chicken & Sausage

Serves: 4   **Cooking time: 30 minutes**

2 links Italian sausage, sweet or hot

4 skinless, boneless chicken thighs, cut into 1-inch pieces

1 clove garlic, minced

1 sprig fresh rosemary, kept whole (with about a 2-inch stem)

1 cup cherry tomatoes, halved

1 cup white wine (dry Umbrian)

1 cup chicken broth

2 Tbsps. butter

1 tsp. salt

1 Tbsp. olive oil

1 tsp. crushed red pepper (optional)

1. Heat olive oil in a Dutch oven over medium heat.
2. Remove and discard the sausage casings, add the sausages to the olive oil, and cook for 2–3 minutes, or until the sausages begin to brown, using two wooden spoons to break them up into crumbles.
3. Add the cut chicken and garlic to the pot and sauté until the chicken begins to brown, 3–5 minutes.
4. Add the cherry tomatoes and fresh rosemary, stirring the ingredients together until the tomatoes begin to release some of their juices, 1–2 minutes.
5. Season with salt (and optional crushed red pepper).
6. Pour in the white wine and chicken broth to deglaze the pan, scraping up the browned bits from the bottom.
7. Cover the pot, reduce the heat to low, and simmer for 7–10 minutes.
8. Remove from heat, add the butter, and allow it to melt.
9. Stir the ingredients together until fully combined.
10. Remove and discard the rosemary sprig.
11. Serve over toasted crusty bread or plain boiled potatoes.

OCTOBER

And for dessert, follow the holy friar's lead. As he lay on his death bed, Francis had only one culinary request that we know of: he wanted some of the "good things" that Blessed Jacoba of Settesoli had served him in Rome. Jacoba was from the ancient and noble Frangipani family, and some think that the good thing in question was *frangipane*, an almond cream named after her kin. Others say that the treat was a Roman version of *mustacciouli*, a chocolate-covered Neapolitan almond pastry. Either way, Saint Francis got his wish and died a happy man: Jacoba arrived just as he finished writing the request and before he had a chance to send it. In honor of this story, some Franciscan communities distribute almond confections during their celebration of the Transitus ("Passing") of Saint Francis, that is, on the evening of October 3. You can cheat and have some on his feast day too. We offer the following simple and sweet treat that comes with a dollop of decadence for a simple saint who offered a lot of sweet consolations.

OCTOBER

Almond & Nutella Cookies
Yields: 20–24 cookies   Cooking time: 30 minutes

1 cup almonds, slightly toasted and crushed

2 cups all-purpose flour

1 cup butter, softened to room temperature

1¼ cups granulated sugar

½ tsp. almond extract

½ tsp. vanilla extract

1 cup Nutella, softened to room temperature

1. Preheat oven to 350°F.
2. Cream butter in a mixer.
3. Add sugar, then flour, almonds, and vanilla and almond extracts as you continue mixing, until ingredients are fully combined.
4. Prepare 2 baking sheets with parchment paper.
5. Roll 2-Tbsp. scoops of dough into balls, then slightly flatten into disks.
6. Place the cookies on the baking sheets about 2 inches apart.
7. Use your fingers to make a small indent or dimple in the middle of each cookie.
8. Use a teaspoon to add a small dollop of the Nutella in the indent of the dough, approximately ½ tsp. of Nutella per cookie.
9. Bake for 15–20 minutes, or until golden brown.
10. Remove and allow to cool before serving.

DINING WITH THE SAINTS

FOOD FOR THOUGHT

Holy personalities are oftentimes characterized as sweet or fiery. Saint Francis was both. Consider the personality that God gave you, and ask yourself how to make it more digestible to others, especially when trying to share the Good News.

OCTOBER 6
SAINT BRUNO

Bruno of Cologne (1030–1101) was a canon and a well-regarded theologian at Rheims when he decided to leave the world. Withdrawing to a mountain not far from Grenoble, France, with six companions, he founded the hermitage of the Grand Charterhouse (or Chartreuse in French) and by extension the Carthusian order, which combines the solitary life of the hermit with the communal life of the monk. Saint Bruno was dragged away from his beloved Chartreuse to become the counselor of Pope Urban II and was never to see it again, although he was permitted to return to solitary life with some of his companions on a mountain in Italy, close enough to the papal court to be called on if necessary.

This famous German beef, which can take up to seven days to marinate and tenderize, speaks to the iconic flavors of Germany's culinary traditions. Roasted meat, deep rich flavors, and a sweet and sour gravy make a celebratory meal that can help us remember the spiritual contributions of this great saint.

German Sauerbraten

Serves: 4–6   Prep time: 4–7 days of marinating   Cooking time: 4 hours

4–5 lbs. beef roast

4 slices of thick-cut bacon, cubed

2 Tbsps. olive oil

2 large onions, diced (yielding about 2½ cups)

2 large carrots, diced (yielding about 1½ cups)

1 large leek, thoroughly immersed in water to remove dirt, washed and chopped

3 cloves garlic, minced

2 large sprigs fresh thyme

2 sprigs fresh rosemary

2 bay leaves

6 whole cloves

1 Tbsp. cracked juniper berries, or ½ cup gin

1 Tbsp. of black peppercorns

2–3 tsps. salt

2 tsps. sugar

3 cups red wine

1 cup apple cider vinegar

½ cup raisins

1 Tbsp. honey

2 tsps. ground ginger

2 Tbsps. flour

1. In a large Dutch oven over medium-high heat, heat the onions, carrots, leeks, garlic, thyme, rosemary, bay leaves, cloves, peppercorns, salt, sugar, apple cider vinegar, juniper berries (or gin), red wine, raisins, honey, and ginger until the liquid begins to boil. Simmer for 8–10 minutes.
2. Remove from the heat, allow to cool, and refrigerate.
3. Add the roast, immersing it in the vegetables and juices, and allow it to marinate for 4–7 days.
4. Remove the meat and pat it dry.
5. Strain all of the liquid from the vegetables and reserve these separately, discarding the bay leaves.
6. Rinse and dry out the same Dutch oven and cook the bacon bits in it over medium-high heat until crispy. Remove the bacon and set aside.
7. In the same pot on medium-high heat, sear the roast on all sides for 3–5 minutes, until the meat is well caramelized. Remove the roast from the pot and set it aside.
8. Turn the heat down to medium-low and return the strained vegetables to the pot.
9. Add the flour, mix well, and cook for about 5 minutes.
10. Return the vegetable liquid to the pot, stirring constantly to avoid any lumps.
11. Return the bacon bits and the beef to the pot, immerse them fully, and cover the pot.
12. Cook for 2½–3 hours, until the meat is cooked and tender, and remove it from the pot and set aside.
13. Put the vegetables and gravy in a blender, or use an immersion blender to blend the mixture to a fine consistency. Pour the entire mixture through a strainer to create a silky gravy and discard the solids caught by the strainer. (You may have to use a spatula to push the juices through the strainer.)
14. Cut the meat into ½–1-inch cubes and pour the gravy on top.

FOOD FOR THOUGHT

While a pressure cooker or even *sous vide* cooking would create this dish in half the time it takes to marinate, there's something to be said about the quality that comes from tradition, even if it's a little less practical. Consider what traditions you enjoy, even the ones that take a lot of time but for you are worth the wait. Thank God for those traditions and don't be tempted to cut corners; celebrate the process and not just the results.

OCTOBER 15
SAINT TERESA OF ÁVILA

When she was a little girl, Teresa (1515–1582) and her brother dreamt of becoming martyrs, and so they set off for the land of the Moors. Their plan for easy access to Heaven was thwarted, however, by an uncle who met them on their way and quickly brought them back to their worried mother. Next they resolved to become hermits, but they could never find enough stones to build their hermitages in the family garden.

Saint Teresa, who had a lovely, self-deprecating sense of humor, recounted these stories later in life. She went on to become a spiritual grown-up of the first rank. Teresa reformed the Carmelite order that she had joined, and she was eventually declared a Doctor of the Church for her deep psychological and spiritual insights into how to become holy.

Saint Teresa died during the night of October 4–October 15. No, that's not a typo. She passed away on the very night that the Gregorian reform of the old Julian calendar deleted ten days from the year 1582. In that singular year, the day after October 4 was October 15.

Despite her asceticism, our saint undoubtedly relished good cuisine. She was known to say, "When it's time to fast, it's time to fast. But when it's time to feast, it's time to feast!" This sweet treat will help us remember the simple and delicious things of life faithfully and joyfully lived in the spirit of this wonderful Doctor of the Church.

Yemas de Santa Teresa
Yields: 8–10 yemas   Cooking time: 10 minutes

the yolks from 6 large eggs

1 cup confectioner's sugar, or slightly more

the peel of ½ lemon

½ cup granulated sugar

1. In a saucepan over medium heat, heat the granulated sugar in 6 Tbsps. of water, stirring until the sugar water starts to boil.
2. Add the lemon peel and continue to simmer, stirring regularly, until it becomes a thicker syrup. Remove and discard the lemon peel and set aside the saucepan of syrup to cool.
3. In a separate mixing bowl, lightly whisk the egg yolks and add them to the syrup after it has cooled.
4. Return the saucepan to the stove on low heat and whisk slowly and continuously for 4–5 minutes, or until the mixture pulls away from the sides of the saucepan and begins to solidify.
5. Pour the mixture onto a plate, allow it to cool, and sift the confectioner's sugar over it.
6. Pinch off a golf-ball-sized bit of the mixture and roll it into your hands, along with the confectioner's sugar.
7. Repeat the process until all the yolk mixture and all the confectioner's sugar are used.
8. Chill the balls for 1½ hours and serve them in individual paper candy cups.

FOOD FOR THOUGHT

Look at your past week of meals and celebrations, and ask yourself if there were times when you fasted and times when you feasted. Life is all about balance. Make sure that you do a little bit of fasting for penitential purposes, like on Fridays, and do some feasting each week as well, especially on holy days like today.

OCTOBER

OCTOBER 17 *(OCTOBER 16)*
SAINT MARGARET MARY ALACOQUE

Saint Margaret Mary Alacoque (1647–1690) was bedridden with rheumatic fever for four years in her childhood. But when she made a vow to enter religious life, she instantly became better. Later in her life, Margaret Mary forgot about her vow and, complying with her mother's wish for her to marry, started attending social events with her brothers. But one night Margaret Mary returned home from a Carnival ball in her finery and had a vision of Jesus, scourged and bloody, reproaching her and telling her how much He loved her because of her vow.

Hesitating no longer, Saint Margaret Mary entered the Visitation Convent and became a nun. Eventually, she received additional visions from Jesus, who instructed her to spread devotion to His Sacred Heart and made Twelve Promises to her for those who kept this devotion, including the grace of final repentance to anyone who receives Holy Communion on the first Friday of nine consecutive months. Despite great resistance, she succeeded in spreading the devotion, and it has remained popular ever since.

Saint Margaret Mary's last name means "to the rooster," and we are happy to honor her sobriquet. Coq au vin was designed to compensate for the toughness of a male chicken, but whether you use a bona fide rooster or a hen, our recipe will not disappoint.

Margaret Mary's Ala Coq au Vin
Serves: 4–6   **Cooking time: 2 hours**

4–6 chicken thighs, skin on and bone in	4–6 strips of bacon, diced
1 tsp. kosher salt	2 cups cremini mushrooms, sliced
1 tsp. black pepper	1 onion, diced

1 large carrot, peeled and diced

2 cloves of garlic, minced

1 Tbsp. tomato paste

2 Tbsps. all-purpose flour

2 cups of red wine, full-bodied and dry

1 cup chicken broth

1 Tbsp. brandy

1 small bunch of fresh thyme

3 Tbsps. butter

2 Tbsps. fresh parsley, minced

1. Preheat oven to 350°F.
2. Season chicken with salt and pepper.
3. In a large oven-safe pot or Dutch oven over medium heat, cook the bacon until crispy. Remove the bacon and set it aside, reserving half of the oil.
4. In the same pot, sear the chicken on both sides until slightly browned, approximately 2 minutes on each side. Remove and set aside.
5. To the same pot, add the carrots, garlic, mushrooms, and onions and sauté until onions become translucent and mushrooms are roasted.
6. Add the butter and flour and stir together until they form a paste.
7. Add the red wine, stir until the flour is fully incorporated in the wine, and simmer until the scent of the red wine is reduced, approximately 4–5 minutes.
8. Add the tomato paste, broth, and brandy. Stir to incorporate the tomato paste.
9. Return the chicken to the pot, top off with the thyme, and cook in the oven, half covered, for about 25 minutes, or until the internal temperature reaches 165°F.
10. Remove the chicken from the sauce to let it rest.
11. Plate some of the vegetables, top with the chicken, and ladle some of the gravy over the entire dish.

FOOD FOR THOUGHT

Saint Margaret Mary Alacoque received messages from both Jesus and the devil. She had to use discernment and even sacramentals, sprinkling holy water on the apparitions she received. We also need to make sure that we are discerning the messages that we receive in prayer. One litmus test is this: if it leads to a greater love of God and neighbor, it is from God; if it does not, to Hell with it.

OCTOBER

OCTOBER 18
SAINT LUKE

Saint Luke the Evangelist is the author of the third canonical Gospel and the Acts of the Apostles. He did not know Our Lord personally, but he was a disciple of Saint Paul and, it is believed, a confidant of Our Lady (and her physician!), which may explain why his Gospel includes so many details about Christ's infancy and childhood that are not found elsewhere.

A very ancient tradition applies the four "living creatures" mentioned in Ezekiel 1 and Revelation 4 (man, lion, ox, and eagle) to the authors of the four canonical Gospels. The symbol for Saint Luke is an ox: oxen were used in Temple sacrifices, and his Gospel opens with Zechariah sacrificing in the Temple (Luke 1). Luke's is also the only Gospel to include the parable of the Prodigal Son, which culminates in the slaying of a fatted calf.

And if a fatted calf is good for a feast, imagine how much better a fatted steer is. Our recipe for steak honors an evangelist whose writings provide much spiritual red meat.

Saint Luke's Sizzling Steak with Herbal Butter
Serves: 2   Cooking time: 30 minutes

1 ribeye steak, 9–12 oz.

1 Tbsp. olive oil

2 tsps. kosher salt

2 tsps. cracked black pepper

1 tsp. olive oil

2 Tbsps. room-temperature butter, plus 2 Tbsps. butter for basting

½ tsp. garlic powder

½ tsp. dried oregano

½ tsp. dried parsley

1. Prepare herbal butter: Mix together garlic powder, oregano, parsley, and the softened room-temperature butter. Form into a square and chill in the refrigerator until the steak is cooked.
2. Season the steak on both sides with salt and pepper and set it aside at room temperature for about 30 minutes before cooking.
3. Preheat the oven to 450°F.
4. In a cast-iron skillet over high heat, heat olive oil to smoking point.
5. Add the steak and cook for 2 minutes on each side, until a caramelized crust forms on both sides.
6. Put the entire skillet in the oven and cook for 6 minutes for a rare steak and 8 minutes for a medium-rare steak.
7. Carefully remove skillet and return it to the stove over medium heat and add the butter.
8. When the butter melts and foams, baste the meat with the melted butter for 2 minutes.
9. Remove the meat from the skillet and allow it to rest on a wire rack.
10. Immediately add some slices of the herbal butter directly to the hot steak to melt gently before cutting the steak and serving it.

FOOD FOR THOUGHT

Saint Luke's Gospel uses a unique phrase to describe the Blessed Virgin Mary. Three times Luke states that "she pondered these things (of Jesus) in her heart" (Luke 2:19, 2:51; see also 11:28). Behold the essence of contemplation! This week, practice pondering Jesus in your heart. In the meantime, as the steak is being served, recite another verse from Luke: "Bring hither the fatted calf.... Let us eat and make merry!" (Luke 15:23)

OCTOBER 22
SAINT JOHN PAUL II

Karol Wojtyła (1920–2005), better known as Pope Saint John Paul II, probably holds the world record for breaking the most world records, at least the most important ones. This charismatic successor of Saint Peter was the first non-Italian pope in 450

years, the most travelled pope in history (129 countries!), the first pope to enter a synagogue on an official papal visit, and the pope who beatified and canonized more persons than all his predecessors combined. The pope's funeral Mass was the single largest gathering of heads of state in world history, with four kings, five queens, and over seventy presidents and prime ministers in attendance; it was also probably the single largest pilgrimage event in the history of Christianity, with four million mourners arriving in Rome to honor their beloved Holy Father and chant "Santo subito!"—sainthood now!

Formerly, Polish cream cake was simply called *kremówka*, but when it was discovered that John Paul II loved this layered pastry from his homeland, it was renamed papal cream cake, or Kremówka Papieska (kreh-MOOF-kah pah-PYESS-kah). Crunchy, sweet, and creamy, our recipe will keep you smiling as you celebrate the memory of a great evangelizer and a great witness to the beauty of our orthodox faith.

Kremówka Papieska

Serves: 2   **Cooking time: 30 minutes**

2 sheets puff pastry dough	3½ Tbsps. cornstarch	2 Tbsps. confectioner's sugar
2 cups milk	1 tsp. vanilla extract	
4 egg yolks	1 Tbsp. butter	2 mint leaves, for garnish
¼ cup sugar	¼ cup raspberries	

1. Cut the store-bought puff pastries into 4-x-6-inch squares and bake according to the directions on the box.
2. In a small saucepan over medium heat, heat the milk, vanilla, and 4 Tbsps. of the sugar.
3. In a separate bowl, combine the cornstarch with the egg yolks and the remaining 4 Tbsps. of the sugar and mix well.
4. Very slowly pour the warm milk over the yolk mixture, whisking continuously to avoid cooking the eggs. Return the mixture to the stove and cook over low heat for 1–2 minutes, or until it forms into a custard texture.
5. Place one piece of the puff pastry on a plate. Pour a thin layer of the pastry cream over the pastry. Layer another puff pastry and add more cream. Add a third and final layer of pastry, then a final layer of cream, and top off with raspberries. Sift confectioner's sugar on top, garnish with a mint leaf, and serve.

FOOD FOR THOUGHT

John Paul II was famous for repeatedly saying, "Be not afraid" (John 6:20). This reassuring admonition reminds us to identify and confront all of the things that cause us fear and to put them in God's hands. If you find yourself in a state of fright, recite Psalm 23: "The Lord is my shepherd, I shall not want."

OCTOBER 25
SAINT MINIATUS

It is believed that Miniatus, or Minias, was either a soldier in the Roman army or a member of Armenian royalty on pilgrimage when he became the first martyr in the city of Florence, Italy, in AD 250. After refusing to sacrifice to the gods, Miniatus was thrown into an amphitheater with a lion or panther, but the beast refused to touch him. He was beheaded instead, and one legend claims that he picked up his head afterwards.

If we were hyper-vegetarians, we would be tempted to say that the animal refused to eat Minias because it wisely preferred vegetables and that Minias had the strength to carry his own severed head because he did too. In any event, it puts us in mind of a dish from the rustic cuisine of Florence, Ribollita Florentina, a combination of winter greens and day-old bread that is favored by the locals. (More than likely, Saint Miniatus enjoyed a similar dish in his day.) Our recipe is a perfect way to make greens taste great, in season and out of season.

Ribollita Florentina
Serves: 2–3   **Cooking time: 40 minutes**

½ cup olive oil, divided

1 cup pancetta (or thick-cut bacon), cubed

4 cups kale, destemmed and shredded

2 cups spinach

2 cups white cabbage, shredded (or substitute any green cabbage)

OCTOBER

2 cups cannellini beans

2 stalks celery, diced

2 carrots, peeled and diced

1 onion, diced

2 cloves garlic, minced

1 zucchini, chopped

1 large potato, peeled and chopped into ½-inch cubes

2 Tbsps. tomato paste

2 tsps. dried basil (or fresh basil, minced)

2 tsps. dried parsley (or fresh parsley, minced)

2 tsps. dried thyme (or fresh thyme, minced)

2 tsps. dried oregano (or fresh oregano, minced)

2 tsps. dried sage (or fresh sage, minced)

1 tsp. dried rosemary (or fresh rosemary, minced)

1 tsp. chili powder

4–6 slices crusty bread

1–2 Tbsps. grated parmesan cheese

1. In a large pot over medium-high heat, heat all but 2 Tbsps. of the olive oil and cook the pancetta until crispy.

2. Add the kale, spinach, cabbage, beans, celery, carrots, onions, garlic, zucchini, and potatoes and stir until the potatoes become soft.

3. Add tomato paste, basil, parsley, thyme, oregano, sage, rosemary, chili powder, and 2 cups of water and stir together.

4. Cover, lower the heat to medium-low, and simmer for 10–15 minutes, stirring occasionally.

5. While it simmers, prepare the bread by lightly brushing it with olive oil before toasting it on a grill pan or in a toaster oven.

6. To assemble this dish, place a piece of the toast on a plate, pour ribollita on top of the bread, and top off with more bread. Drizzle with olive oil and parmesan cheese and serve.

FOOD FOR THOUGHT

Veggies are good for us. In fact, it is a general rule of health that we should be eating more of what grows in the ground than of what walks on it. And as you contemplate how to incorporate more healthy greens into your diet, figure out what "spiritual vegetables" you should be adding to your plate as well (for example, more daily prayer or weekly adoration).

OCTOBER 31
ALL HALLOWS' EVE

I n the early Middle Ages, the Church in Ireland had to deal with the Celtic festival of Samhain (the Lord of the dead in Celtic mythology) on October 31. The Druids believed that infernal spirits roamed freely on this night, and they responded to this threat on the principle "If you can't beat 'em, join 'em." Consequently, they disguised themselves as various kinds of phantoms to escape harm and tried to appease evil spirits by offering them food and wine.

The Church was gradually able to wean the Celts from their heathenish ways, replacing their ghoulish camouflage with pious masquerades of the angels and saints in processions on All Hallows' Eve and replacing the food offerings with "soul cakes" made on Halloween and offered to the poor in memory of the faithful departed. The original intention of "souling" was doubly charitable, ensuring that the poor would be fed on this day, in exchange for which the poor would pray for the donor's dead loved ones. Eventually, the practice became more frolicsome, as groups of young men and boys began going from house to house and asking for food, money, and ale in addition to cakes. On this night the Irish, incidentally, also enjoy boxty, a potato bread or dumpling. (We should mention that All Hallows' Eve was traditionally a day of fasting and complete abstinence from flesh meat.)

At the other end of Christendom, November 1 was once a Roman festival in honor of Pomona, the goddess of fruits and orchards whose signature treat was apples. The association survives in the old Halloween custom of ducking for apples.

Of the two options, soul cakes or apples, we choose apples. (If your preference is for soul cakes, don't worry: there is no definitive recipe for a soul cake, so you can bake whatever you want.) Our Caramel Apple Pops are easy to make and easier to eat than whole caramel apples.

Caramel Apple Pops
Serves: 4   **Cooking time: 1 hour**

1 Granny Smith apple
½ lemon, juiced
½ cup light corn syrup
1 cup brown sugar, tightly packed
2 Tbsps. unsalted butter

⅛ tsp. salt
½ tsp. vanilla extract
2–4 Tbsps. candied sprinkles or chopped nuts, or some roughly chopped popcorn
1½ cups heavy cream

1. Run the apple under hot water for 1–2 minutes to wash away the waxy coating.
2. Cut it into 4 equal-sized wedges and trim away the core.
3. Carefully insert a 6-inch skewer into the center part of each apple wedge so that it doesn't break the apple, making it the shape of a popsicle stick, but with an apple wedge.
4. Rub the apple wedges with lemon juice to prevent them from turning brown and put them in the refrigerator until you're ready to dip them in the caramel sauce.
5. In a saucepan over medium-high heat, combine the heavy cream, corn syrup, brown sugar, butter, and salt.
6. Attach a candy thermometer to the saucepan to get an accurate temperature reading, and when the mixture begins to bubble and reaches 235–240°F, remove from the heat, add the vanilla, and mix very gently, as too much stirring can create bubbles that will prevent the caramel from sticking to the apples.
7. Allow this mixture to cool for 10–15 minutes.
8. Carefully dip the apple wedges into the caramel sauce and allow the excess to drip off completely.
9. After the excess caramel has dripped off the apple, immediately add some candied sprinkles, chopped nuts, or chopped popcorn.
10. Enjoy immediately or set in the refrigerator for 10–15 minutes, until the caramel is set.

FOOD FOR THOUGHT

Dressing up in saints' costumes is one way to take back Halloween, but it is not the only way. Think about what statement you want to make during a holiday that in some ways has taken a turn for the worse. But don't forget good old-fashioned trick-or-treating. Be sure to have good candy ready for the little ones knocking at your door (nothing healthy, and no candy corn! If they want to eat something waxy, they can go home and munch on a candle). As the trick-or-treaters are walking away, you can put a new spin on the old custom of souling: instead of their praying for you, say a silent prayer for them, their family, and their departed loved ones. And if you are the trick-or-treater (or the chaperone of one), you can pray for the candy-givers and their deceased just like folks did in the Middle Ages.

CHAPTER 11

November Saints

NOVEMBER 1
ALL SAINTS' DAY

T his great feast honors *all* the souls in Heaven, both the canonized saints recognized by the Church and the uncanonized saints currently unknown to us. According to Pope Urban IV, the holy day is also to compensate for any negligence in celebrating the saints' feasts from the previous year.

In some parts of Europe (Germany, Austria and Switzerland, Slavic nations, Hungary, and some Latin countries), the traditional treat for today is Saints' Cake. The Austrian Allerheiligen-Striezel (All Saints' Cake), which is a braided bread, is one such example. Think of the yeast as the leaven of holiness that turns sinful humans into holy friends of God, and the braiding as the tight-knit communion of saints.

All Saints' Cake (Allerheiligen-Striezel)
Serves: 4–6   Cooking time: 2 hours

2–2¼ tsps. packaged dry yeast

¼ cup warm water

4 cups all-purpose flour

1 pinch salt

⅔ cup warm milk

⅔ cup sugar

½ cup butter, melted

1 egg, separated

1 cup golden raisins

1 Tbsp. sugar

2 tsps. lightly toasted walnuts, chopped

1. In a large mixing bowl, dissolve yeast in warm water and set aside until yeast begins to bloom, approximately 10 minutes.
2. Sift the flour into the water mixture and add salt, warm milk, sugar, butter, egg yolk, and raisins. Mix all the ingredients together until a dough is formed.
3. Pour out the dough onto a surface area dusted with flour.
4. Divide the dough in half and roll into 2 long thick noodles, around 1 inch thick.

5. Braid the two dough noodles together, pinch the ends of the noodles, and tuck them under the dough.
6. Preheat oven to 300°F.
7. Let the dough rise for 30 minutes.
8. Bake for 45–50 minutes.
9. Remove from the oven, sprinkle the chopped walnuts and sugar on top, return to the oven, and cook for another 10–15 minutes.
10. When the bread is baked and golden brown in color, remove it from the oven and let it rest for 10–15 minutes before cutting and serving.

FOOD FOR THOUGHT

If you were a saint, what would you be a patron saint of? Once you have your answer, become a saint for that cause.

NOVEMBER 2
ALL SOULS' DAY

After celebrating the Church Triumphant in Heaven, the Church Militant on earth turns her thoughts to the Church Suffering in Purgatory and prays for the speedy delivery of the poor souls from their painful purification. Many customs surround All Souls' Day, chief among them a visit to the final resting place of one's dearly departed. In many cultures, that visit includes bringing food and drink and offering a libation at the grave, although the Church, at least in some places, frowns upon the latter practice as a pagan holdover. Traditional dishes include English soul cakes (again; see October 31), Italian Eggs in Purgatory(!), Italian Bones of the Dead cookies, Italian *fave dei morti* (beans of the dead—actually, they're almond treats), Spanish and Mexican *pan de muerto* (bread of the dead), Mexican chicken mole (see November 23), and Swiss Dry Bones cookies. As an American alternative, we propose Southern soul food: fried chicken and buttermilk biscuits.

Fried Chicken & Hot Honey Buttermilk Biscuits
Serves: 4–6   **Cooking time: 45 minutes**

THE FRIED CHICKEN

4 lbs. chicken legs

3–4 cups buttermilk

2 tsps. cayenne pepper

3 tsps. salt, divided

2 tsps. garlic powder

2 cups all-purpose flour

1 cup panko bread crumbs

1 tsp. pepper

3 tsps. garlic powder, divided

3 tsps. cayenne pepper, divided

1 tsp. onion powder

1 tsp. paprika

4 cups canola or vegetable oil, or more as needed to cover the chicken in a Dutch oven, for frying

1. In a large bowl, whisk together the buttermilk, 2 tsps. cayenne pepper, 2 tsps. garlic powder, and 2 tsps. of the salt.
2. Wash and clean the chicken, pat it dry with paper towels, and discard the paper towels.
3. Immerse the chicken in the buttermilk mixture and marinate it for 45 minutes to 1 hour.
4. Put the 4 cups oil, or more if you need more to have enough to cover the chicken, in a Dutch oven, and heat it on medium-high heat to 350°F.
5. Combine the flour, panko bread crumbs, pepper, 1 tsp. garlic powder, 1 tsp. cayenne pepper, onion powder, paprika, and remaining tsp. of the salt and whisk together.
6. Remove the chicken from the buttermilk, shake off the excess buttermilk, and completely coat the chicken in the flour and panko mixture.
7. Carefully place the chicken into the hot oil and gently swirl it so that it doesn't stick to the bottom.
8. Cook in batches of 3–4 pieces at a time, making sure the chicken is completely immersed in the oil when cooking.
9. Cook each batch for 15–20 minutes, depending on the size of the chicken parts, making sure the internal temperature of the chicken reaches 165°F.
10. Place chicken on a wire rack to drain, or on a plate lined with paper towels, and sprinkle another pinch or two of salt on the chicken.

THE HOT HONEY BUTTERMILK BISCUITS
Serves: 4–6   **Cooking time: 45 minutes**

2½ cups all-purpose flour, plus more for work surface and hands

2 Tbsps. baking powder

1 tsp. salt

½ cup cold unsalted butter, cubed

1 cup cold buttermilk

2 more Tbsps. buttermilk, combined with 2 Tbsps.

melted butter to make a wash for the biscuits

4 Tbsps. honey

1 tsp. hot sauce, your favorite brand

1. Preheat oven to 425°F.
2. In a food processor, combine the flour, baking powder, and salt. Pulse until the mixture forms coarse crumbles.
3. Pour this flour mixture into a large bowl, add the cup of buttermilk, and mix gently to create a shaggy and crumbly dough.
4. Prepare work surface with flour and pour the rough dough out onto it.
5. Make sure your hands are well floured. Add a little extra flour to this sticky dough and knead it gently, folding it back on itself. Repeat the process 3–4 times, until the ingredients are fully incorporated.
6. Form the dough into a rectangle about 1 inch thick.
7. Use a 2½–3-inch biscuit cutter to cut rounds in the dough. To avoid sealing the sides of the biscuits, do not twist the cutter and lift the rounds, but instead simply press the cutter into the dough and, when all the biscuits are cut, remove the dough around the biscuits.
8. Place the biscuits close together in a cast-iron skillet or on parchment paper on a baking sheet, making sure the biscuits' sides are touching each other.
9. Brush the buttermilk-and-melted-butter wash on all the biscuits.
10. Bake 15–20 minutes, or until the biscuits are golden brown.
11. While they are baking, combine the honey and hot sauce together.
12. Remove the biscuits from the oven and brush them with the honey and hot sauce.

FOOD FOR THOUGHT

Praying for the faithful departed is a pious and practical tradition for people who take their faith seriously. We do this by praying for the faithful departed after we eat (see the Introduction) and as we pass by a cemetery. The most popular prayer for the dead is: "Eternal rest grant unto them, O Lord, and let perpetual light shine upon them. May they rest in peace. Amen." The Church grants a partial indulgence for the souls of the faithful departed every time it is piously said.

NOVEMBER

NOVEMBER 4
SAINT CHARLES BORROMEO

Charles Borromeo (1538–1584) was a giant of the Catholic Reformation (known in the history books as the Counter-Reformation). An Italian of noble birth, he became a cleric at the age of twelve and a cardinal at twenty-one. As archbishop of Milan, Saint Charles personally aided victims of a plague and did penance for the people by processing barefooted in public with a rope around his neck (which is why he is featured this way in Christian art).

Milan's Ossobuco is one of the most famous examples of Lombardian cuisine. Like Saint Charles Borromeo, it is refined, nourishing, and faithful to tradition.

Ossobuco alla Milanese
Serves: 4   **Cooking time: 2 hours**

4 cross-cut veal shanks, 1½–2 inches thick

1 cup of flour, seasoned with a pinch of salt and pepper

2 Tbsps. olive oil

2 medium-sized onions, diced

3 celery stalks, diced

1 large carrot, diced

2 cloves of garlic, sliced

1 small bunch of thyme

2 bay leaves

2 Tbsps. tomato paste

1 cup white wine

1 cup chicken stock

½ cup dried porcini mushrooms soaked in 1 cup of hot water

2 tsps. salt

2 tsps. black pepper

1 tsp. fresh parsley, minced

1 lemon, zested and juiced

1 clove garlic, finely minced

1 Tbsp. olive oil

1. Preheat oven to 350°F.
2. In a Dutch oven or oven-safe pot, heat 2 Tbsps. olive oil over medium heat.
3. Combine the flour, salt, and pepper in a separate dish and dredge the shanks in the flour mixture on all sides.

4. Sear the veal shanks by carefully placing them in the hot oil for about 2–3 minutes on each side, then remove and set aside.

5. To the same pot, add the onions, carrots, celery, garlic, and tomato paste and mix together until the onions become translucent, approximately 3–4 minutes.

6. Add the white wine, stock, dried porcini mushrooms, 1 cup of hot water, and thyme. Mix all together and heat until it comes to a simmer.

7. Return the veal shanks to the pot and slightly immerse them in the liquid.

8. Cover the pot and cook in the oven for 1½ hours.

9. Remove the lid and cook for another 20–30 minutes, until the sauce is thickened.

10. In the meantime, make the gremolata by combining the parsley, lemon zest and juice, and 1 tsp. olive oil in a food processor and pulsing until the ingredients form a chunky paste.

11. Carefully remove the shanks, ladle some of the juices, and drizzle a little of the parsley-and-lemon mixture on top of the veal.

FOOD FOR THOUGHT

Saint Charles was a true reformer, not so much by inventing new things but by bringing out the original beauty of a thing, in his case, the beauty of the Church. Think of something in your life that needs reformation and ask Saint Charles's intercession to help return it to its original form and beauty.

NOVEMBER 11
SAINT MARTIN OF TOURS

Saint Martin (ca. 316–397) was a Roman soldier who was on fire with Christian zeal even before he was baptized. As a catechumen, he saw a poor beggar shivering in the cold and tore his military cloak in two, giving him half. (The Roman army made you pay for half of your uniform, so Martin gave the half that he had paid for.) That night Jesus Christ appeared to him in a dream with the half-cloak and said, "Martin the catechumen hath clothed Me."

Martin eventually became a monk. When the townspeople of Tours tried to trick him into becoming their bishop, the holy man hid from them, only to be betrayed by a flock of honking

NOVEMBER

geese. Whether this story is true or not, goose became the main course of medieval celebrations of "Martinmas" (Saint Martin's Day), and this culinary tradition even influenced the celebration of the first Thanksgiving. The Pilgrims, who were introduced to the Martinmas goose during their stay in Holland, used North American turkeys for their banquet only when they could not find enough geese.

According to an old English proverb, you must ask Saint Martin to dine with you when have goose or you will not get a goose the next year. And to ask Saint Martin to dine is "to share your goose with someone who has none, as Martin did his cloak."[1]

In Germanic countries, the Martinmas goose is eaten with sauerkraut, and in Sweden the bird is stuffed with apples and prunes (which flavor the meat and are discarded before serving); the finished goose is accompanied with cinnamon apples.

Roast goose is a rare red meat bird, which means you can safely eat the breast meat when it's slightly pink and medium-rare. Our recipe brings out the flavors of the goose and pairs naturally with roasted cabbage.

If goose is not your thing, turn either to the roast duck recipe for Michaelmas (September 29), or you can serve pork. In the Middle Ages, it was customary to slaughter swine on or before Martinmas in preparation for winter. The custom led to several proverbs. In Spain, when predicting that someone would get his comeuppance or meet his Maker, folks would say *A cada cerdo le llega su San Martín* ("Every pig has its Saint Martin's Day"); in England, the equivalent adage was "His Martinmas will come, as it does to every hog." In the Rhineland, roasted suckling pig is the main course of choice for Saint Martin's Day; in the Swiss canton of Jura, the *repas du Saint Martin* includes everything but the oink of the recently butchered pigs.

Goose (Martinsgans) with Roasted Cabbage
Serves: 6–8   **Cooking time: 3 hours**

THE GOOSE

8-lb. goose
1 Tbsp. salt
1 small bunch fresh thyme

2 tsps. marjoram, dried (or, if fresh, minced)
2 apples, cored and cut into wedges

1 Tbsp. butter, at room temperature and soft
2 tsps. all-purpose flour

NOVEMBER

1. Preheat oven to 350°F.
2. Salt the skin and cavity of the goose.
3. Rub the cavity with the marjoram and stuff it with apples.
4. Cover bottom of roasting pan with warm water.
5. Place goose on a roasting rack breast-side up and prick it all over with a fork to allow the juices to run out.
6. Cook, basting throughout the cooking process with water and juices from the bottom of the roasting pan, for 2½–3 hours, or until the internal temperature reads 140°F for medium-rare, 165°F for well-done, and the skin is crispy.
7. Remove the goose from the roasting rack, set it aside, and allow it to rest 10 minutes before carving.
8. Make the gravy: Skim the fat off the pan juice, discard the fat and pour the juice into a saucepan, and heat it for 10–15 minutes over low heat. In a separate bowl, combine the butter and flour together. Add the flour paste to the pan juices, whisking together to avoid lumps.

THE ROASTED CABBAGE

½ head green cabbage, shredded

1 clove garlic, minced

1 Tbsp. olive oil

1 Tbsp. butter

2 tsps. red wine vinegar

1 Tbsp. mayonnaise

2 tsps. mustard

¼ cup beer

1 tsp. salt

2 tsps. sugar

1 tsp. black pepper

½ cup light beer

1. In a large sauté pan on medium heat, heat the olive oil and butter.
2. When the butter is melted, add the garlic and cabbage and cook until the cabbage starts to wilt and brown.
3. Add the red wine vinegar, mayonnaise, mustard, vinegar, salt, pepper, sugar, and beer and cook until most of the liquid has evaporated.
4. Serve hot or cooled to room temperature.

NOVEMBER

FOOD FOR THOUGHT

A prayer to Saint Martin: May his intercession for us delay our own Martinmas.

NOVEMBER 15
ALBERT THE GREAT

Albertus Magnus (d. 1280) is probably most famous for being the teacher of Saint Thomas Aquinas, but Albert, who was a Dominican friar, professor at the universities of Paris and Cologne, and bishop of Ratisbon, Germany, deserves our admiration for more than just having taught someone else. Albert had an encyclopedic mind and was a brilliant natural scientist; in some ways, for example, his work on how species are adapted to their environment rivals that of Darwin. Chesterton claimed he was the founder of modern science because he did more than anyone else to turn alchemy into chemistry and astrology into astronomy. That may be an exaggeration, but Albert, who was called "the Great" even during his lifetime, appropriated the spirit of scientific inquiry from Aristotle, purified it of its pagan bias, and added a new openness to experimentation and inductive reasoning.

Albert was not canonized until December 16, 1931, when Pope Pius XI declared him a saint and a Doctor of the Church and assigned his feast to November 15. Ten years later to the day, Pope Pius XII made him the patron saint of natural scientists (Albert is also a patron of medical technicians, pharmacists, and students). At a time when scientific breakthroughs were ushering in new weapons of mass destruction and the name of science was being sullied by Nazi ideology and iniquitous experimentation, the Holy Father wisely held up this German son of the Church as an inspiration for the "peaceful and cautious use of the things of nature."[2] Decades later, Pope Benedict XVI remarked, "St. Albert the Great reminds us that there is friendship between science and faith and that through their vocation to the study of nature, scientists can take an authentic and fascinating path of holiness."[3]

While others called him Great, Albert referred to himself as "Albert of Lauingen" after his hometown in Bavaria, Germany. Semmelknödel is a traditional Bavarian bread dumpling that uses what may be considered a discardable ingredient (crusty old bread) and gives it new life. Sounds like a metaphor for sanctity! As a side dish, Semmelknödel also gives new life to leftover meats and vegetables.

Semmelknödel
Serves: 4–6 (as a side dish)
Cooking time: 1 hour

2 cups of crusty white bread, cubed and left to sit out for a few days to get hard (Note: do not use croutons, which are already double-baked)

1 cup hot milk

1 Tbsp. butter

½ yellow onion, minced (yielding approximately ¼ cup)

4 strips thick-cut bacon, diced

3 Tbsps. fresh parsley, minced

2 eggs, beaten

1 tsp. salt

1 tsp. black pepper

½ tsp. nutmeg

½ cup bread crumbs, as needed

1. Put the hardened cubed bread in a large bowl.
2. Pour the hot milk over the bread and set it aside to soften for 20–25 minutes.
3. In a sauté pan over medium heat, melt the butter and cook the onions until they are translucent. Do not brown or caramelize the onions. Add the onions in melted butter to the bread and milk mixture.
4. In the same saucepan, cook the diced bacon until crispy, drain the grease, and add the bacon to the mixture.
5. Season with salt, pepper, nutmeg, and parsley. Knead the mixture together with your hands until the ingredients are fully incorporated and form a dough with a soft and chunky consistency. If the dough is too wet, add some bread crumbs. Do NOT use flour to bind the mixture.
6. Wet your hands with water and form the dough into balls the size of tennis balls.
7. Refrigerate the dough balls for about 1 hour.
8. In a large, deep pot over medium-high heat, bring water to a simmer, not a full boil.
9. Use a large spoon to carefully lower the balls into the simmering water and cook for 15–20 minutes.
10. Remove the balls with a slotted spoon and serve them as a side dish.

NOVEMBER

FOOD FOR THOUGHT

The title "Great" is given to only a few saints. But the fact is, as Saint John Paul II reminded us, we are not built for mediocrity but for greatness. Ask yourself how you can be great in the art of holy living and then make resolutions to work towards that goal. And while you're at it, pray that scientists around the world use their field as "an authentic and fascinating path of holiness."

NOVEMBER 16
SAINT GERTRUDE THE GREAT

As far as we can tell, this is the only time in the calendar, old or new, that the faithful are treated to back-to-back Greats. No doubt this is an invitation to double down on our merrymaking.

Gertrude (1256–ca. 1302) was a Benedictine nun of the monastery of Saint Mary at Helfta in Saxony, Germany, which she entered, possibly as an orphan, at the tender age of four. She received an excellent education under Saint Mechtilde of Hackeborn, another extraordinary and talented woman. A voracious learner, Gertrude excelled in all the liberal arts and was interested in a variety of subjects ranging from singing to making miniatures. But in Advent of 1280, she began to feel that her learning was motivated by vanity. Jesus relieved her of this anxiety on January 27 through a vision. Gertrude saw a youth lead her by the hand "to guide her through the tangle of thorns that surrounded her soul." When she looked at the youth's hands and saw the imprint of the Holy Wounds, she knew that it was her Savior.

Rededicating herself to her monastic vocation and turning her attention from the liberal arts to theology, Gertrude wrote extensively in order to assist both the wise and the unlearned. Unfortunately, only a few of her writings survive, but they were enough to influence the spirituality of, among others, Teresa of Ávila (who chose her as her role model), Saint Francis de Sales, and Dom Guéranger.

Gertrude is also considered one of the great mystics of the Middle Ages. She had a special concern for the souls in Purgatory and was rewarded with frequent visions about their condition. She also once saw Jesus Himself offering the Mass.

At the age of forty-six, her body worn out and riddled with pain, Gertrude passed into eternal life in November of 1301 or 1302. Appropriately, she died in the month during which the Church is especially solicitous of the souls in Purgatory.

Centuries later, King Philip IV of Spain petitioned Rome for her to be declared patroness of the West Indies, and his petition was granted. In Peru, Gertrude's feast is celebrated with great pomp, and there is a town in New Mexico named after her, Santa Gertrudis de lo de Mora.

Why did the good king want Gertrude to be the patron saint of the West Indies? We don't know, but it affords us the opportunity to enjoy the dishes of this marvelous region. Tonight, let the island of Jamaica offer up her riches for the great Gertrude. Although Jamaican Jerk Chicken is certainly not what Gertrude ate growing up, she definitely inspired the jerks around her with the spice and zest of her own life.

Jamaican Jerk Chicken

Serves: 4–6   **Cooking time: 1 hour**

3–4 lbs. chicken leg quarters (thighs and drumsticks)

1 medium onion, coarsely chopped

3 scallions, chopped

1 scotch bonnet pepper, chopped (be careful not to touch your eyes after cutting this hot pepper)

1 Tbsp. five-spice powder

1 Tbsp. allspice berries, coarsely ground

1 Tbsp. black pepper

1 tsp. dried thyme

1 tsp. ground nutmeg

1 tsp. salt

½ cup soy sauce

1 Tbsp. vegetable oil

1. Mix all of the ingredients except the chicken in a food processor until all of the ingredients are fully incorporated into a loose paste.
2. Pour the mixture into bowl, add the chicken, and marinate overnight (or at least 5 hours).
3. Prepare the grill to medium heat.
4. Cook the chicken skin-side down for 10–15 minutes with the grill covered.
5. Turn chicken over and cook uncovered for another 10–15 minutes, or until the internal temperature is 165°F.

NOVEMBER

FOOD FOR THOUGHT

Spice tolerance is different for everyone. Remember, you can always add spice, but you can't take it away. Consider some of the challenging people in your life and approach them with a milder manner before creating too much heat and spice. Then, meditate on these words of Pope Benedict XVI about the life of this talented and pious woman:

> It seems obvious to me that these are not only things of the past, of history; rather St. Gertrude's life lives on as a lesson of Christian life, of an upright path, and shows us that the heart of a happy life, of a true life, is friendship with the Lord Jesus. And this friendship is learned in love for Sacred Scripture, in love for the Liturgy, in profound faith, in love for Mary, so as to be ever more truly acquainted with God himself and hence with true happiness, which is the goal of our life.[4]

NOVEMBER 19 *(NOVEMBER 17)*
SAINT ELIZABETH OF HUNGARY

Elizabeth (1207–1231) was married to Blessed Louis of Thuringia at the age of fourteen and bore him three children. Although the marriage had been arranged, the couple grew to love each other deeply. Elizabeth was renowned for her extraordinary charity to the poor, which her husband gladly supported—up to a point. Once, he came home to find his wife taking care of a leper in their bed! Understandably, the duke was a bit miffed until he saw a vision of our crucified Lord lying there instead of the leper.

Elizabeth was widowed at the age of twenty when the plague took her dear husband. Her in-laws treated her badly, but instead of complaining she moved to a tiny cottage and spent the last years of her short life serving the sick and poor, dying at the age of twenty-four. Her care for the less fortunate knew no bounds. As one of her biographers relates,

One day in winter a sick woman asked her for some fish; Elizabeth ran immediately to a neighboring stream, invoking thus the Divine Provider of all good: "Lord Jesus Christ, if it be your will, send me some fish for your suffering one." And having searched the water she found therein a large fish, with which she hastened to gratify her patient.[5]

Our recipe for Hungarian Seafood Soup honors both Elizabeth's piscatorial efforts for the poor and her earthly homeland.

Hungarian Seafood Soup (Halaszle)
Serves: 4 **Cooking time: 1 hour**

1 lb. fish carcasses

1 lb. carp steaks (or substitute any other white fish), 4 steaks

2 medium-sized onions, cut into rings

1 red bell pepper, diced

2 large tomatoes, peeled and quartered

1 large carrot, peeled and chopped

2 ribs celery, diced

1 Tbsp. Hungarian paprika

½ tsp salt

½ cup dry white wine

1. To a large pot, add the fish carcasses, tomatoes, peppers, onions, celery, carrots, and just enough water to cover the ingredients. Cover the pot, bring to a boil, and cook on low heat for 30 minutes.
2. Use a slotted spoon to remove the vegetables, being careful not to scoop up any bones or other pieces of the fish carcasses.
3. Strain the liquid through a fine mesh strainer or sieve. Discard any remaining pieces of the fish carcass but reserve any remaining vegetables.
4. Clean the pot and return the liquid and vegetables to it. Add 4 cups of water and the white wine and bring to a boil.
5. Season with salt and paprika.
6. Bring to a simmer, gently add the fish steaks, and cook for 30 minutes, being careful not to break the fish by excessive stirring.
7. Serve with crusty bread or boiled potatoes.

FOOD FOR THOUGHT

Saint Elizabeth had the opportunity to dine on the richest and best ingredients, but she chose to eat with the poor and to fish for them. She was a real friend to many, but especially to those who hungered for companionship.

NOVEMBER 23
SAINT CLEMENT

Pope Saint Clement I (d. ca. 99) was the third successor of Saint Peter and an "Apostolic Father," that is, a Father of the Church who learned at the feet of the original apostles. According to an old legend, Clement was banished to work in the stone quarries of modern-day Ukraine and, after converting many of his fellow prisoners to Christianity, was sentenced to die by being tied to an anchor and thrown into the Black Sea.

Oranges and lemons
Say the bells of St. Clement's.

Thus begins an old English nursery rhyme about church bells in and around London. The church in the jingle, it is speculated, is either St. Clement Danes or St. Clement Eastcheap, both of which are close to wharves where citrus fruit would arrive from sunnier climes. The clementine, which is a cross between a willowleaf mandarin orange and a sweet orange, is named not after our saint but after its creator: Brother Marie-Clément Rodier, C.S.Sp., was a French missionary in Algeria who helped run an orphanage. When Brother Clément successfully bred this new variety of mandarin orange in 1902, the orphans christened it the clementine.

We think that Pope Saint Clement would be pleased with this charming example of Catholic charity and service, and we also think that he would like our Clementine Chicken Salad. Our recipe enriches the classic creamy concoction with clementine sweetness, citric freshness, and a dash of paprika pungency.

Clementine Chicken Salad
Serves: 4   **Cooking time: 30 minutes**

2 precooked chicken breasts, cubed

2 clementine oranges, peeled, segmented, and the segments cut in half

2–3 Tbsps. pecans, chopped

½ cup mayonnaise

1 Tbsp. mustard

1 tsp. paprika

½ tsp. salt

½ tsp. pepper

2 Tbsps. fresh cilantro leaves

1 head bib lettuce

1. In a bowl, combine the precooked chicken, mayonnaise, mustard, paprika, salt, and pepper and mix until well combined.
2. Add the halved clementine segments and pecans and gently fold all together.
3. Divide the lettuce leaves on 4 separate plates to create lettuce cups. Divide the chicken salad evenly among the plates. Sprinkle cilantro leaves atop the chicken and serve with a crusty roll.

FOOD FOR THOUGHT
"The Epistle of Clement" was written by today's saint to the church in Corinth. It is easy to find online and makes for interesting reading, establishing as it does the apostolic authority of the clergy at a very early date in Church history.

NOVEMBER 23
BLESSED MIGUEL PRO

It's not our fault that November 23 has two great saints with great culinary possibilities. José Ramón Miguel Agustín Pro Juárez (1891–1927) was a Mexican Jesuit priest martyred by the anti-Catholic regime of Mexico in what Graham Greene called the "fiercest persecution of religion anywhere since the reign of Elizabeth." Miguel's Jesuit confrères described him as a sparkling conversationalist who was both playful and prayerful. After studying and being ordained in Europe, Father Miguel returned to Mexico, where his beloved Church had been forced underground. He ministered to small groups of Catholics in secret, celebrating the Mass and administering the sacraments; he even disguised himself in a policeman's uniform to

administer the viaticum to prisoners. On one occasion, Miguel was scheduled to celebrate Mass at someone's home when he found the place surrounded by police. Undaunted, he approached the sergeant in charge, flashed his wallet quickly in the man's face, and identified himself as a high-ranking detective. After curtly interrogating the frightened sergeant, he went into the house, celebrated Mass (much to the joy of the people inside), and came back out, admonishing the sergeant to watch out for the renegade priest.

Father Pro's earthly ministry ended when he was arrested on a trumped-up charge of trying to assassinate the president of Mexico, condemned without trial, and executed by firing squad. After blessing and forgiving his executioners, he held his arms out in the shape of the cross and shouted the battle cry of the Cristero rebels resisting the government: *¡Viva Cristo Rey!*—"Long Live Christ the King!" The Mexican government filmed his execution, and the footage is included in the closing credits of the 2012 film *For Greater Glory*.

Mole (pronounced MOE-lay) is a spicy Mexican sauce served with meat or poultry. Although Native Americans had been making a similar sauce for centuries, it is thanks to the cook of a convent in the city of Puebla, the capital of the Mexican state of Puebla de los Angeles, that we have mole today. Maria del Perpetuo Socorro (named after Our Lady of Perpetual Help) was preparing Sunday dinner for Archbishop Manuel Fernández de Santa Cruz when she decided to add unsweetened chocolate, peanuts, sesame seeds, and cinnamon. We think Blessed Miguel would be pleased with Pro Chicken Mole: the mole to honor his Mexican heritage and the country for whose soul he fought, and the chicken to point out ironically that he was anything but. Our recipe can help you cook mole like a real pro.

Pro Chicken Mole

Serves: 4–6   **Cooking time: 1½ hours**

3–4 lbs. previously poached chicken, shredded

10 dried chiles anchos, stems and seeds removed

8–10 dried chiles guajillos, stems and seeds removed

2 dried chiles chipotles, stems and seeds removed

5 cups chicken broth, divided

½ cup raisins

5 Roma tomatoes

1 medium white onion, cut into thick slices

4 serrano peppers, stems removed

10 cloves garlic

¼ cup slivered almonds

¼ cup pepitas

½ cup sesame seeds, divided

1 tsp. anise or fennel seeds

2-inch cinnamon stick, broken in half

2 tsps. oregano

½ cup roasted peanuts (or substitute ¼ cup creamy peanut butter)

10–12 saltine crackers

2 corn tortillas, toasted

½ Tbsp. ground cumin

1 tsp. salt, divided, plus more to taste

½ tsp. pepper

4 Tbsps. olive oil or grapeseed oil

1 3-oz. disk of Mexican chocolate, broken into pieces

2 Tbsps. brown sugar, or more to taste

1. Put 4 cups of water in a saucepan over high heat and bring the water to a boil.
2. Heat a separate saucepan on medium heat for 3–5 minutes. Add the de-stemmed and de-seeded dried ancho, guajillo, and chipotle peppers and toast them for a few minutes on each side.
3. Add the peppers to the pot of water and boil for about 15 minutes.
4. Transfer the chilis to a blender, add 3 cups of the chicken broth, the cumin, and ½ tsp. of the salt and blend. Pour through a strainer, discard the pepper mash, and reserve the liquid.
5. To a separate bowl, add the raisins and cover with hot water and set aside.
6. To a large pan over medium heat, add the almonds, pepitas, sesame seeds, anise or fennel seeds, cinnamon stick, and oregano and toast for 5–6 minutes, stirring often to avoid burning.
7. Transfer these ingredients to a blender or food processor and process into a powder.
8. Preheat the oven to broil. Line a baking sheet with aluminum foil and add the tomatoes, serranos, onions, and garlic. Place on a rack in the middle of the oven and broil for 6 minutes, then turn over to broil for another 6 minutes on the other side.

NOVEMBER

9. Add these roasted vegetables to the powdered almond-spice mixture in the blender. Add the peanuts, crackers, corn tortillas, raisins, pepper, the remaining ½ tsp. of the salt, and the remaining 2 cups of the chicken broth. Blend until smooth and set aside.

10. In a Dutch oven or heavy-bottomed pot over medium heat, heat the olive oil. Add the liquid reserved from the toasted chilis, cover, and cook for 20 minutes, stirring occasionally. Add the mix from the blender, stir well, and bring to a light boil.

11. Add the Mexican chocolate, brown sugar, remaining chicken broth, and the cooked chicken and continue cooking for 1 hour.

12. The sauce will darken as it cooks. At this point you may want to add more salt, to taste. Toast the remaining sesame seeds and use them to garnish the mole.

13. Serve with warm tortillas, rice, beans, and a fresh salad.

FOOD FOR THOUGHT

To recognize that Christ is King requires us to see ourselves as servants. How do we serve Christ today and every day? When we serve Him well, we may not be martyred or need to proclaim *¡Viva Cristo Rey!*, but our actions will speak those words clearly.

NOVEMBER 24 *(DECEMBER 14)*
SAINT JOHN OF THE CROSS

Juan de Yepes y Álvarez (1542–1591) was from a family of *conversos*, Jews who had converted to Catholicism under pressure from the Spanish Crown. He entered the Carmelites and, along with Saint Teresa of Ávila, became a great reformer of that order and a founder of the Discalced Carmelites. Saint John of the Cross suffered terribly for his reforming efforts (he was brutally imprisoned and tortured for months by fellow Carmelites), but he survived and endured to become a great spiritual master, poet, mystic, and Doctor of the Church. Saint John of the Cross's most famous work—and one of the greatest works of Spanish literature—

is *The Dark Night of the Soul*, a masterpiece about the difficulties in making spiritual progress towards God.

This saint reminds us of the passionate love that God has for us, a love that led Jesus to become our Passover lamb who takes away the sins of the world. This roasted lamb leg, bone in, is a classic Spanish dish.

Cordero Asado
Serves: 8–10　　　　**Cooking time: 2½ hours**

½ suckling lamb or a bone-in leg of lamb (approximately 9–11 lbs.)

½–¾ cup olive oil or melted lard

2 tsps. fresh rosemary, finely minced

1 Tbsp. salt

1. Preheat oven to 400°F.
2. In a small saucepan, heat olive oil or lard and set aside.
3. Trim any excess fat from the lamb and discard it.
4. Score the lamb with a few slits about ¼ inch deep.
5. Season lamb with salt and rosemary, coating all sides.
6. Place lamb in a roasting rack, or any oven-safe dish.
7. Put in the oven to roast and baste with the oil or lard every 20–30 minutes. Cook for generally 30 minutes per pound, to an internal temperature between 145 and 160°F, until the lamb is golden-brown and the meat is tender.
8. Serve with roasted potatoes.

NOVEMBER

FOOD FOR THOUGHT

Saint John of the Cross saw himself as God's beloved. Do you know how much God loves you? Try this: think of something that you love about yourself and thank God for it. Next, imagine that you don't actually possess this lovable quality. Guess what? God still loves you! That's how much He loves you.

NOVEMBER 25
CATHERINE OF ALEXANDRIA

Saint Catherine (282–305) was a noble young woman from Alexandria who consecrated her virginity to the Lord and who, like Saint Catherine of Siena, had a mystical vision in which she saw a ring being placed on her finger by Christ. Catherine upbraided the Roman emperor Maximinus for his persecution of Christians, and the emperor responded by assembling seventy pagan scholars to refute her. The learned Christian maiden, however, converted them to the faith instead, which is why she is now the patron saint of philosophers. The emperor then tried to execute her on a spiked wheel, but when she ascended the gallows the wheel was destroyed by lightning and the executioner killed. The account of her legend ends by stating that she was beheaded.

Traditionally, Catherine is a popular lady. Because she defeated the philosophers in a debate, she is a patroness of several professions or activities involving education and the law. Because she was almost executed on a spiked wheel, she is invoked by anyone remotely connected to wheels or wheel-like devices, including carters, seamstresses, weavers, wool spinners, milliners, and potters. Because she was beheaded, she is invoked against head ailments such as headache, migraine, and brain tumors. Because of her virginal marriage to Christ, she is called upon as a protector of purity, a matchmaker for unwed girls, and a patroness of childcare and nurses. Catherine was even occasionally asked to protect against shipwreck, probably for no other reason than that she had a reputation for powerful intercession. Finally, as one of the Fourteen Holy Helpers, she is invoked against sudden death, the kind that her tormentors suffered when they tried to kill her on that wheel.

In Estonia, on the vigil of the feast, *kadrisants* or *kadris* (Catherine beggars) go door-to-door begging for food and supplies in exchange for songs and blessings. In this respect modern-day Estonia is not that different from medieval England, when "Katterners" would "go kattering," begging for apples and beer while serenading homes with such memorable ditties as this:

> Cattern and Clemen be here, here, here,
> Give us your apples and give us your beer.[6]

Katterning or catterning is similar to the practice of souling on All Hallows' Eve (see October 31).

As the goal of catterning implies, one cannot celebrate on an empty stomach. In England, "Cattern cakes" made with caraway seeds were baked by lace-makers who invoked Saint Catherine as their patron.[7] In French Canada, unmarried girls would make "Saint Catherine's taffy" and give it to eligible boys. The holiday is called "Taffy Day" by some French Canadians. In northern France a heart-shaped cake called Coeur de Sainte Catherine (Saint Catherine's Heart) was given to a *catherinette* (an unmarried woman at or beyond the age of twenty-five), though we do not think the saint would mind if the whole family enjoyed the treat.[8] Here is the recipe.

Le Coeur de Sainte-Catherine (Saint Catherine's Heart Cake)
Serves: 4–6   **Cooking time: 1 hour**

1¼ cups all-purpose flour

1 cup brown sugar

2 Tbsps. cornstarch

2 Tbsps. baking powder

¼ tsp. salt

½ tsp. ground ginger

½ tsp. cinnamon

½ tsp. nutmeg

¼ tsp. allspice

¼ tsp. ground cloves

¼ tsp. ground ginger

½ cup whole milk

2 large eggs at room temperature

1 tsp. vanilla

½ cup butter at room temperature

¼ cup unsweetened applesauce

1 apple, peeled, cored, and cut into small cubes

½ cup chopped walnuts

1. Preheat oven to 350°F.
2. Grease a heart-shaped cake pan (or a cake baking pan of any shape) with butter.
3. Sift all the dry ingredients together in a large mixing bowl.
4. In a separate bowl, whisk together the eggs, milk, and vanilla.
5. In a stand mixer or hand mixer, whip the butter until it becomes light and fluffy.
6. In the same bowl as the butter, alternately add small amounts of the dry ingredients and the wet ingredients until all of the ingredients are fully incorporated.
7. Using a spatula, fold in the applesauce, apples, and walnuts.
8. Pour the batter into the buttered pan.
9. Cook in the oven for 35–40 minutes, or until a toothpick inserted comes out clean.

NOVEMBER

FOOD FOR THOUGHT

What fills your heart with joy and what breaks it with grief? Whatever the answer, pray to be like Saint Catherine, a person of heart and encouragement. To "encourage," by the way, literally means to "put your heart" into something or someone.

NOVEMBER 30
SAINT ANDREW

Andrew (d. 60) was a disciple of Saint John the Baptist and the first disciple of Our Lord, the younger brother of Saint Peter who introduced his older sibling to Jesus, and the apostle who introduced the boy with the fishes and loaves to Jesus for one of His Eucharist-foreshadowing miracles (John 6:8). According to tradition, Andrew preached the Gospel in Byzantium and other areas south of the Black Sea before being crucified in Greece on an X-shaped cross.

Saint Andrew is the patron saint of several countries including Scotland; his feast day is Scotland's national day, and his cross is the saltire on Scotland's flag. The traditional Scottish meal for "Andermas," as Saint Andrew's Day was once called, is sheep's head, although you can also enjoy haggis (see June 10). Appropriately, Andrew's name means "manly," for these foods are not for the faint of heart. We suspect that most readers will prefer their mutton in the form of a gyro, a delicious lamb wrap from Greece that is easier to buy than make. This, too, is appropriate: Saint Andrew was martyred in Patras, Greece, and he is the patron saint of that city.

Still, we can't resist following a suggestion made in the old *Feast Day Cookbook* and testing your intestinal fortitude with a Brunswick stew, which is traditionally made with squirrel meat. It was customary in England to hunt squirrel on Saint Andrew's Eve (November 29), leaving plenty of time to prepare the critters for dinner the next day. But if you are feeling squirrely about this choice (sorry, we couldn't resist), you can substitute rabbit or chicken.

NOVEMBER

Whatever the meat, Brunswick stew is excellent. There is a reason why the states of Virginia, North Carolina, and Georgia vie for the honor of being the home of this early American contribution to world cuisine.

Brunswick Stew
Serves: 8   **Cooking time: 1 hour**

2 lbs. precooked squirrel meat (or substitute cooked and shredded chicken breasts)

6 Tbsps. unsalted butter

1½ cups onions, chopped

3–4 garlic cloves

2 large potatoes, peeled and cut into cubes (yielding approximately 3 cups)

1 cup lima beans

2 cups frozen corn kernels

1 cup frozen okra, diced

3 cups chicken stock

2 cups diced tomatoes

½ cup ketchup

1 Tbsp. Worcestershire sauce

2 Tbsps. brown sugar, tightly packed

1 tsp. salt

1 tsp. black pepper

1 tsp. cayenne pepper

1. To a Dutch oven or heavy-bottomed pot, add the butter and melt over medium heat.
2. Add the onions and garlic and sauté until the onions become translucent.
3. Add the corn, okra, potatoes, lima beans, tomatoes, and chicken stock, cover the pot, and cook approximately 10 minutes, until the potatoes are tender.
4. Add all the other ingredients and spices and mix well.
5. Simmer the stew, uncovered, for 30 minutes, or until the liquids are evaporated and the stew is thickened.
6. Serve with rolls and coleslaw.

NOVEMBER

FOOD FOR THOUGHT
Saint Andrew was the first to be called by Jesus Christ and the one who introduced his brother Peter to Him. When you came to your own sense of faith, did you share it with someone? Saint Andrew reminds us that the Good News enjoins us to tell others, starting with our own families.

CHAPTER 12

December Saints

DECEMBER 3
SAINT FRANCIS XAVIER

The Spanish-born Saint Francis Xavier (1506–1552) became one of the first seven founding Jesuits when he was won over by his classmate Saint Ignatius of Loyola in Paris. Francis was sent to India, where he is said to have converted more people to the faith than any other person in history except the apostle Saint Paul. Saint Francis Xavier also conducted missions in Indonesia and Japan and died at the age of forty-six, as he was trying to enter into China, his final dream as a missionary.

Like Saint Ignatius of Loyola, Saint Francis hailed from the Basque region of Spain, where this Basque-style chicken is a local favorite.

Pollo a la Vasca
Serves: 6–8   **Cooking time: 45 minutes**

½ lb. chorizo sausages

2 Tbsps. olive oil

3 chicken breasts, cut into 1-inch cubes

½ tsp. salt

½ tsp. black pepper

1 jar roasted red peppers

1 large onion, thinly sliced

5 cloves garlic, minced

1 14–16 oz. can or jar of diced tomatoes

½ cup pitted black olives, drained and chopped

½ cup pimiento peppers

½ cup sherry

2 tsps. paprika

1 tsp. crushed red peppers

1 cup artichoke hearts, canned or from a jar

1. In a Dutch oven or heavy-bottomed pot over medium heat, cook the olive oil and chorizo sausages. When the chorizo is browned, remove and set it aside.
2. To the same pot add the chicken breasts, season with salt and pepper, and cook until browned on each side. Remove and set aside.
3. Add the onions and garlic and sauté for 2 minutes or until the onions become translucent.

4. Add all the other ingredients and mix together, cooking until it creates a little broth.
5. Return the chicken and chorizo to the pot, mix together, and lower the heat to simmer for another 30 minutes or until the sauce has thickened.
6. Serve with crusty bread or boiled potatoes.

FOOD FOR THOUGHT

In Rome's Church of the Child Jesus, there is a reliquary containing the right arm of Saint Francis, a vivid reminder of the thousands of baptisms that he personally performed. It is true that the spirit is willing while the flesh is weak, but it is also true the flesh can do amazing things when animated by a zealous spirit.

DECEMBER 4
SAINT BARBARA

According to the stories that have come down to us, Barbara (ca. third century) was a beautiful maiden whose father imprisoned her in an effort to shield her from the outside world. Barbara nonetheless converted to Christianity while her father was away, and when he returned he angrily handed her over to the authorities, who condemned her to death by beheading. Barbara's wicked father personally carried out the sentence, but on his way home he was struck dead by a bolt of lightning and consumed in flames. One of the Fourteen Holy Helpers, Barbara is invoked against fever and sudden death.

Some parts of central Europe observed a charming custom in which a maiden broke off a branch from a cherry tree and placed it in a vase of water. If the branch, called the *Barbarazweig*, blossomed on Christmas Eve, the maiden was sure to find a husband within the year.

Don't worry: we will not ask you to eat twigs tonight. Barbara was a Greek from Heliopolis, Phoenicia (present-day Lebanon). This dish is inspired by Greek and Lebanese cuisine.

DECEMBER

Beef Kafta

Serves: 6–8   **Cooking time: 1 hour**

¼ cup parsley

1 small onion, quartered

1 lb. ground beef

2 tsps. allspice

½ tsp. cumin

½ tsp. cinnamon

½ tsp. ground coriander

½ tsp. turmeric

½ tsp. cayenne pepper

½ tsp. salt

½ tsp. black pepper

1 Tbsp. olive oil

1. Preheat your oven to 400°F or your grill to medium heat.
2. In a food processor, blend the onions and parsley together. Put in a strainer, squeeze out any excess liquid, and discard the liquid.
3. Return the mixture to the food processor and add all of the other ingredients except the olive oil. Blend together to form a thick and slightly chunky paste.
4. Pour the ingredients into a bowl to begin molding the meat mixture into 1-inch oblong shapes. They can either be formed around a skewer or simply shaped and placed on a baking sheet.
5. Brush olive oil on each of the meat kaftas.
6. Cook for 6–8 minutes on each side using an indoor stovetop grill pan or an outdoor grill.
7. Serve with yogurt and pita bread.

FOOD FOR THOUGHT

Saint Barbara is a patroness against thunderstorms because of her father's explosive death, but we can also imagine her as a model of mild composure. We could all use fewer storms and more calm in our lives—for example, when we're stuck in traffic, waiting in a long line at the grocery store, or trying to talk to difficult people, including those closest to us. With a dad like hers, Barbara certainly understands our predicament.

DECEMBER

DECEMBER 6
SAINT NICHOLAS

Saint Nicholas, bishop of Myra (270–343), is called the Wonderworker by Eastern Christians. There is a medieval legend that when the Alexandrian heretic Arius took the floor at the Council of Nicaea and went on and on about how Jesus Christ was not consubstantial with the Father, Nicholas, unable to bear Arius's heretical prattling any longer, walked up to him and slapped him. (As one meme puts it, "Deck the halls? How about deck the heretic?") The story goes on to assert that Nicholas was imprisoned for striking a bishop, but that night Jesus Christ and the Blessed Virgin Mary visited him in jail, congratulated him for defending the truth, and liberated him.

Before that, when he was a layman, Nicholas saved three dowry-less maidens from prostitution by throwing three bags of coins down their chimney. As a result, he became the patron saint of the poor, prostitutes, brides, and newlyweds, and, of course, the future Santa Claus. Nicholas holds dozens of other patronages as well, but he is best known as a patron saint of children, in part because of his patronage of the young maidens but also because of a gruesome story about an innkeeper who killed three boys, dismembered them, and pickled their remains in a barrel. Nicholas visited the inn, and after calling the innkeeper to repentance, reassembled and resurrected the boys. In France, the repentant innkeeper became Saint Nick's sidekick, Père Fouettard, or "Father Whipping," who gives out lumps of coal and beatings to the naughty while Nicholas distributes gifts to the nice.

Thanks be to God, there are no traditions about eating pickled meat tonight on Saint Nicholas's Day. Rather, because Saint Nicholas is a great patron of children and visits them on the eve of his feast and leaves treats in their shoes, there are a number of sweets to refresh the saint on his journey. In Poland, if there is a red sunset on Saint Nicholas's Day, it is because the angels are busily baking the saint's honey cakes (*ciastka miodowe*); in Germany there are at least two treats named after the saint and served on his feast day: *Nikolausschnitten* (candy) and *Klauskerl* (Saint Nicholas Breadman). But we are going to land on Holland's spiced hard biscuit: the *speculaas*.

241

Speculaas (Saint Nicholas Cookies)

Yields: approximately 20 cookies   **Cooking time: 1 hour**

2 tsps. fennel seeds, ground finely

1 tsp. cinnamon

2 tsps. nutmeg

2 tsps. ground cloves

2 tsps. coriander

2 tsps. anise

1 tsp. lemon zest

1 tsp. orange zest

1 tsp. allspice

½ cup butter

2½ cups cake flour

1 cup sugar

½ tsp. baking powder

1 egg

1. In a stand mixer or using a hand mixer, cream the butter, sugar, and egg until light and fluffy.
2. Sift all of the other dry ingredients together, add them to the mixture in small batches, and continue mixing until a dough is formed.
3. Allow it to rest overnight in the refrigerator, or for a minimum of 5 hours.
4. Pour out the dough on a floured surface and, using a floured rolling pin, roll it out as thinly as possible.
5. Preheat the oven to 350°F and line a baking sheet with parchment paper.
6. Use a cookie cutter or cookie molds to cut out different shapes.
7. Use a spatula to place the cookies on the baking sheet, spaced about 1 inch apart.
8. Bake in the oven for 15–20 minutes, or until golden brown.
9. Allow the cookies to cool on a cookie rack for a few minutes before serving.

FOOD FOR THOUGHT

'Tis better to give than receive. Consider the nonmaterial gifts that you give to people. Saint Nicholas shows us that the best way to truly bless people is with the best gift of all, faith in Jesus Christ.

DECEMBER

DECEMBER 7
SAINT AMBROSE

We move from one great bishop of the early Church, who allegedly smacked a heretic, to another, who smacked down an emperor and an empress. Saint Ambrose (335–397) was the governor of Aemilia-Liguria in northern Italy when he addressed the faithful in Milan as they were electing a new bishop. The crowd suddenly cried out, "Ambrose for bishop!" though he hadn't even been baptized. Ambrose went from being a catechumen to a bishop in a mere nine days. As the chief shepherd of Milan he energetically defended the Church from heresy and imperial encroachment. He browbeat the emperor Theodosius into doing public penance for a massacre he had authorized at Thessalonica, and he stared down Empress Justina by staging a sit-in and refusing to hand over his church to her beloved heretical Arians. Ambrose also found time to receive the great Saint Augustine (August 28) into the Church and to compose several magnificent hymns.

Ambrose is one of the few canonized saints credited with creating a dish. After he noticed that there was not enough meat to feed the poor, he came upon the idea of beating the meat flat and coating it with egg and breadcrumbs; in other words, he invented "meat-extending," as it was called during the rationing days of World War II. The pulpit in the cathedral of Milan has a carving depicting Ambrose's delicious invention. Today his recipe is called Cotoletta alla Milanese.

Whether or not the story is true, Cotoletta alla Milanese is perhaps *the* signature dish of Milan, with deep ties both to the city and to the Catholic faith. The recipe is at least as old as the year 1148, when it is mentioned as a staple of the monks in Milan's Basilica of Saint Ambrose.

DECEMBER

Cotoletta Alla Milanese

Serves: 4   Cooking time: 30 minutes

THE VEAL

4 scalloped veal filets, thinly cut or pounded thin

2 eggs

1 cup all-purpose flour

2 cups bread crumbs (Italian seasoned)

¼ cup olive oil

1–2 tsps. salt, plus 1 more pinch

1–2 tsps. pepper, plus 1 more pinch

1. Season the veal filets with 1–2 tsps. each of salt and pepper and coat them with flour.
2. Prepare the egg wash by whisking together the 2 eggs with 2 Tbsps. of water.
3. Shake off excess flour and dip the filets into the egg wash.
4. Shake off the excess egg and coat both sides of the veal with the bread crumbs.
5. Set the veal aside in the refrigerator for a few minutes.
6. Heat the olive oil in a pan over medium heat and place the veal gently in the oil and cook for 2–3 minutes on each side, or until golden brown. Remove the veal from the pan, set it aside, and immediately add a pinch of salt and pepper to the top of the veal.

THE SAFFRON AIOLI

1 pinch saffron

1 egg yolk

2 tsps. lemon juice and zest

½ cup olive oil

pinch salt

pinch pepper

1. Put the saffron, egg yolk, salt, pepper, lemon juice, and zest in a bowl.
2. Whisk the ingredients together while slowly drizzling in the olive oil, until the mixture has a creamy consistency.

THE COTOLETTA

1. Serve the veal with a dollop of the aioli. You can also add some fresh greens and garnish with a slice of lemon.

DECEMBER

FOOD FOR THOUGHT

Saint Ambrose knew how to make his resources last for the benefit of the poor. Tonight, let us reflect on how we can be more frugal in our lives, both for the sake of our families and for the sake of the less fortunate.

DECEMBER 8
THE IMMACULATE CONCEPTION
OF THE BLESSED VIRGIN MARY

On December 8, 1854, Pope Pius IX solemnly defined what had already been in the Catholic drinking water since time immemorial, namely that the Blessed Virgin Mary, by a special proactive application of the graces won by her Son's victory on the cross, was preserved from original sin, thereby making her womb a fitting place for the Son of God and her flesh a fitting source for His. Mary is the only human being besides Adam, Eve, and Jesus Christ to come into this world without original sin, but she is not alone in receiving the graces of the cross prior to the first Good Friday. By a special preapplication of grace, *every* holy person before the crucifixion, from Abel to John the Baptist, is redeemed by the Blood of the Lamb prior to Its actual shedding; the difference in Mary's case is that it was applied to prevent not only actual sin but original.

In 1847, the Holy See declared Mary, under the title of the Immaculate Conception, the patroness of the United States of America, in response to a request from the U.S. bishops, and in May 1942 Pope Pius XII extended this patronage specifically to American Catholic soldiers. Other countries (and a large number of U.S. dioceses) have likewise had Our Lady of the Immaculate Conception declared their patron saint.

The Mother of God, who bore the Incarnate Lamb of God in her womb, is typically represented as dressed in blue (a symbol of purity). And she is, as we have just mentioned, the patroness of the United States, where beef is a national favorite. Putting this all together, we present to you a beef-lamb burger with blue cheese and American barbeque sauce.

Barbeque Blue Cheeseburgers

Serves: 4 **Cooking time: 30 minutes**

1 lb. ground beef

¼ lb. ground lamb

1 onion, minced

1 clove garlic, finely minced

1 tsp. salt

1 tsp. black pepper

1 tsp. dried thyme

2 Tbsps. crumbled blue cheese

2 Tbsps. barbeque sauce, any brand of your choice

4 hamburger buns, lightly toasted

1. Preheat oven to broil.
2. In a large bowl, combine the ground beef, ground lamb, garlic, onions, salt, pepper, and thyme, mix well with your hands, and form into 8 patties.
3. Heat an oven-safe pan over high heat, place the patties in the pan, and cook for 3–5 minutes.
4. Flip the patties, immediately place the pan in the oven, and broil the patties for another 3–5 minutes. Remove the pan from the oven and top off the patties with an evenly distributed amount of barbeque sauce and crumbled blue cheese.
5. Return to the oven and cook for another 1–2 minutes.
6. Remove the pan from the oven and the patties from the pan, let them rest for a few minutes, place them in the buns, and serve with your favorite condiments.

FOOD FOR THOUGHT

Have a cookout and invite not just your friends but also people who aren't a part of your regular social group. This is good practice for the eternal banquet in Heaven, and it may provide an evangelizing opportunity to explain the beautiful doctrine that Catholics celebrate today.

DECEMBER

DECEMBER 12
OUR LADY OF GUADALUPE

We know that you were feasting to honor the Mother of God a mere five days ago, but so what? Our Lady of Guadalupe deserves her own celebration. The Blessed Virgin appeared attired as an Aztec princess to an Indian convert named Juan Diego on a hill near Mexico City on December 9, 1531. When the bishop asked for proof of the apparition's authenticity, Juan Diego went to the hill and gathered Castilian roses (which are not native to Mexico and were out of season) in his tilma, or cloak. When he unfolded his tilma before the bishop, the flowers fell to the floor, revealing on the tilma a miraculous image of the Virgin. Within twenty years, nine million native Americans converted to Catholicism, approximately the same number in Europe that left the Church because of the Protestant Reformation. (Coincidence?) Our Lady of Guadalupe is now revered as the Queen of Mexico and Empress of the Americas, Protectress of Unborn Children, and heavenly Patroness of the Philippines.

There are many outstanding Mexican dishes we could choose to honor Our Lady of Guadalupe, but tonight try Tacos Al Pastor (Tacos Shepherd-Style) for the Mother of the Good Shepherd who is the Supreme Pastor of our souls—and because Juan Diego was a shepherd by occupation. (Another coincidence?)

DECEMBER

Tacos Al Pastor

Prep time: 3–4 hours**Cooking time: 20 minutes****Serves: 4–6 people**

2–3 lbs. pork butt or loin (or thin-cut pork chops)

½ onion, roughly chopped

6 oz. pineapple juice

½ pineapple, peeled, cored, and diced into small pieces

½ cup orange juice

¼ cup distilled white vinegar

2 Tbsps. ancho chili powder

4 cloves garlic, minced

1 chipotle pepper

1½ tsps. salt

1 tsp. pepper

1 tsp. dried oregano

2 limes, cut into wedges

½ cup freshly chopped cilantro

1 small red onion, diced

12 tortillas, corn or flour

1. Slice the pork into thin strips and place it in a large bowl or a resealable plastic bag.
2. To a blender, add the pineapple juice, chopped onions, orange juice, white vinegar, chipotle, chili powder, garlic, salt, and oregano and blend to make the marinade.
3. Put the pork in ¾ of the marinade and refrigerate for 3–4 hours.
4. Make the sauce: put the remaining ¼ of the marinade in a small pot and cook until reduced by half.
5. Heat a skillet or grill to high heat. Working in small batches, sear each slice of pork until it is cooked through, 2–4 minutes on each side.
6. Set aside the pork and let it rest for 5 minutes.
7. Add the diced pineapple to the hot pan and cook until charred.
8. Return the pork to the pan to warm.
9. Serve the meat up hot on a warmed tortilla, topped with the sauce, the freshly chopped cilantro, the grilled pineapple, some diced red onion, and a lime wedge.

FOOD FOR THOUGHT

Shepherds are people who have the difficult task of leading their flock to verdant pastures and still waters. In these turbulent times, it is important to recognize and maybe even create our own areas of refuge and refreshment. Consider inviting your priest, pastor, or spiritual shepherd to dine at your home to give him a little rest from his labors.

DECEMBER 13
SAINT LUCY

Lucy of Syracuse (283–304) was a Christian maiden whose prayers to Saint Agatha miraculously cured a malady from which her mother was suffering. When the governor of Syracuse found out about Lucy's faith, he ordered her to be defiled in a brothel. But the soldiers could not move her an inch, even when they tied her to a team of oxen. They then tried to burn her on the spot, but after getting the wood ready they were unable to light it. Finally, Saint Lucy was felled by a sword.

A later tradition is that Lucy was tortured and that her eyes were gouged out; a different version is that she gouged out her own eyes when a suitor took a lusty interest in them. Either way, Lucy is most famously portrayed in Christian art holding a tray containing her two eyes (actually, we should say two of her eyes, because another pair miraculously grew back). Understandably, she became the patron saint of the eyes and of the blind.

In medieval times, Saint Lucy's Day was a great holy day, perhaps because it fell soon after the winter solstice and was a harbinger of the return of longer days and more light (this was before the Gregorian calendar moved the winter solstice to December 21). Lucy's name means "light" in Latin, and there are many charming customs that play upon this theme, such as having the youngest daughter, decked in a wreath of candles, present her mother with pastries in bed for breakfast. In Sweden, there is a pastry called Lussekatter and a ginger snap called Lucia Pepperkakor. Lucy's native Syracuse honors her with a wheat porridge called *cuccìa*.

Our own recipe hearkens to these traditions, with an eye towards her memorable martyrdom (get it?).

....

Eyes-of-Saint-Lucy Buns
Serves: 6–8   Cooking time: 3 hours

½ cup raisins

2 Tbsps. Marsala wine

1¾ cups warm milk (115°F)

1 package active dry yeast

¾ cup sugar

6 tablespoons unsalted butter, melted and then cooled

1 egg, plus 1 more for the egg wash

½ tsp. salt

6–6½ cups unbleached all-purpose flour

¼ cup coarse sugar

DECEMBER

1. In a small bowl, combine the raisins and Marsala wine and set aside.
2. In a separate larger bowl, combine the warm milk and yeast and allow the yeast to dissolve and bloom, approximately 10 minutes.
3. To the milk mixture, add the sugar, butter, 1 egg, and the salt and mix together until all the ingredients are fully incorporated.
4. Add the flour one cup at a time, stirring it in and then kneading until the dough is smooth and no longer sticks to your hands. Place the dough in a buttered bowl, cover it with plastic wrap, and let it rise until it doubles in size.
5. Turn the risen dough onto a floured board and knead it again until smooth.
6. Divide dough into 20 equally sized pieces and roll each piece under the palm of your hand into an 8-inch-long rope, 1 inch thick.
7. Shape the dough ropes into a figure eights, and place a raisin in the center of each of them to represent Saint Lucy's eyeballs.
8. Place the figure eight buns on a parchment-lined baking sheet, spaced at least 2 inches apart.
9. Cover with a rag and allow the buns to rise, approximately 25–30 minutes.
10. In the meantime, preheat the oven to 370°F.
11. Beat the remaining egg with 1 Tbsp. of water to make the egg wash, and brush the wash evenly over each bun. Sprinkle coarse sugar evenly over each one.
12. Bake for 30–35 minutes, until golden brown.
13. Remove the buns from the oven and allow them to cool on a baking rack.

FOOD FOR THOUGHT

Custody of the eyes is a hallmark of sanctity. Review your week and ask yourself if you allowed your eyes to wander towards things that are not godly, and ask for the grace to help you see through the eyes of God.

DECEMBER

DECEMBER 16 *(AUGUST 2)*
SAINT EUSEBIUS OF VERCELLI

As if in anticipation of her celebration of the birth of the God-Man, the Church celebrates several saints in December who were stalwart foes of Arianism, the heresy that denied that Jesus Christ is true God and true man. One of these early heroes is Saint Eusebius (283–371). Born in Sardinia, Eusebius became the bishop of Vercelli in northern Italy. He suffered greatly for his opposition to the Arian heresy and for his defense of Saint Athanasius of Alexandria, so much so that the Church traditionally honors Eusebius as a martyr, even though he died an old man in his bed (after years of painful exile).

This hearty thickened "soup," historically a peasant's dish, captures the bold flavors of Eusebius's native Sardinia.

Zuppa Gallurese
Serves: 4   **Cooking time: 1 hour**

4½ cups of lamb, chicken, or beef broth

1 loaf of day-old bread, about 1 lb., cut into slices and left out to dry for a few hours

1 cup grated pecorino cheese

1 cup grated fontina cheese

¼ cup fresh parsley leaves, minced

1 tsp. black pepper

1. Preheat oven to 350°F.
2. In a large saucepan over medium heat, warm the broth until it begins to simmer.
3. Cover the entire surface of a rimmed baking dish with bread, making sure there are no gaps in the bread surface.
4. Sprinkle the pecorino cheese over the bread, then sprinkle with black pepper and parsley.
5. Lay another layer of bread and another layer of pecorino cheese, and again sprinkle with black pepper and parsley.
6. When all of the pecorino cheese and bread are used up, slowly ladle the hot broth onto the bread until it is wet but not drowned.

7. Use a spatula to make sure the bottom layer is wet and there is no broth pooled beneath it. Note: You may not use all of the broth, depending on the weight and thickness of the bread.
8. Sprinkle the fontina cheese on top of the bread mixture.
9. Bake in the oven for 40–50 minutes, or until the cheese has melted and is golden.
10. Remove the pan and let the dish rest about 10 minutes before cutting into the "soup" and serving it.

FOOD FOR THOUGHT

Telling the truth is difficult to do when it may result in backlash and loneliness, as it did for Saint Eusebius. It takes a confident but humble person to tell the truth effectively. This week consider what "white lies" you have told and what sins of omission you have made; then take mental steps to avoid these sins in the future.

DECEMBER 21 *(JULY 3)*
SAINT THOMAS THE APOSTLE

The apostle famous for his doubting is, fittingly, the first apostle to affirm explicitly the divinity of Jesus Christ. Rebounding from his incredulity about the resurrection, Thomas proclaimed, "My Lord and my God" (John 20:24–29). Along with the refutation of Arianism by saints we celebrate in December, Saint Thomas's belief that Jesus is true God primes the pump nicely for the great festival celebrating the birth of the God-Man.

Saint Thomas is hailed as the apostle of India because it is believed that he spread the Gospel to that faraway land and created the ancient church called the "Saint Thomas Christians." According to one tradition, it was in India that Thomas, an experienced carpenter, was commissioned to build a palace for a local king but spent the money instead on the poor, so that the monarch would have an eternal abode in Heaven. The king was

DECEMBER

not pleased by this allegorical application of his expenditures and threw Thomas into jail. Saint Thomas escaped and is today the patron saint of architects.

Later Thomas drew the ire of another king by baptizing members of his court or his family. The king's soldiers apprehended the saint and killed him with lances in Mylapore, near Chennai, in AD 72. "Saint Thomas's Mount" is a little hill in the suburbs of Chennai believed to be near the place where he was martyred. And the San Thome Basilica in Mylapore contains some of his relics, although the majority of his remains were transferred to the city of Edessa (in Turkey) on July 3 of AD 232.

The feast of Saint Thomas was celebrated on December 21 in the Roman Rite from the time it was introduced into the calendar in the ninth century until 1969, when it was moved to July 3, the anniversary of the translation of the saint's relics to Edessa. Some Thomas Christians, such as the Syro-Malabar Church, celebrate Saint Thomas's feast on July 3, while others, such as the Malankara Orthodox Church, celebrate three feasts: July 3 (the translation of his relics), December 18 (the day he was lanced), and December 21 (the day he died). And the Byzantine Rite's feast of Saint Thomas is October 6.

There is an old superstition for Saint Thomas's Day that has inspired our choice for the night. If a German baker stopped kneading the dough for Kletzenbrot or Hutzelbrot to run out and hug the trees in the orchard, they were guaranteed to bear much fruit in the coming year. Our recipe for Kletzenbrot (Fruit Loaf) is a different take on the fruitcake many Americans still enjoy (or joke about) at Christmastime, combining the sweetness of fruit and the crunch of nuts with the spice of India, and emerging from the cooking process not as a hard brick-like loaf but as a delicious pudding.

Saint Thomas's Kletzenbrot
Serves: 4   **Cooking time: 30 minutes**

½ cup chopped walnuts, toasted

1 Tbsp. olive oil

½ onion, finely minced (yielding ¼ cup)

3 apples, diced into ½-inch cubes

½ cup dried cranberries

2 tsps. yellow curry powder

¼ cup brown sugar

1 tsp. turmeric

1 tsp. salt

3 Tbsps. cider vinegar

2 tsps. fresh ginger, grated

DECEMBER

1. In a large sauté pan on low heat, toast the chopped walnuts for about 5 minutes, continuously stirring the nuts in the pan to avoid burning them. Remove the walnuts from the pan and set aside.
2. In the same pan, heat the olive oil, add the onions, and cook until they are translucent, approximately 3–5 minutes.
3. Add the curry powder and turmeric and cook for 1 minute, until fragrant.
4. Add the chopped apples, cranberries, brown sugar, ginger, salt, cider vinegar, and ½ cup water to the pan. Cover and bring to a boil.
5. Lower the heat and move the lid slightly off the pan in order to let the steam escape.
6. Cook for about 10–15 minutes, or until the liquid has almost evaporated.
7. Remove from the heat, fold in the walnuts, and serve as a side dish to roasted meats.

FOOD FOR THOUGHT

We sometimes think of fruit as only sweet. But spicing up fruit to make it more interesting highlights its sweetness. Difficult situations can either make us bitter or angry, when they should be testing our sweetness. Think of a challenging person or situation and talk to God about how a little more sweetness on your part could make a difference for the better.

For December 24 through 31, see chapter 14, Advent, and chapter 15,
The Twelve Days of Christmas.

PART II

The Liturgical Seasons (The Temporal Cycle)

CHAPTER 13

The Ember Days

T he Ember Days, which have been making a minor comeback in Catholic circles in recent years, fall on the Wednesday, Friday, and Saturday of the same week and occur in conjunction with the four natural seasons of the year. Autumn brings the September Embertide, also called the Michaelmas Embertide because of its proximity to the feast of Saint Michael on September 29. Winter brings the December Embertide during the third week of Advent, spring brings the Lenten Embertide after the first Sunday of Lent, and summer heralds the Whitsun Embertide in the week after Pentecost.

Fasting and partial abstinence from the flesh of warm-blooded animals during the Ember Days were enjoined on the faithful from time immemorial until the 1960s. The association of fasting and penance with the Embertides has led some to think that their peculiar name has something to do with smoldering ash or embers. But the English name is probably derived from their Latin title, the Quatuor Tempora, or "Four Seasons."

And it is that Latin title that inspired, of all things, the name of a popular Japanese cuisine. In the sixteenth century, when Spanish and Portuguese missionaries settled in Nagasaki, Japan, they sought ways of making tasty meatless meals for the Ember Days and started to batter and deep-fry shrimp. The idea caught on with the native population, who applied the process to a number of different seafoods and vegetables already in their diet. The Japanese localized the Latin *tempora* and called it tempura.

Fried foods are delicious, but much depends on the batter, which can range from unpleasantly heavy to perfectly crispy and addictive. Happily, the Japanese have perfected the crunch factor with their tempura batter. Our version is great any time, but especially on days of abstinence.

Temporal Tempura
Serves: 4–6   **Cooking time: 1 hour**

1 carrot, peeled and cut into thick planks

1 Japanese eggplant, cut into circles 1 inch thick

2 cups broccoli florets

15–20 small portobello mushrooms, washed, patted dry with a paper towel, and halved

1 large egg

1 cup ice water

½ cup all-purpose flour

½ cup rice flour

canola or vegetable oil for frying

salt to taste, after frying

1. Cut the vegetables into bite-sized pieces.
2. In a separate bowl combine egg, all-purpose flour, rice flour, and ice water and whisk together until ingredients are fully combined to make the tempura batter.
3. Pour enough oil into a Dutch oven or a heavy-bottomed pot to fill it halfway to the top. Put on medium-high heat until it reaches a temperature of 350°F.
4. In batches, gently dip the vegetables into the tempura batter, gently shake off the excess batter, and carefully lower the battered vegetables into the hot oil using tongs or a slotted spoon. Fry each ingredient for 3–5 minutes, occasionally stirring the pot, until golden brown.
5. Remove the vegetables from the hot oil and place them a wire rack or on a plate lined with paper towels.
6. Add a pinch of salt to the vegetables immediately after they've been fried.
7. Serve as is or accompanied with your favorite dipping sauce.

FOOD FOR THOUGHT

The Ember Days once served as a quarterly spiritual checkup, an opportunity to reflect on the state of one's soul and recalibrate. They also invited the faithful to meditate on and give thanks for the beauty of each of the four natural seasons. There's a time and a place for everything under the sun, as Qoheleth says in the book of Ecclesiastes. A healthy spiritual life is an organized life that includes spiritual exercises appointed throughout the day. But a healthy soul is also ready to say yes to God's unexpected demands or challenges. This week, work daily prayer time into your schedule, but also be responsive to God's schedule for you.

CHAPTER 14

Advent

Advent, the four-week period preceding Christmas, is a curious season. It awaits the coming of the Messiah, who already came two thousand years ago. It celebrates the first coming of Jesus Christ, who came in humility as a baby in Bethlehem, in order to prepare for His Second Coming, when He will come in glory as a Judge from the East. In churches, the penitential colors of violet and rose (okay, purple and pink) are used, and some hymns of joy (like the "Gloria in excelsis") are suppressed; outside churches, once can find caroling in the streets, Yuletide drinks, and seasonal sweets.

Speaking of which, no other time of year and no other holiday have inspired so many culinary customs around the world. We would have to write another book to cover all the international options for Advent and Christmas. Oh wait, we already did. (See Mike's *Why We Kiss under the Mistletoe: Christmas Traditions Explained*.)

In this chapter, instead of cataloguing all the breads, cakes, pastries, cookies, gingerbread, fruitcake, main courses, and side dishes of the season, we keep things simple with three practical suggestions: a classic holiday treat from Greece, England's famous fig pudding, and an easy and delicious way to observe the tradition of a meatless meal on Christmas Eve.

A TREAT FOR ADVENT AND CHRISTMAS

Christians are so giddy with joy around Christmas that they start playing with their food, making it resemble cherished details of the Christmas story. English mincemeat pie was once rectangular in shape and made to resemble the manger and the infant Jesus. *Stollen,* a popular bread baked in Germany since the Middle Ages, is made with folds of dough that are meant to remind us of the swaddling clothes in which Mary wrapped her newborn Son.

But perhaps the gold medal goes to the *Diples* ("folds") of Greece, known in English as "Christ's Diapers." These cinnamon-spiced, fried puff pastries are a delicious distraction from the stress of holiday preparation.

Christ's Diapers (Diples)

1 package puff pastry
½ cup sugar
1 tsp. salt

¼ cup cinnamon
½ cup crushed nuts of your choice (sliced almonds or crushed walnuts)

¼ cup honey   ½ cup of confectioner's sugar

1 cup melted butter

1. Cut the store-bought puff pastry in half and use a floured rolling pin to flatten the halves.
2. Preheat oven to 375°F.
3. Sprinkle one half with sugar, cinnamon, a light drizzle of honey, and a light but even layer of nuts.
4. Layer the other puff pastry on top and gently press gently together.
5. Lightly brush some of the melted butter on the top side of the puff pastry.
6. Cut the puff pastry into pieces approximately 1½ inches wide by 4–5 inches long, and roll the pieces semi-tightly.
7. Brush on more butter.
8. Bake in the oven for 15–20 minutes, or until golden brown.
9. Remove and rest on a baking rack.
10. Dust confectioner's sugar on top and serve.

FOOD FOR THOUGHT

We broach heresy when we forget that God truly became man, like us in all things but sin. A diaper may not sound appetizing, but it is a vivid reminder of Jesus's complete humanity. Perhaps that is why one of the most cherished relics in Croatia's Dubrovnik Cathedral is (allegedly) one of Jesus's diapers.

THE FIRST SUNDAY OF ADVENT

A nglicans and Episcopalians call the Sunday *before* Advent "Stir Up Sunday" and use the day to begin stirring up their Christmas or plum pudding (which takes weeks to mature properly). On the other hand, and for historical reasons that are unclear, Catholics call the first Sunday *of* Advent "Stir Up Sunday" and begin their puddings on that day. Both Sundays are appropriate insofar as each has a Collect or entrance prayer in its service that opens with the words "Stir up."

The process of making a traditional Christmas pudding has come to abound in allegory and harmless superstition. It should be stirred from East to West to commemorate the journey of the

ADVENT

Magi; it should have thirteen ingredients in honor of Christ and His apostles; every member of the family and every guest should stir the pudding while secretly making a wish. The stirring represents the arousal of our hearts for the Lord's coming, while the richness of the pudding represents the good things that He brings with Him from Heaven. There is even a little poem to accompany the task:

Stir up, we beseech thee,
The pudding in the pot;
And when we get home
We'll eat the lot.

Christmas pudding may include any number of good luck tokens, such as a coin for prosperity, a thimble for luck (or another year of spinsterhood!), a button for another year of bachelorhood, and a ring for marriage, with each of these blessings going to the person who finds the relevant object in his or her piece. Just make certain to tell everyone to look for it, so that no one will choke on his new destiny.

As for the more edible side of the pudding, ingredients include currants, sultanas or raisins, sugar, lemon rind, nutmeg, cinnamon, bread crumbs, eggs, and suet (because the latter is no longer common in U.S. grocery stores, American recipes usually have butter instead). But the most famous addition is warmed brandy poured onto the pudding and set ablaze when it is time to serve it. Some recipes include brandy as one of the ingredients to be stirred in, in the hope that it will keep the pudding from molding as it is maturing for four weeks. But much to Mike's dismay, Father Leo assures him that alcohol is not a perfect preservative. Better to refrigerate or even freeze, and then thaw and reheat.

Fig Sticky Pudding

Serves: 4   **Prep time: 30 minutes**   **Cooking time: 1½ hours**

2 cups pitted dates

1 cup chopped figs or fig preserves

2½ cups water

1 tsp. baking soda

1 cup sugar

2 eggs

2½ cups of self-rising flour

⅓ cup dark chocolate chips

4 scoops vanilla ice cream

2 cups brown sugar

3 cups heavy cream, divided

¾ cup butter, plus another ½ cup butter at room temperature to grease the ramekins

1 cup fresh figs, sliced, for garnish

mint leaves, for garnish

1. Preheat oven to 350°F.
2. Add dates, figs or fig preserves, and water to a medium saucepan over medium heat, bring to a boil, and cook 2–4 minutes. Stir in baking soda and use an immersion blender, or put in a food processor to purée.
3. In a stand mixer or hand mixer, cream butter and sugar until light and fluffy. Add eggs one at a time and beat well.
4. Fold in the flour, the puréed mix, and the chocolate chips.
5. Butter 4 individual ramekins.
6. Fill the ramekins half full with the batter and bake for 25–30 minutes.
7. Prepare the sauce by combining the brown sugar, ¾ cup butter, and 2 cups heavy cream over low heat and simmer.
8. When the pudding is cooked, remove from the oven and let stand for 15 minutes.
9. Whip the remaining 1 cup of cream.
10. Serve the pudding in the ramekins after cutting a cross on the top of each and pouring on 1–2 Tbsps. of the sauce.
11. Serve with a small scoop of vanilla ice cream, a few slices of fresh figs, and a dollop of whipped cream and mint.

DECEMBER 24
CHRISTMAS EVE

THE MEATLESS MEAL

For centuries, the Christmas Eve dinner was one of the most important family meals of the year and a time to extend hospitality to those who had no families of their own. Steeped in ritual and expectation, the dinner straddled the fence between the penitence of Advent and the joy of Christmas. Because December 24 was a day of fasting and of abstaining from the meat of warm-blooded animals, it was long the custom to have a special seafood meal the night before Christmas.

In many parts of Italy, Christmas Eve supper, or *cenone*, consists of twelve courses in honor of the apostles, but the content of those courses varies from region to region and family to family. In southern Italy, the meal is called the Feast of the Seven Fishes. One national favorite is *capitone*, eel sautéed in onion and shallots; another is *fritto misto* or "mixed fry," deep-fried fish, vegetables, or fruit. Other courses can consist of pasta with a meatless sauce such as gorgonzola or anchovy. In Abruzzi (in southern Italy), the feast includes *insalata di arance*, a salad made with orange slices and black pepper marinated in olive oil.

Portugal observes the meatless tradition with *bacalhau*, or salt cod, although some regions prefer *polvo*, or octopus.

ADVENT

A traditional Mexican meal has a "salad of the Good Night" (*ensalada de Nochebuena*), marinated fish (*seviche*), and fried cakes (*buñuelos*). Armenians, on the other hand, have a simple meal of fried fish, lettuce, and boiled spinach, for according to legend this was what Our Lady ate the night that Christ was born.

In Provence (southern France), the *gros souper* (big supper) consists of *aioli*, a delicious garlic mayonnaise, served with fish, snails, and vegetables. For dessert there are thirteen different treats: fruits, nuts, chocolates, and so forth. In some places thirteen is considered a lucky number because it is the sum of Christ and the apostles.[1]

In Slavic lands, the Christmas Eve meal ("Wigilia" in Polish) cannot begin until the first star in the night sky is sighted; it is usually the responsibility of the youngest child to keep watch for it. Stalks of grain are placed in the four corners of the room for a bountiful harvest, and hay is spread out under the tablecloth in honor of the manger. In Poland, the meal begins with grace and the breaking of a rectangular Christmas wafer called *opłatek* ("offering"). The father breaks off a piece and passes the remainder to the rest of the family until everyone has a piece. As the wafer is passed around, prayers are said for loved ones. The ritual symbolizes the unity of the family in Christ, as well as forgiveness and reconciliation. In parts of the Ukraine a wheat porridge called *kutia* serves a similar function. The twelve-course meal in honor of the apostles can consist of soups like borscht, and fish like herring and carp: some Poles buy a live carp a couple of days ahead of time and let it swim around in their bathtub for maximum freshness. For dessert, they enjoy a compote made of twelve different fruits (again in honor of the apostles).

We're still chuckling about the Greek treat of "Christ's Diapers," and so tonight we honor the seafood traditions of Christmas Eve with a dish that evokes Christ's swaddling clothes. *Salmon en papillote* is French for salmon wrapped in parchment paper. It is not only a surefire hit, but relatively stress-free as well—an important consideration on a hectic day like December 24.

Salmon en Papillote

Serves: 4   **Prep time: 20 minutes**   **Cooking time: 10 minutes**

4 pieces of parchment paper, 18 x 15 inches each

4 pieces of boneless, skinless salmon, 4–6 oz. each

2 cups sliced sweet onion

2 cups shredded carrots

4 garlic cloves, minced

16 spears asparagus, trimmed to 5 inches

1 Tbsp. salt, divided

1 Tbsp. black pepper

½ cup grapeseed oil

4 lemons, cut into slices ½ inch thick

2 Tbsps. butter

2 Tbsps. green onions, chopped, for garnish

1. Preheat oven to 450°F.
2. Mix together onions, carrots, and garlic in a bowl with half the grapeseed oil, season with 1 tsp. salt and 1 tsp. pepper, divide into 4 parts, and pile 1 of the 4 parts on one end of each piece of parchment paper.
3. Season the asparagus with 1 tsp. salt, 1 tsp. pepper, and the remaining oil and lay it on top of the onions and carrots.
4. Place the salmon on top of the vegetables, add the butter, season with the remaining 1 tsp. salt and 1 tsp. pepper, and top with lemon slices.
5. Fold the other half of parchment over the fish and, starting from one end, fold and crimp the paper. Right before you seal it tightly, add in a little water to keep the fish moist.
6. Place the packages on a baking sheet and bake for 8–10 minutes.
7. Remove from oven, top with green onions, and serve.

The Twelve Days of Christmas

DECEMBER 25
CHRISTMAS DAY

CHRISTMAS

" **A**nd Mary brought forth her firstborn son, and wrapped him up in swaddling clothes, and laid him in a manger; because there was no room for them in the inn" (Luke 2:7).

The great feast of the Nativity of Our Lord Jesus Christ has long served as an occasion for special dishes. The traditional Christmas Day dinner varies according to nationality, but it is generally marked by hearty and delicious dishes.

Réveillon, which comes from the French word for "to awaken," is used to denote Christmas Eve and also the meal enjoyed in the wee hours after returning from Midnight Mass. Great French foods such as oysters, *boudin* (blood sausage), and roast turkey would grace the table, while in French Canada there would always be a delicious pork pie called *tourtière* and a green ketchup called "chow chow." The dinner is traditionally concluded with a pastry called a *bûche de Noël* (Christmas log).

The English have preserved the medieval tradition of eating geese and plum pudding, but by the time Dickens wrote *A Christmas Carol* in 1843, they had also adopted the American custom of roast turkey. England is also famous for its mincemeat pie. During the Middle Ages these large meat pies were rectangular to resemble the manger in Bethlehem, with a hump in the middle to signify the infant Jesus. These pies were so closely associated with Catholicism that when the Puritans abolished the celebration of Christmas in the seventeenth century, they also forbade mincemeat pies. From that point on the pies have been made in a circular shape and have grown smaller, sweeter, and less carnal. Today's mince pies contain no meat and are roughly the size of a cookie.

Geese and turkey are popular Christmas dishes in many parts of continental Europe, while the Scandinavians prefer some kind of pork, such as ham or spareribs. That goes for Icelanders too, but they also like ptarmigan, a game bird similar to grouse.

The main Christmas dish in Greece is roast turkey but with a Mediterranean twist: it is stuffed with rice and chestnuts.

Germans enjoy goose, rabbit, duck, *Krustenbraten* (crispy pork roast), potato dumplings, and sausage stuffing. Jamaicans, on the other hand, prefer curry goat, while New Zealanders like lamb roasted or barbecued in an underground pit.

We offer two options for a main course. Our Prosciutto-Wrapped Beef Tenderloin combines two crowd-pleasers (prosciutto and tenderloin) and throws in the flavor of umami mushrooms. Pair it with a hearty red wine like a cabernet sauvignon or merlot, and you will have a Christmas dinner to remember. And don't forget to tell your guests that the prosciutto wrapping is in honor of baby Jesus's swaddling clothes!

Another outstanding choice, perfect for larger gatherings, is our Baked Ham with Brown Sugar and Pineapple. As we noted above, Scandinavians are particularly fond of Christmas ham, but the pineapple in our recipe also brings the flavors of Hawaii to the table. An international dish for a universal feast! And be sure to listen to Bing Crosby and the Andrews Sisters' "Mele Kalikimaka" as the ham is being served.

CHRISTMAS

Prosciutto-Wrapped Beef Tenderloin
Serves: 6–8 **Prep time: 1 hour**

1 center-cut beef tenderloin

1 oz. dried porcini mushrooms

2 Tbsps. fresh rosemary, finely chopped

1 8-oz. package of sliced prosciutto (6–8 slices)

2 tsps. kosher salt

2 tsps. black pepper

1 Tbsp. sugar

2 Tbsps. olive oil, divided

2 cloves garlic or 2 Tbsps. shallots, finely chopped

¼ cup red wine

2 tsps. cold butter, chopped into cubes

1. Preheat the oven to 400°F.
2. Take the tenderloin out of the refrigerator and trim it of all silver skin.
3. Sprinkle the tenderloin with the sugar, lightly rub it in, and let sit for 2–3 minutes.
4. Process three quarters of the mushrooms, the rosemary, and the pepper in a food processor to a coarse mix.
5. Take the remaining quarter of the mushrooms, put them in ¼ cup of water, and rehydrate for 5 minutes.
6. Mince the rehydrated mushrooms and put them and the coarse mushroom mix into a bowl with just enough olive oil to make a paste. Mix and reserve.
7. Once the beef starts to look shiny, season it with salt and pepper and let it sit for 2 minutes.
8. Rub the rest of the olive oil (except 1 tsp., which you should reserve for the gravy) all over the tenderloin, wrap it in the prosciutto, and tie it with butcher's twine to hold it all together.
9. Sear the wrapped tenderloin over medium-high heat in a cast-iron skillet or oven-proof pan with a little olive oil until the prosciutto is a nice caramelized color, but not burnt. You are only starting the cooking process; this should only take about 5 minutes.
10. Take the beef out of the skillet, let it rest for 2 minutes, and crust it with the mushroom-rosemary paste. Add additional olive oil to the skillet, put the meat back in the skillet, and put the skillet back in the preheated oven.
11. Roast the meat for 30 minutes, or until it reaches an internal temperature of 125°F.
12. Cover the beef with foil to keep it from cooling off and place it on a wire rack over a baking sheet to rest.
13. Make the gravy: Pour the liquid from the skillet into a bowl. Return the skillet to the heat, add the remaining tsp. of the olive oil, sauté the chopped garlic or shallots, and then add in the red wine to deglaze the pan, making sure to scrape up all the brown bits on the bottom. Once the liquid has mostly evaporated and the pan is almost dry, add back in the drippings from the mushrooms and beef. Return to a boil again just briefly to thicken, then remove from the heat, add in the butter, and swirl the pan to finish the sauce. Taste and season with salt and pepper as needed.

Baked Ham with Brown Sugar and Pineapple
Serves: 8–10   Cooking time: 4 hours

15 lbs. bone-in ham

2 cups brown sugar, tightly packed

1 tsp. cloves, crushed or ground

20-oz. can of pineapple rings in pineapple juice

1 box wooden toothpicks

1. Preheat the oven to 350°F.
2. Remove the ham from the package, rinse it, and dry with a paper towel.
3. Add the cloves and brown sugar to a bowl and mix together.
4. Drain the pineapple slices, reserving the juice from the can.
5. Place 4–5 slices of pineapple in the bottom of a roasting pan. (Do not use the rack, just the roasting pan.)
6. Place the ham on the pineapple and score the entire top of the ham crosswise in a diamond pattern, with cuts about 1 inch apart and on a diagonal.
7. Rub the cloves over the entire ham.
8. Place pineapple rings on the entire surface of the ham, affixing with toothpicks if necessary.
9. Pour pineapple juice into the roasting pan, about 2 inches deep, and discard the excess juice.
10. Wrap the entire ham with aluminum foil and bake for 3 hours, approximately 15 minutes per pound, or until the internal temperature reaches 145°F.
11. After 3 hours, carefully remove the aluminum foil, baste the ham with the juices in the roasting pan, and cook for another 30 minutes uncovered.
12. Allow the ham to rest 15 minutes before carving it into slices.

CHRISTMAS

FOOD FOR THOUGHT
From the winter wonderland of Scandinavia to the tropics of Hawaii, Christmas touches the hearts of all believers. And how could it not? As Eastern Christians proclaim: "Christ is born: Glorify Him!"

DECEMBER 26
SAINT STEPHEN

Saint Stephen, one of the first seven men ordained a deacon by the guidance of the Holy Spirit, is called the protomartyr, for in being stoned to death by order of the Sanhedrin, he was the first disciple of Christ to shed his blood for the faith (Acts 7:57–59). Stephen is a model of that divinely infused love known in the Christian tradition as *agape* or *caritas*, the gift of God which in English we call "charity." The divine origin of charity cannot be overemphasized, for it is by no human love that someone can follow the example of our Savior and forgive the men murdering him. Yet as Saint Luke tells us, as Stephen was dying he fell to his knees and cried out in a loud voice, "Lord, lay not this sin to their charge."

Our Leftover Stone Soup hearkens to Stephen's manner of martyrdom and helps relieve overburdened refrigerators the day after Christmas. We'd like to say that it kills two birds with one stone, but that would be in poor taste.

By a strange twist of history, Saint Stephen is the patron saint of horses. In former times, farmers in Europe would decorate their horses and bring them to church for a blessing. Afterwards, the family would go on a "Stephen's ride" in a wagon or sleigh. It was also customary to bless hay and oats on this day, and in some parts of Poland folks would throw oats at the priest after Mass in imitation of Saint Stephen's stoning!

Another Polish custom (one less likely to freak out your priest) is to bake the Horseshoes of Saint Stephen (*podkovy*), delicious pastries that are shaped like a horseshoe and filled with jam, poppy seeds, or ground nuts.

Leftover Stone Soup

Serves: 8–10   **Cooking time: 30 minutes**

1 large smooth stone, scrubbed and washed clean (to be removed at the end of the cooking process)

4 quarts chicken broth

1 tsp. olive oil

2 cups leftover meats, cubed (ham, turkey, chicken, or beef)

2 cups leftover starch (rice, mashed potatoes, or cubed roasted or baked potatoes)

2 cups leftover vegetables, cubed (squash, carrots, brussels sprouts, beans)

1 cup leftover leafy greens (spinach, or even lettuce from a salad)

2 cloves garlic, minced

1 onion, minced

2 tsps. soy sauce

1 tsp. black pepper

2 tsps. leftover herbs, minced (basil, oregano, parsley, or sage)

1. In a large pot, heat olive oil over medium heat.
2. Add the stone and tell your children that you will add things to make the stone "taste better."
3. Sauté the leftover meats in the olive oil until they develop some char or caramelization.
4. Add the fresh onions and garlic and sauté until onions are translucent.
5. Add the leftover vegetables and the potatoes or rice and mix together.
6. Season with soy sauce, black pepper, and leftover minced herbs.
7. Add the chicken broth and bring to a boil.
8. When the broth is boiling, add the leafy greens until soft and tender, approximately another 5 minutes.
9. Remove the stone, wash it clean, and set aside.
10. Ladle the soup into individual bowls.

Horseshoes of Saint Stephen (Podkovy)

Yields: 14–16 horseshoes   **Cooking time: 1 hour and 20 minutes**

½ cup potato starch

¾ cup butter

1½ cups flour

½ cup sugar

pinch of salt

½ cup milk chocolate chips

2 Tbsps. cream

1. Pour sugar, potato starch, and salt into the bowl of a stand mixer and mix together.
2. Add the butter and continue mixing it all together.

3. Add the flour in small batches to form a dough.
4. Knead the dough, divide it into about 14 balls, and place them on a greased baking dish.
5. Cover with plastic wrap and refrigerate for about 1 hour.
6. With your hands, roll each dough ball into an 8-inch noodle.
7. With a floured rolling pin, flatten the dough noodle to make a flat strip. Cut away any uneven pieces so that you have a flat, long, rectangular dough.
8. Form the strip of dough into a curve, the shape of a horseshoe, and poke small holes every inch around the horseshoe to replicate the nails to the horse's hooves.
9. Place the horseshoe-shaped dough onto a cookie sheet lined with parchment paper.
10. Preheat the oven to 350°F and bake for 15 minutes.
11. Cool on a baking rack.
12. In a separate, microwave-safe bowl, combine the cream and chocolate chips. Microwave for 1 minute, stir the melting chocolate chips and warm cream together to form a chocolate glaze, and use a spoon to scoop some of the glaze over top of the horseshoe cookies.

FOOD FOR THOUGHT

Saint Stephen's feast is the traditional occasion for the abundance of Christmas to be shared with the less fortunate. It was on this day that the poor boxes of the church were emptied and their contents distributed to the needy—hence the term "Boxing Day." Do something nice for the poor today, like giving a homeless person some food or warm clothes. Then say a prayer for the less fortunate before wassailing in gratitude for the blessings God has given you.

DECEMBER 28
HOLY INNOCENTS

"herod, perceiving that he was deluded by the wise men, was exceeding angry; and sending killed all the men children that were in Bethlehem, and in all the borders thereof, from two years old and under, according to the time which he had diligently inquired of the wise men" (Matthew 2:16–17).

From what we can tell, the Roman Rite has always kept the feast of "Childermas" (Children's Mass) on December 28, ever since it first began to be celebrated in the fifth century. The Western Church presents an interesting array of saints on December 26, 27, and 28. Stephen is a martyr by will, love, and blood; John the Evangelist a martyr by will and love (but not blood, because he died a natural death); and the Holy Innocents are martyrs by blood alone. Indeed, because these children died not only for Christ but instead of Him they are called *flores martyrum*, the "flowers of the martyrs." To paraphrase Saint Augustine, "They are the first buds of the Church killed by the frost of persecution."[1]

The Twelve Days of Christmas are a time of topsy-turvy customs where social ranks and pecking orders are inverted in giddy imitation of the grandest inversion of all, the fact that Almighty God humbled Himself to be born a Man in a chilly and malodorous stable.

In the Philippines and some Spanish-speaking countries, Childermas is the equivalent of April Fools' Day, a time of pranks and practical jokes called *inocentadas*. And, of course, all of Christendom once abstained from servile work on this day—along with the other twelve days of Christmas.

Today, come up with your own topsy-turvy, prankish, leisurely customs. A good snort of an adult beverage might help with the creative process.

Blancmange ("white eating") is a medieval dessert said to have been invented by Bavarian chefs to honor the Holy Innocents. Although this claim has been disputed, the symbolism works. Almonds have been associated with infancy and childhood (they were a favorite to give to children as treats). The whiteness of the cream can be seen as a symbol of innocence, and if you sprinkle it with strawberry or cherry sauce, you have a reminder of the blood that King Herod spilled.

Blancmange
Serves: 4–6   **Cooking time: 30 minutes**

5 cups fresh raspberries, plus 1 more cup for decoration

5 tsps. gelatin powder, divided

1½ cups hot water

2 Tbsps. all-purpose flour

¾ cup milk

¾ cup and 2 Tbsps. sugar

⅔ cup almond meal

2 cups heavy cream

2 tsps. vanilla extract

½ cup confectioner's sugar

1. Blend the 5 cups raspberries in a food processor or with an immersion blender until smooth and pour them through a fine mesh strainer or sieve.
2. In a separate bowl, combine the gelatin powder with the hot water, whisk until the powder is completely dissolved, and set aside.
3. To a large saucepan, add the flour, milk, sugar, and almond meal and heat on medium-high, stirring frequently until it starts to boil.
4. After 2–3 minutes of boiling, remove from the heat and add the heavy cream, vanilla extract, and the raspberries-and-gelatin mixture. Whisk together until everything is fully combined.
5. Pour the mixture into a large gelatin mold and refrigerate for at least 6 hours, preferably overnight.
6. When ready to serve, dip the gelatin mold pan in a bowl of hot water for 30 seconds to help release the dessert, put a large plate on top, and flip it upside down.
7. Decorate with fresh raspberries and a dusting of confectioner's sugar.

CHRISTMAS

FOOD FOR THOUGHT
In the topsy-turvy spirit of the Twelve Days of Christmas, Childermas is a time to honor the baby of the family. In some monasteries and convents, the youngest member of the community would be abbot or abbess for the day and receive congratulations and have "baby food," such as hot cereal, served to them for dinner. In the family, the youngest child received special honors, even becoming master of the household. Not all customs, however, bode well for the young 'uns. In some places, children awoke to a spanking from their parents to remind them of the sufferings of the Holy Innocents. Consider how you might adapt these customs in your own family this Childermas—perhaps by letting the kids take charge of cooking and serving dinner tonight.

DECEMBER 31
SAINT SYLVESTER (AND SAINT BASIL)

According to the Byzantine calendar, January 1 is the feast of Saint Basil the Great. On the vigil of his feast, Greeks enjoy Saint Basil cake, or *Vasilopita*. The father steps outside at midnight and smashes a pomegranate for good luck. He then cuts the *Vasilopita*. The first piece is dedicated to Jesus Christ and the second to the Church, while additional pieces are for absent loved ones. Finally, those present each get a piece, beginning with the oldest. Even the baby must have some to ensure good luck for the New Year. And the person who gets the piece with the coin in it is guaranteed good fortune.

This charming tradition is inspired by a legend about the saint. The Roman prefect of Cappadocia had demanded an exorbitant tax from the population, and so the people sadly gathered their valuables to give to him. Saint Basil, however, appealed to the prefect and had the tax repealed. Since the people could not be sure whose valuables among the collection were whose, Basil advised them to make small pies. The saint then put the valuables into the pies, and each person miraculously received what was originally his.

In the Roman Rite, on the other hand, the Church celebrates the feast of Saint Sylvester. Saint Sylvester was supreme pontiff during the reign of Constantine, the Roman emperor who ended the persecution of the Church. One legend even claims that Sylvester baptized Constantine after the latter was miraculously cured of leprosy.

There is a simple reason why the saint's feast falls on this day: after twenty-one years of service to God as pope, Sylvester died and was buried on December 31, 335. That said, there is something appropriate about preparing for the new civic year (at a time when our hearts are filled with hope for "peace on earth") by honoring the first bishop of Rome to assume the throne of Peter during a time of civic peace.

Sylvester's feast is so closely tied to December 31 that in many countries New Year's Eve is known as Sylvester Night (*Silvesterabend* or *Silvesternacht* in German). In Germany, carp or herring salad is the traditional New Year's Eve meal. In Scandinavian countries, it is roast beef, baked potatoes, *risgrynsgröt* (rice porridge), and *kringler* (a kind of donut). In Austria, *Krapfen*, apricot-jam doughnuts, are traditionally eaten when the clock strikes twelve, and in Spain and other Spanish-speaking areas it was considered good luck to eat twelve grapes at the twelve strokes of midnight.

Our recipe takes a cue from Saint Basil's name as well as from this Spanish custom. Some of Fr. Leo's great-grandparents were Spaniards, and so he feels an obligation to toast them. And since we'll be drinking bubbly grapes this evening, why not also enjoy grapes in a savory dish that is easy to cook on a hectic night of revelry and remembrance?

Basil-Seasoned Chicken with Roasted Grapes
Serves: 4　　　　　Cooking time: 30 minutes

2 chicken breasts, fileted to yield 4 pieces	1 tsp. black pepper
½ cup basil leaves, minced	2 Tbsps. all-purpose flour
2 cloves of garlic, minced	¼ cup chicken broth
3 Tbsps. butter, divided	2 cups seedless grapes, red or white, halved
3 tsps. salt, divided	

1. Lightly pound the chicken filets into thin cutlets, season with pepper and 2 tsps. salt, and dredge with flour.
2. Melt 2 Tbsps. butter in a nonstick pan over medium heat and add the garlic and minced basil leaves. Sauté until garlic and basil become fragrant.
3. Shake off excess flour from the chicken and discard the flour. Add the chicken to the pan, cook each side for 3–4 minutes, remove from pan, and set aside.
4. Add the grapes to the pan and cook for 1–2 minutes, or until the grapes take on some color and emit some of their juices.
5. Add the chicken broth and heat until it begins to lightly boil. Turn off the heat and add the remaining 1 Tbsp. of butter and 1 tsp. of salt and slowly stir together to make a light sweet and savory sauce.
6. Scoop some of the sautéed grapes and sauce and pour over the chicken.
7. Serve with rice or potatoes.

FOOD FOR THOUGHT

A popular practice on New Year's Eve is toasting, which can be seen as a profoundly Christian custom. A toast engages all five bodily senses: the touch of the glass, the sound of the clinking, the smell of the bouquet or nose (with wines and whiskies), the sight of the drink and of the person with whom you are toasting (it's very important to make eye contact during a toast), and, of course, the taste. Finally, the toast itself— that is, the spoken wish—takes these earthly dimensions and sanctifies them in what is basically a prayer. Tonight, thank God for the goods of the earth from the past year. And for the toast, paraphrase Saint Thomas More, who once wished a friend a New Year of "godly prosperity."

JANUARY 1
FEAST OF THE CIRCUMCISION/ MARY, MOTHER OF GOD

Over the centuries, January 1 in the calendar of the Latin Church came to be a combination of three feasts: the Octave Day of Christmas, the Maternity of the Blessed Virgin Mary, and the feast of the Circumcision of Our Lord—which, according to the New Testament, took place on the octave of His birth (Luke 2:21). Today, in the post–Vatican II calendar, January 1 is known as the Octave of the Nativity and the Solemnity of Mary, Mother of God.

In Coventry, England, godparents give their children Godcakes, along with a blessing for the New Year. These baked puff pastries in the shape of an isosceles triangle are meant to honor the Holy Trinity.

CHRISTMAS

But with our eye ever towards the practical, we propose a champagne-infused vinaigrette that can be made from leftover New Year's Eve champagne. While traditional cultures would use this time to make sweet pastries as a continuation of the Christmas season, secular cultures have used this day to begin resolutions. Our recipe, drizzled over your favorite salad, is a perfect way to combine the sweetness of the celebration and the desire for a healthy start to the New Year.

Champagne-Infused Vinaigrette
1 clove garlic, finely minced
2 Tbsps. Dijon mustard
½ cup champagne
½ lemon, zested and juiced
2 Tbsps. honey

½ tsp. salt
½ tsp. black pepper
2 dashes hot sauce
½ cup extra virgin olive oil

1. Add the champagne to a small saucepan over high heat, bring to a boil, turn down to low, and simmer for 2–4 minutes.
2. Remove the champagne from the heat and set aside to cool.
3. To a large bowl, add the garlic, mustard, honey, salt, pepper, and hot sauce and whisk together.
4. Add the cooled champagne, lemon zest, and lemon juice and whisk together.
5. In a thin stream, add the extra virgin olive oil while continuing to whisk. The vinaigrette should thicken and become creamy looking.
6. If the vinaigrette is too thick, add a tablespoon of water. If too thin, add a tablespoon of oil and whisk vigorously.
7. Pour over your favorite healthy (or not so healthy) salad.

CHRISTMAS

FOOD FOR THOUGHT
What was your New Year's resolution last year? How did you do? If you didn't fare as well as you had hoped, do not despair. An aspiring saint (and please God, we are all aspiring saints) does not see January 1 as a "miracle day" but as just another day to start again, even if the restart may not fully take until a few weeks or a few months later. Do not be discouraged on this great day of celebration and fresh hope.

CHAPTER 16

Epiphany and the Time Thereafter

JANUARY 6 *(SUNDAY BETWEEN JANUARY 2 AND 8)*
EPIPHANY

The great feast of the Epiphany, which is a holy day of obligation in most countries, celebrates the visit of the Magi to the newborn King in Bethlehem, and thus it celebrates the fact that Jesus Christ came to save not only the Jews but the Gentiles (represented by the Magi, Zororastrian priestly scholars). The Magi are also called the Three Kings, in accordance with two Old Testament prophecies that describe kings from Tharsis, Arabia, and Sheba bringing to the Messiah presents (Psalm 72:10) such as gold and frankincense (Isaiah 60:3–6).

King Cake is a favorite in many Catholic cultures. A small object is put in a cake. Traditionally, it was a coin; more recently, it is a small figurine of the infant Jesus. Whoever finds the object in his piece of the cake is king of the merry party. In Austria, Germany, France, England, and Canada, the King Cake contained a bean and a pea; finding the bean made one a king, while the pea made one a queen.[1]

In Mexico, Rosca de Reyes, or Kings' Day Bread, is a wreath-shaped loaf with cinnamon, anise seed, vanilla extract, and dried fruit. The dinner guest who finds baby Jesus in his slice must make the tamales for the next gathering. A similar custom exists in Spain. Roscón de Reyes is a delicious cream-filled oval pastry with a hidden bean and a surprise. Whoever finds the surprise gets good luck for the year; whoever finds the bean has to buy the next *roscón*.

But we have a simpler option. The Three Wise men brought gifts that can translate to ingredients: something golden, something fragrant, and something oily. This recipe combines three ingredients—golden yellow bell peppers, savory fragrant bacon, and melted cheese—for an amazing Epiphany-inspired brunch.

Bacon-Wrapped Golden Bell Peppers and Eggs
Serves: 4   **Cooking time: 20 minutes**

2 golden yellow bell peppers

4 eggs

1 cup of grated cheddar cheese

8 strips of bacon

4 pinches of salt

4 pinches of pepper

1. Cut away the stem and a small part of the bottom of each yellow pepper so that you can remove the seeds while keeping the circular shape.
2. Cut each pepper in half so that you have four circles of pepper.
3. In a large frying pan, layer 2 strips of bacon in the shape of an "X."
4. Place one pepper circle on top of the bacon, so that the center of the "X" cross of the bacon is in the middle of the circle, with the open side of the pepper up, so the pepper is like a cup.
5. Turn the heat to medium-high and cook the bacon partially, until the bacon fat starts to render.
6. Carefully crack an egg into the center of the pepper, making sure the egg stays inside the pepper.
7. Add a pinch of salt and pepper to the egg.
8. Use tongs to fold up the bacon, almost wrapping the bell pepper cup with the bacon.
9. After 1–2 minutes, use a spatula to carefully flip the pepper and egg.
10. Add 1 Tbsp. of cheese on top of the upside-down pepper, egg, and bacon cup.
11. Cover the pan and cook for another 1–2 minutes, or until the bacon is crispy and the egg is cooked through.
12. Carefully remove the pepper-and-egg mixture and dab it with a paper towel to absorb the extra grease before serving.

FOOD FOR THOUGHT

In some parts of the world, Epiphany is called "Little Christmas" because it is the final day for exchanging Christmas gifts. In the Irish counties of Cork and Kerry, it is also called "Women's Christmas." Irish men do all the household chores today, while their womenfolk hold parties or go out with their friends, with pubs and restaurants holding special "Ladies' Night" attractions. Children also give special gifts to their mothers and grandmothers on this day. Use your imagination to apply these customs to your own situation: for instance, perhaps Dad and the kids make the brunch today and let Mom relax.

EPIPHANY

FEBRUARY 2
CANDLEMAS

When does the Christmas season end? There is no clear answer to this seemingly simple question. For most Americans, it seems to peter out about halfway through Christmas Day itself, after the last present has been opened or when the credits roll at the end of *It's a Wonderful Life*. In medieval and early modern Europe, in contrast, the festivities were just getting started on Christmas Day and would not end until Epiphany (January 6). And since for most of its history the feast of Epiphany was celebrated as an octave (eight days), some would extend the celebration to January 13. In Sweden and Norway, January 13 is also Saint Knut's Day, when it is time for one last party before the Christmas decorations come down: "Twentieth day Knut, Driveth Yule out," as an old saying has it.[2] In the Philippines, Christmastide ends on January 9 with a spectacular procession and day-long celebration of the feast of the Black Nazarene, a seventeenth-century black wooden statute of Jesus carrying the cross. And because of some stubborn holdouts who refused to accept the reformed calendar of Pope Gregory XIII (AD 1582), southwest England observes Twelfth Night on January 17, the date determined by the Julian calendar.

Finally, some folks insist that the season lasts forty days, beginning on December 25 and ending on February 2, the feast of the Purification of the Blessed Virgin Mary. Hence the Robert Herrick poem commanding Christmas revelers to put away their holiday decorations on the night of February 1:

> Down with the rosemary, and so
> Down with the bays and mistletoe;
> Down with the holly, ivy, all,
> Wherewith ye dress'd the Christmas Hall.[3]

Even if all good things must come to an end, we sympathize with the impulse to keep the merriment going. In the modern Catholic and Anglican calendars, February 2 is the feast of the Presentation of Jesus Christ. In the Byzantine Rite kept by the Eastern Orthodox and Eastern Catholic Churches, it is the Meeting of the Lord. But for most of the Roman Catholic Church's history, February 2 was the feast of the Purification of the Blessed Virgin

EPIPHANY

Mary. All three feasts highlight something that took place when Mary and Joseph brought Jesus to the Holy Temple forty days after His birth (Luke 2:21–40)—and February 2 is forty days after December 25. The new Catholic and Anglican feast recalls that Jesus, a firstborn male, was "redeemed" or consecrated to the Lord in conformity with the Mosaic Law.[4] The Byzantine feast focuses on the meeting of Simeon and Anna with the long-awaited Messiah. And the old Roman Catholic feast emphasizes that Mary presented herself at the Temple to be ritually purified from childbirth according to the Law of Moses. The feast of the Purification, incidentally, is nicknamed Candlemas ("Candle Mass") because the day was marked in the Middle Ages with a great blessing of candles and a procession after Mass.

On this day we celebrate the boldness and the beauty of light, which gives us hope and awakens us. This lemon meringue is a perfect dessert that highlights the brightness of the lemon, like the golden color of the sun, while the puckering tartness wakes up our taste buds like a clear dawn piercing through the curtains.

Lemon Meringue Pie

Serves: 4–6   Cooking time: 45 minutes

1 store-bought pie crust

½ cup cornstarch

1¼ cups sugar, plus 6 Tbsps. for the meringue

¼ tsp. salt

2 cups boiling water

3 eggs, separated

1½ tsps. lemon zest

½ cup lemon juice

1. Preheat the oven to 350°F.
2. Boil 2 cups of water.
3. Mix cornstarch, 1¼ cups sugar, and salt in a saucepan, slowly stir in the boiling water, turn the heat on medium-high, and cook approximately 15 minutes, stirring occasionally, until thick.
4. Whip the egg yolks until light, add to the mixture in the saucepan along with the lemon rind and lemon juice, and cook 2 minutes, stirring constantly.
5. Add the butter, allow to cool slightly, then pour into the store-bought pie crust.
6. Beat the egg whites until foamy, then gradually add in 6 Tbsps. sugar.
7. Continue beating until the meringue stands up in stiff peaks.
8. Spread it on top of the pie filling, to the edges.
9. Bake for 15 minutes, remove from the oven, and cool in the refrigerator.

EPIPHANY

287

FOOD FOR THOUGHT

Light is a beautiful gift, but it is not always welcome, especially when you're trying to get more sleep. Consider the brightness of your own personality or your way of interacting with others. Do we give the light that sustains hope, or does our light emanate accusation and criticism, like a policeman's interrogation lamp in a 1930s gangster movie? Renew your commitment to imitate Jesus Christ, the light who shineth in darkness, which enlighteneth every man that cometh into this world (John 1:5 and 9).

EPIPHANY

CHAPTER 17

Mardi Gras or Carnival

In the traditional calendar of the Roman Rite, there is a season that acts as a bridge between the residual Yuletide joy of the Time after Epiphany and the coming austerity of Lent. Known as Septuagesima or Pre-Lent, this bridge begins three Sundays before Ash Wednesday, which is roughly seventy days before Easter: hence the name Septuagesima, or "seventy" in Latin.

Although the season of Septuagesima is not in the post–Vatican II calendar, it continues to exert an influence, since it is Septuagesima that backhandedly gives us Carnival, better known in the United States (or at least in New Orleans) as Mardi Gras. In the weeks leading up to Lent (and in the days prior to refrigeration), Christians needed to get rid of all the foods that they would not be allowed to consume during the forty-day Great Fast, and centuries ago that was quite a long list: not only flesh meat but all dairy products were once forbidden. And the closer Lent approached, the more urgently these food items needed to be consumed. Ironically, the pre-Lenten excesses and glittering pageantry we associate with Mardi Gras in New Orleans or the *carnevales* in Brazil and Venice can be traced to voluntary fasting prior to Lent. This history is present in the very word "carnival," a Catholic neologism that means "reduction" (*levare*) of "meat" (*caro/carnis*)—or, according to other authorities, saying goodbye (*vale*) to meat (*carne*).

There are hundreds of ethnic dishes that were inspired by this pre-Lenten time. Of the many culinary candidates worthy of mention, pączki is particularly interesting, first because it is relatively well known in several regions of the United States and second because it has a rather peculiar and zealous group of devotees, including its own lobby, the National Pączki Promotional Board. Pączki (pronounced PAUNCH-key) is a Polish pastry, similar to a jelly donut, that is traditionally eaten in the weeks immediately leading up to Lent. As with many pre-Lenten foods, the idea of making pączki was to get rid of all the dairy products in the home before Lent began, since the old Lenten fast, which was much stricter than it is now, once prohibited eating anything that came from an animal.

Our unique recipe for Pączki Meat Pockets honors the tradition of finishing up the dairy products, but it also allows us to enjoy some meat before we say goodbye to it. The result is the best of both worlds: a wonderfully wanton combination of pancake and meat, sweetness and savoriness.

Pączki Meat Pockets
Yields: 15 pancakes   Cooking time: 1 hour and 30 minutes

3 cups flour

1 cup milk, warmed

4 egg yolks

3 Tbsps. butter, melted

2¼ tsps. dry yeast (one packet)

⅓ cup sugar

2–4 Tbsps. rum

4–5 cups of canola or vegetable oil, for frying

1 lb. ground beef

½ onion, minced

2 cloves garlic, minced

½ tsp. salt

½ tsp. pepper

1. Add the ground beef, onion, garlic, salt, and pepper to a large pan and cook over medium heat until brown. Pour the meat into a bowl and set aside.
2. In a separate bowl, combine the flour, warm milk, sugar, and yeast. Mix well, cover with a kitchen towel, and set aside for 30 minutes, until the mixture becomes foamy and bubbly.
3. Add the flour, egg yolks, melted butter, and rum and mix together.
4. Turn out the dough onto a floured surface and knead for about 5 minutes. Cover with a cloth and allow to rest in a warm place for about 45 minutes.
5. Flour your board and rolling pin and gently press the dough to an approximately 1-inch thickness.
6. Use a biscuit cutter or a large glass to cut out 3–4-inch-wide rounds.
7. Pour enough oil into a large pan to fill it halfway and heat it to about 340–350°F.
8. Carefully place each dough round in the oil and fry for about 2–3 minutes on each side, then remove from the pan onto a cooling rack or a plate lined with a paper towel.
9. Once cooled down, cut the pastry in half and fill it up with a little of the ground beef, or add jelly and fruit to make a sweet dish.

DRUNKARDS' THURSDAY, THE THURSDAY BEFORE LENT

Syrian Christians call this day Drunkards' Thursday. For them, it is the high point (or low point, depending on your point of view) of Carnival indulgence. Their go-to meal is roast lamb and appetizing stuffed grape leaves called dolmas. Our recipe combines the two beautifully, and you can freeze the leftovers for later snacking. In fact, we won't tell anyone if you make these well before Drunkards' Thursday and enjoy them during all of Pre-Lent.

Lamb & Rice Dolmas (Stuffed Grape Leaves)
Yields: 40–50 dolmas   Prep time: 1 hour   Cooking time: 1 hour

1 16-oz. jar of grape leaves (approximately 60–70 leaves)

1½ cups of short-grain rice, soaked in 3 cups of water for 20 minutes

3 Tbsps. olive oil

1 large onion, finely chopped

1 lb. ground lamb

1 tsp. salt

1 tsp. pepper

2 tsps. allspice

1 tsp. cumin

4 Roma tomatoes, cut into rounds

½ cup fresh parsley, chopped

½ cup fresh dill, chopped

½ cup fresh mint leaves, chopped

4–5 cups chicken broth, warmed

2 lemons, juiced

1. Soak the rice in 3 cups of water for 20 minutes.
2. Meanwhile, drain the water from the grape leaves, rinse them in a colander, separate them, and lay them out on plates or sheet pans.
3. To a large skillet over medium heat, add 1 Tbsp. of the olive oil and sauté the onions until they are translucent.
4. Add the ground lamb, salt, pepper, allspice, and cumin and cook until the lamb is browned, approximately 8–10 minutes.
5. Drain any excess fat from the pan and set it aside.
6. Drain the water from the rice, put it in a large mixing bowl with the meat, fresh herbs, and 1 Tbsp. of the olive oil, and mix until all the ingredients are fully incorporated.
7. Grease the bottom of a heavy cooking pot with the remaining 1 Tbsp. of olive oil.

8. Arrange a few grape leaves to cover the bottom of the pot.
9. Arrange the tomato slices on top of the grape leaves to cover as much of the bottom of the pot as possible.
10. Stuff the rest of the grape leaves individually by laying the leaf rough-side facing you, then adding a heaping tablespoon of the rice-and-meat mixture in the center of the leaf and folding in the sides and rolling up the leaf.
11. Repeat the process until all of the stuffing is used.
12. Arrange the stuffed grape leaves in layers over the tomatoes and grape leaves in the pot.
13. Add the warmed chicken broth, cover the pot, and cook over medium heat for 30 minutes.
14. Uncover the pot, pour the lemon juice over the leaves, and continue to cook for about 30 more minutes over low heat until the rice is fully cooked and the liquid is almost evaporated.
15. Cover the entire top of the pot with a large plate and carefully pour out any excess liquid.
16. Turn the entire pot over onto that same plate, remove the grape leaves that were at the bottom of the pot (and are now on top of the dolmas), and serve.

THE FRIDAY BEFORE LENT (AND FRIDAYS DURING LENT)

Ponti, Italy, has a peculiar tradition. On the Friday before Lent, its inhabitants like to make a thousand-pound polenta and a six-thousand-egg-omelet.

Since that might be a bit much for your family, turn instead to our salmon steaks. Technically, Catholics are called to abstain from flesh meat every Friday of the year unless they substitute some other form of penance. Our flavorful and filling salmon steaks meet all the requirements of Friday abstinence but take the bitterness out of penance.

Salmon Steaks
Serves: 4   **Cooking time: 30 minutes**

4 salmon steaks
1 Tbsp. olive oil
1 Tbsp. butter

1 tsp. salt
1 tsp. black pepper
1 tsp. garlic powder

1 tsp. dried oregano	2 tsps. mustard
2 Tbsps. mayonnaise	1 tsp. lemon juice

1. Preheat oven to 400°F.
2. In a small bowl, combine mustard, mayonnaise, and lemon juice, mix together, and set aside.
3. Season the salmon steaks with salt, pepper, garlic powder, and oregano on both sides.
4. Heat olive oil in a large oven-safe pan over medium heat, place the salmon in the hot oil, and cook for 5 minutes.
5. Turn the steaks over, add butter, and cook until it melts and turns frothy. Baste the steaks for 2 minutes.
6. Divide the mayonnaise mixture in four, place one portion on top of each steak, and spread it out over the entire salmon.
7. Place in the pan in the oven and cook for 5 minutes, or until the mayonnaise starts to brown and bubble.
8. Remove the pan from the oven and the steaks from the pan and serve them with potatoes, rice, or even a salad.

FOOD FOR THOUGHT

We follow various schedules in our lives, but sometimes we forget to keep a schedule in our spiritual lives. We convince ourselves that we can pray throughout the day, but we fail to take the time to pray. Consider how you can use this last Friday before the start of Lent to schedule meals according to the letter and the spirit of the upcoming season.

QUINQUAGESIMA SUNDAY, THE SUNDAY BEFORE LENT

Quinquagesima Sunday is so named because it is roughly the fiftieth day before Easter. Quinquagesima is also called *Dominica Carnevala* ("Meat-Reduction Sunday"), for it was after this Sunday that the faithful centuries ago began to abstain voluntarily from flesh meat—but before they did, they gorged on what they could before the austerity of the Great Fast.

Before Vatican II, it was common to have a pancake breakfast after Sunday morning Mass. You can revive this tradition, or you can empty your freezer of your favorite meats.

Do you have pork chops in the fridge? If so, you are in luck. Our recipe for Pork Chops with Sautéed Apples is an easy-to-cook and easy-to-eat meal perfect for a Sunday gathering. It's fuss-free, tasty, and celebratory. Moreover, it is a reminder that Sundays during Lent are still mini-celebrations of Easter (as is every Sunday), which means that you can still use this recipe on any Sunday in good conscience.

Pork Chops with Sautéed Apples
Serves: 4   Cooking time: 20 minutes

4 ½-inch-thick pork chops, bone in

½ cup of flour

1 tsp. salt

1 tsp. black pepper

1 tsp. garlic powder

1 tsp. onion powder

1 tsp. dried oregano

1 Tbsp. olive oil

1 Tbsp. butter

2 Granny Smith apples, diced

1 Tbsp. sugar

1 Tbsp. vinegar

1 Tbsp. fresh cilantro leaves

1. To a large ziplock bag, add the flour, salt, black pepper, garlic powder, onion powder, and dried oregano and shake the bag to combine the flavors.
2. Add the pork chops to the bag and shake to evenly coat the pork chops.
3. In a large pan over medium heat, heat the olive oil.
4. Add the pork chops to the pan and cook for 4–5 minutes, or until the edges of the pork start to brown.
5. Flip the pork chops over, add the butter, and continue to cook until it melts and gets frothy.
6. Baste the pork chops for another 3–5 minutes.
7. Remove the pork chops and set aside.
8. To the same pan, add the apples, sugar, and vinegar and sauté until the apples become tender.
9. Place the apples on a serving platter and put the pork chops on top, garnished with a sprinkle of cilantro leaves.

FOOD FOR THOUGHT

While abstinence from meat and dairy is no longer required of the faithful during the Sundays of Lent as it once was, you can keep to the spiritual meaning of the season by truly making Sunday a day of rest. An easy, pre-prepped meal is the best way to serve your family while keeping to the spirit of the Lord's Day.

SHROVETIDE

Not all Christian customs of Septuagesima involve merriment and feasting. While the Latin countries had Carnival, the countries of northern Europe had Shrovetide. The verb "to shrive" is Old English for a priest's hearing confession; hence, Shrovetide was a time for the faithful to go to confession and be "shriven" in preparation for Lent. While this period originally encompassed the entire week preceding Lent, it is more common to hear of Shrove Sunday, Monday, and Tuesday, the three days leading up to Ash Wednesday. Needless to say, this custom is an excellent way to prepare for Lent.

Of course, not even the sternest of northern believers could resist every impulse to blow off a little steam. While "to shrive" might refer to sacramental absolution, "to shrove" means "to keep Shrove-tide; to make merry."[1] Large sporting events were popular during Shrovetide (according to legend, the world's first soccer match took place on a Shrove Tuesday, between the Britons and the Romans), and in Ireland getting married during Shrovetide was considered good luck, perhaps because weddings were forbidden during Lent.

COLLOP MONDAY, MONDAY BEFORE LENT

A collop meant a strip of meat; eventually it came to refer to a strip of bacon. The English tradition was to have eggs and collop (in other words, bacon and eggs) on this day. Our recipe for Pork Belly with Honey Soy Glaze restores the original meaning of collop while adding a little zest to the final days before Lent.

Pork Belly with Honey Soy Glaze

Serves: 4–6   **Cooking time: 3 hours**

2 lbs. pork belly

1 Tbsp. white vinegar

2 Tbsps. salt

1 Tbsp. black pepper

1 Tbsp. garlic powder

2 Tbsps. honey

1 Tbsp. soy sauce

2 tsps. fresh grated ginger

2 Tbsps. fresh cilantro leaves

1. Preheat the oven to 350°F.
2. Wash and dry the pork belly.
3. Use a small knife or fork to poke holes throughout the skin.
4. Rub the entire pork belly with white vinegar.
5. In a large bowl, combine the salt, pepper, and garlic powder and mix together.
6. Spread the seasoning over the entire surface of the pork belly.
7. Place the pork belly on a baking rack so that it lies as flat (not curved) as possible.
8. Place the baking rack on a rimmed baking sheet and pour 1–2 cups of water into that dish.
9. Place the baking sheet with the baking rack and pork belly in the oven and cook for 2½ hours.
10. In the meantime, in a small bowl, combine the honey, soy sauce, and ginger.
11. After the 2½ hours, brush the honey-and-soy glaze on the pork belly skin.
12. Turn the oven to low broil and cook the pork belly for another 10 minutes, or until the pork skin is crispy and slightly bubbled.
13. In a small saucepan over medium heat, bring to a light simmer the remaining glaze as a dipping sauce for the pork belly.

FOOD FOR THOUGHT

Spiritual diets are an important part of the faith. We Catholics have no dietary restrictions, but we do have dietary disciplines. As you prepare for Lent, consider the spiritual dietary disciplines that you will make during the upcoming season. Be thoughtful about your choices, since Lent is more than just giving up chocolate: it is training to be a spiritual soldier for the Kingdom of Heaven.

MARDI GRAS,
THE DAY BEFORE ASH WEDNESDAY

Ah, Shrove Tuesday, Fastern's E'en, or Fat Tuesday (Mardi Gras in French). Whatever you call it, today is the final hurrah and the last chance to consume the comestibles once forbidden during a traditional Lent. In England, the last of the dairy products would be used to make pancakes, which gave the day yet another nickname: Pancake Tuesday.

Venice, Italy, has elaborate masquerade parties, while Brazil is (in)famous for its Carnival bacchanalia.

Stateside, when most Americans think of Mardi Gras, they think of New Orleans. Louisianians were perfecting fusion cuisine long before the term was coined. French, Spanish, West African, and Choctaw influences led to the creation of Cajun cuisine in the southwest rural part of the state as well as to the creation of Creole cuisine in the urban center of New Orleans, resulting in classics such as filé gumbo, jambalaya, boudin balls, and étouffée.

Our Prompt Succor Shrimp Étouffée (see January 8) captures the flavor of New Orleans and makes an excellent main course. And for dessert, our Bananas Foster is difficult to beat. This flambé dish, a New Orleans favorite, is sure to please and impress, but make sure that you have a lid nearby to cover the pan in case the flames get a little too dramatic!

Bananas Foster
Serves: 2 people (dessert)   Cooking time: 10 minutes

2 bananas, peeled and cut into long quarters
2 Tbsps. butter
1 tsp. cinnamon

¼ cup brown sugar
¼ cup brandy or rum
vanilla ice cream

1. In a stainless-steel pan over medium-high heat, melt the butter.
2. Add the cinnamon and brown sugar and allow those ingredients to melt and come together.
3. Add the rum and continue to cook.
4. When the mixture starts to bubble, use a stick lighter to ignite the fumes.

5. When the flames die down, add the bananas and gently coat them with the sugar-and-rum glaze.
6. Cook for 1–2 minutes more, until the bananas are cooked, soft, and fully covered with the glaze.
7. Serve warmed bananas covered with the glaze and topped with scoops of vanilla ice cream.

FOOD FOR THOUGHT

On this day, many parishes burn the leftover palms from last year's Palm Sunday to create the ashes that will be used for Ash Wednesday. Similarly, you can write down your faults and failures from the past year and throw the paper into a fire as you resolve to work on these failings and go to confession more often over the next forty days.

CHAPTER 18

Lent and Holy Week

I n the old, old days, Catholic cookbooks had two categories: "fat days," when no fasting or abstinence was required, and "meager days," on which it was prohibited to consume the flesh of a warm-blooded animal and even dairy products. In this chapter we provide some "meager" recipes for Lent (though not all are dairy free) before turning in the next to the fat goodies of Eastertime.

Lent is an excellent time to pare down, and our recipes and suggestions are designed to help you turn to a life of holy yet tasteful simplicity.

THE DAYS OF LENT

I t is ironic that the Great Fast, as Lent is still called in the East, is the mother of so many foods. We start with the most famous, and perhaps the most surprising.

In early Christianity, the pretzel was not a Super Bowl Sunday snack but a Lenten treat. In the 400s, when Lent meant total abstinence from all meat and dairy products, Roman Christians made a simple bread out of flour, water, and salt. And to reward children for their good behavior, they gave them these simple treats, called *pretiola* or "little rewards," from which came the German *Brezel* or *Prezel* and our "pretzel." These little rewards even came shaped as a child's arms in prayer (forearms crossed and hands on the shoulders).

While the Irish enjoyed champ (mashed potatoes) during Lent and the Maltese *Kwareżimal* (Lenten almond cakes), the Polish relished a good dish of *kotlety z grzybów*, large slices of mushroom that look like meat. Our Cream of Mushroom & Barley Soup hearkens back to this tradition.

And then there are those masters of cuisine, the chefs and cooks of France. We include here a new twist on an old French recipe from 1643. This vegetable soup with fish broth is simple, hearty, and Lent-friendly. It also provides an opportunity to use some almost-turned vegetables as well as old bread to create a delicious meal with a heaping of history.

Cream of Mushroom & Barley Soup
Serves: 4–6   **Cooking time: 30 minutes**

3 cups fresh mushrooms (either a mix or all one type of mushroom works well)

2 cloves garlic, minced

1 shallot, minced

2 Tbsps. canola or vegetable oil

1 Tbsp. all-purpose flour

4 quarts vegetable broth

1 tsp. salt

1 tsp. pepper

2 tsps. fresh thyme

2 cups barley

2 tsps. sherry wine

1. Cook barley according to package and set aside.
2. In a large pot on high heat, heat the oil, add the mushrooms, and cook until they start to brown.
3. Add the shallots, garlic, and thyme and sauté for 1–2 minutes.
4. Add the all-purpose flour and mix. Cook for 1–2 minutes.
5. Deglaze the pot by adding 1 cup of vegetable broth at a time and gently whisking to avoid lumps. Continue pouring the broth until it is all used.
6. Add the cooked barley and stir until the soup is fully heated.
7. Drizzle with the sherry.

Fish Day Soup (Soup de Santé)

Serves: 4–6 **Cooking time: 30 minutes**

2 Tbsps. canola or vegetable oil

½ Tbsp. flour

4 cups of fish broth

1 cup celery, diced

1 cup endives, chopped

1 cup spinach

1 cup of green cabbage, shredded

2 onions, sliced into thin strips

½ cup white wine

1 tsp. salt

½ tsp. pepper

1 Tbsp. fresh parsley, minced

4–6 slices of day-old French bread (one per person)

1. Heat the oil in a large pot over medium-high heat.
2. Add the vegetables and sauté for 1–2 minutes.
3. Add two cups of water, bring to a boil, and cook until the vegetables are tender.
4. In a small bowl, combine 2–3 Tbsps. of water with the flour, mix together to form a roux, and add to the pot.
5. Add the fish broth and all of the seasonings and allow the soup to come together to a light simmer.
6. Place a piece of French bread in each serving bowl and ladle the vegetables and soup on top of the bread.
7. Sprinkle with parsley for garnish.

FOOD FOR THOUGHT

Remember, man, that thou art dust, and unto dust thou shalt return.

ASH WEDNESDAY

The beginning of Lent in the Roman Rite remains a day of fasting and total abstinence from the flesh of a warm-blooded animal. We will pass over the curious historic exceptions to this rule, which included aquatic birds, beaver tail (it's so fishlike!), and in some parts of Michigan, muskrat (yum!). Oh, and there is also capybara, the world's largest rodent, which has inspired the following doggerel:

You'll enjoy capybaras to eat;
Venezuelans proclaim them a treat.
Those of Catholic bent
May consume them for Lent
If a fine rodent burger's their meat.

Even during Lent, we don't want to ruin your appetite, so instead of muskrat or capybara, we recommend more palatable options for Ash Wednesday. Austria has *Fastenbrezel* (a cinnamon-flavored bread baked on straw), and England has Hasty Pudding (made in haste because it is inappropriate to cook for a long time on Ash Wednesday), but we recommend our own Chickpea, Tuna, and Cabbage. This hearty salad can be served cold or as a warm main course, heated in a sauté pan. Even though it is technically a "meager" meal, it will make you feel full on the most meaningful Wednesday of the year.

Chickpea, Tuna, and Cabbage
Serves: 4   **Cooking time: 30 minutes**

1 15-oz. can chickpeas, drained and rinsed

1 can tuna, drained

2 cups green cabbage, shredded

2 cloves garlic, minced

½ tsp. red chili pepper flakes

2 Tbsps. olive oil, divided, plus a little extra for the end of the cooking process

1 lemon, zested and juiced

2 Tbsps. fresh parsley, minced

2 Tbsps. fresh mint, minced

1 tsp. salt

1 tsp. black pepper

1. In a large sauté pan over medium-high heat, heat a little of the olive oil and sauté the green cabbage and garlic until the cabbage is soft and slightly caramelized. Remove from the pan and set aside.
2. To the same sauté pan, add a little more oil and the chickpeas and cook for 2–3 minutes, until warmed through.
3. Add the can of tuna and cabbage and toss all together.
4. Add the red chili peppers, the lemon juice and zest, parsley, mint, salt, and pepper.
5. Mix all of the ingredients together until warmed through.
6. Garnish with a drizzle of the remaining olive oil.
7. Serve with a crusty piece of bread, either warm or after being chilled in the refrigerator for a few hours.

FOOD FOR THOUGHT

On this first fast day of the Lenten season, reflect on how we are always called to feast on spiritual foods. Indeed, one of the goals of bodily fasting is to gain a healthy detachment from earthly goods so that our souls can feast more readily on heavenly things. And on a practical note, be sure to drink lots of water when you fast, for the sake of both body and soul.

LENT

LAETARE SUNDAY, THE FOURTH SUNDAY OF LENT

ost folks remember this Sunday as the one (along with Gaudete Sunday in Advent) when the priest wears "pink" vestments. Just don't say that to the priest or he'll never wear them again (priests are *men*, after all). The technical name for this beautiful liturgical hue is rose, and as a lighter shade of the penitential color of violet, it evokes the penitence of the season but with an added dimension of joy. Although there are a number of historical reasons for this practice, the one given by Pope Innocent III (1216) is the most relevant to our concerns: "On this Sunday, which marks the middle of Lent, a measure of consoling relaxation is provided so that the faithful may not break down under the severe strain of the Lenten fast but may continue to bear the restrictions with a refreshed and easier heart."[1]

And *Dining with the Saints* is all about refreshing and easing the heart. Laetare Sunday is also known as Mothering Sunday. The Epistle reading in the old Roman Rite (Galatians 4:22–31) refers to "the Jerusalem that is above" as our mother. In England, this was the day on which apprentices and students were released from their duties in order to visit their "mother church," the church in which they were baptized. This little holiday also enabled them to visit their mums and bring them gifts: the original Mother's Day! One such gift, still enjoyed in England today, is the Simnel Cake. The seventeenth-century poet Robert Herrick penned the following verses in honor of the occasion:

> I'll to thee a simnel bring
> 'Gainst thou go a-mothering;
> So that, when she blesses thee,
> Half that blessing thou'lt give me.[2]

Our recipe—which, in a "consoling relaxation" from the old rules for Lent's "meager days," includes an entire cup of butter—is so good that you may be tempted to skip all the mothering and keep the cake for yourself. And if you add eleven dough balls to the cake, you will be honoring the original design (the number eleven represents the Twelve apostles, minus Judas).

Simnel Cake

Serves: 4–6   **Cooking time: 2 hours**

THE ALMOND PASTE

1¾ cups almond flour

1½ cups powdered sugar

white of 1 large egg

½ tsp. salt

2 tsps. almond extract

1. Combine the almond flour and powdered sugar in a stand mixer on medium speed.
2. Add the egg white, salt, and almond extract, and mix until the ingredients are fully combined.
3. Remove the almond paste mixture and form it into a ball, then press into a log, wrap in plastic, and refrigerate for 1 hour.

THE CAKE

1 cup of butter at room temperature

2 cups sugar

4 eggs

2 cups sifted flour, plus a little more for the lemon and/or orange peel

¼ cup lemon and/or orange peel

1 cup golden raisins

1. Preheat the oven to 325°F.
2. Use a stand mixer to make the batter, combining the sugar and butter and mixing until soft and smooth.
3. Add the eggs, one at a time, and continue to mix.
4. Sift the flour and add it to the mixture a little at a time.
5. Dust the peel and the raisins with a little flour and incorporate them into the batter.
6. Line a round cake tin with wax paper and pour in half of the dough.
7. Slice the almond paste thin and use the slices to cover the surface of the batter.
8. Add the remaining batter on top of the almond paste layer and put the cake pan into the oven.
9. Bake for 45–60 minutes, until the point a toothpick inserted in the cake comes out clean.
10. Serve with whipped cream or white icing combined with a few drops of almond extract.

LENT

FOOD FOR THOUGHT

There is Christian joy even in penance, but today we rejoice that we can see the Easter light at the end of the Lenten tunnel. Are you more joyful over the fact that the disciplines of Lent are coming to an end or that we are drawing closer to the resurrection of Jesus Christ? It is okay if the answer is both.

PASSION SUNDAY, THE FIFTH SUNDAY OF LENT

In the traditional calendar, it was on the fifth Sunday of Lent that the Church turned her attention more explicitly to the suffering and death of Jesus Christ and veiled the sacred images in the church. "Passion" nowadays denotes a strong emotion, but it used to signify suffering. The common denominator between the two is that a strong emotion pulls you hither and thither, and thus you are experiencing or "suffering" this tug of war like a leaf blown by the wind.

Passion Sunday is also known as Carling Sunday because it was on this day that, during a famine in Newcastle, England, a ship arrived with a cargo of these hard gray or brown peas. When they weren't being consumed, carlings were put in one's shoe during Lent for mortification. (Ouch!) We won't stop you from embracing this old tradition, but you may want to turn instead to our recipe for Chickpea, Tuna, and Cabbage (see Ash Wednesday).

Another option on this day is frumenty, a medieval dish that was traditionally served on Passion Sunday. According to legend, this porridge made from boiled grain was what Joseph served his brethren when he hosted them, giving Benjamin five times as much (see Genesis 43:34).

But since it is Sunday, we thought a nice dessert was in order. Our Passion Fruit Cream is the perfect topping for any cake. You can choose any cake recipe from this book—or another dessert, such as Madeleine Cookies (see July 22)—but we also allow you to cheat and use a store-bought dessert such as angel food or pound cake.

Passion Fruit Cream
Yields: topping for 4–6 desserts   **Cooking time: 15 minutes**

1 cup passion fruit   2 Tbsps. sugar
1 cup heavy cream

1. Whip the heavy cream and sugar until it forms whipped cream.
2. Fold in the fresh passion fruit.
3. Add a heaping dollop of this cream to any store-bought dessert.

FOOD FOR THOUGHT

Passion fruit was named after the Passion of Our Lord because of the plant's distinctive flower. When Jesuit missionaries discovered *Passiflora* in Paraguay in the sixteenth century, they saw in its exquisite features an allegory of Our Lord's suffering and death. The flower's five sepals and five petals call to mind the ten apostles (minus Judas and Saint Peter). The corona (a double row of colored filaments) represents the crown of thorns, while the vine tendrils symbolize the flagella used in the scourging. The five stamens represent the Five Wounds, and the three spreading styles the nails that transfixed Christ's hands and feet. The column of the flower betokens the pillar of the scourging, the fragrance signifies the spices the women brought to the tomb, the round fruit recalls the world that Christ's death redeemed, and the red spots on some species hearken to the drops of blood that Jesus shed.

What a rich example of the Catholic sacramental imagination—that is, of seeing all creation as a divine sign that eloquently points to its Creator, even in the smallest details. This week, put on your sacramental goggles and try to see the fingerprints of our loving God everywhere and in everything.

LENT

PALM SUNDAY

P alm Sunday commemorates Jesus Christ's triumphant entry into Jerusalem, when throngs of people laid palm branches and even their own clothes on the path before Him and proclaimed "Hosanna to the Son of David! Blessed is He that cometh in the name of the Lord." It is customary on this day to have palm leaves blessed and to take them home and keep them as a sacramental. In Spain, Palm Sunday was called *Pascua Florida* because it was the custom to bless flowers as well as palms on this day. Initially the name applied only to Palm Sunday, but over time it was applied to Easter and its Octave as well. Thus when Ponce de Leon first spotted the coast of Florida on March 27, 1513 (Easter Sunday), he had a name for the new land ready at hand.

Today was called Fig Sunday in parts of England because everyone ate figs for the occasion. There is a tradition that Our Lord snacked on these fruits after His entry into Jerusalem, but another reason may be that the day after He entered, He cursed a fig tree for not satiating His hunger, even though it was the wrong season for figs (see Mark 11:12–14).

Jesus is not the only one who may have trouble finding fresh figs during the spring. Even in our own day, when modern agribusiness can provide watermelons in January, fresh figs, which bruise and spoil easy, are a rarity at the grocery store this time of year. Dried figs, on the other hand, are available year-round and may be your best bet for observing this custom. Heck, even Fig Newtons would work.

As for the main course, we recommend our Hearts of Palm Pasta. Not only is this dish an obvious tie-in to today's Sunday, but since heart of palm was once one of the most expensive ingredients on the market because of the difficulty of procuring it, it also evokes the kingship of Our Lord. Heart of palm has a light vegetal quality, with a crunchy and yet soft exterior, and tastes like a combination of white asparagus, young coconut, and celery. And you can think of the bow tie–shaped farfalle pasta as tiny little palm leaves spread out in front of the King.

Hearts of Palm Pasta
Serves: 4–6   **Cooking time: 30 minutes**

1 lbs. farfalle pasta

2 Tbsps. olive oil

2 cups hearts of palm, cut into ⅛-inch pieces

2 cloves garlic, minced

¼ cup white wine

1 cup heavy cream

2 Tbsps. fresh parsley, minced

1 tsp. salt

½ tsp. pepper

½ cup parmesan cheese

1. Cook pasta al dente: according to package directions, but subtract 2 minutes from the cooking time. Reserve ½ cup of the starchy water, then drain the rest.
2. In a large sauté pan over medium heat, heat the olive oil.
3. Add the hearts of palm and garlic and cook until fragrant.
4. Add the white wine and cook for 2 minutes.
5. Add the heavy cream, parsley, salt, and pepper, and bring the ingredients to a simmer.
6. Add the pasta to the pan and toss, adding some of the starchy water, a little at a time, until the desired consistency, which should be just creamy enough to coat the pasta.
7. Add the parmesan cheese and mix together before serving.

FOOD FOR THOUGHT

Palm Sunday is in a sense the original feast of Christ the King. Today, let us renew our loyalty to Our Sovereign Lord and pray that we not end up like the fickle crowd in Jerusalem, praising Jesus one day and condemning Him the next.

HOLY THURSDAY

One of the holiest days of the year is known by several names. Although in English-speaking countries it is usually known as "Holy Thursday," its official liturgical title is "Thursday of the Lord's Supper." The holy day is also sometimes called "Maundy Thursday" after something that took place during the Last Supper, the washing of the feet. (*Mandatum*, whence "maundy" is derived, is the opening word of John 13:34 in Latin: *Mandatum novum do vobis*, or "A new commandment I give you.") And in some countries, the day is

LENT

known as "Clean Thursday." Public penitents were not allowed to bathe during Lent as a part of their penance, but on this day they finally got to hit the showers before they were welcomed back into the Church by the bishop. The idea caught on, and soon everyone was bathing (a rare occurrence!) on Holy Thursday in preparation for Easter.

But the most perplexing name for the feast is "Green Thursday," in the German, Slavic, and Hungarian languages. Is it a corruption of the German *grünen*, meaning to mourn, or is it indeed from *grün*, the German word for green? Is it derived from the custom of eating bitter greens like dandelions in imitation of the bitter herbs of the Jewish Passover? Or did the odd name *cause* the culinary custom?

Whatever the answer, several cultures have a tradition of eating some greens, or nothing but greens, on this day. In France and New Orleans, for example, it was considered good luck to make a soup from seven different greens on Holy Thursday. Our Godly Green Soup proudly stands in this tradition.

But if going green is not your thing, bake yourself some Judases, or *Jidáše*. The Czech cookies are shaped like a rope to recall how Judas hanged himself after betraying Our Lord (Matthew 27:5). If that sounds a bit macabre, just be grateful that the Czechs did not create a treat inspired by the description of Judas's death in the Acts of the Apostles 1:18, or we would be eating Exploding Guts Cookies.

Godly Green Soup
Serves: 4–6   **Cooking time: 45 minutes**

2 Tbsps. olive oil, plus extra for end of cooking process

1 green pepper, chopped

1 cup green cabbage, chopped

1 cup kale leaves, minced

1 bunch spring onions, chopped

2 cups spinach

2 Tbsps. oregano

2 Tbsps. fresh parsley

2 cloves garlic

1 cup of small potatoes, peeled and boiled

4 quarts vegetable broth

1 tsp. salt

1 tsp. black pepper

1. To a large pot over high heat, add 2 Tbsps. of olive oil.
2. When it starts to smoke, add the bell pepper, green cabbage, kale, and spring onions. Sauté until the vegetables begin to soften and are lightly blistered.
3. Add the spinach, oregano, parsley, and garlic, mix together, and cook for 2–3 minutes.
4. Add the potatoes and broth and bring to a simmer.
5. Use an immersion blender to blend all of the ingredients together to a light creamy consistency.
6. Serve with crusty bread and another light drizzle of olive oil on top of the soup.

LENT

FOOD FOR THOUGHT

This is the night on which Our Lord was betrayed by a kiss (in fact, the kiss of peace used to be omitted on this night because the bitter aftertaste of the "Judas kiss" was too fresh on the minds of the faithful). Think about the people with whom you share a kiss, and pray that you will all be sincere in your affections and never use a sign of love as an act of insincerity.

GOOD FRIDAY

Good Friday is known as a day of fasting. In contemporary Church discipline, it is one of the only two mandatory days of fasting left on the calendar (Ash Wednesday being the other). In former times, Good Friday was the occasion for far more rigorous observances. The Irish kept what was known as the Black Fast, in which nothing, except perhaps for a little water or plain tea, was consumed until sundown. And in the second century the Church is said to have kept a forty-hour fast that began on the hour when Christ died on the cross (3:00 p.m. Friday) and ended on the hour that He rose from the dead (7:00 a.m. Sunday).

But despite its link to fasting, Good Friday is also associated with several foods. In Greece it is customary to have a dish with vinegar added to it, in honor of the gall Our Lord tasted on the cross. In some parts of Germany, one would eat only *Spätzle* (dumplings) and stewed fruit. In other areas of central Europe, vegetable soup and bread would be eaten at noon and cheese with bread in the evening. At both meals people would eat standing and in silence. The custom, widespread in Catholic countries, of marking every new loaf of bread with the sign of the cross took on a special meaning on Good Friday. In Austria, for instance, *Karfreitaglaib*, bread with a cross imprinted on it, was eaten on this day.

But the most famous Good Friday bread is the hot cross bun. According to legend, Father Rocliff, the priest in charge of distributing bread to the poor at Saint Alban's Abbey in Hertfordshire, decorated buns with a cross in honor of Our Lord's Passion. The custom endured well into the nineteenth century and spread throughout England, where hot cross buns were sold on the streets, as the nursery rhyme tells us, for "one a penny, two a penny." Today, hot cross buns are available during all of Lent.

Several pious superstitions grew up around hot cross buns, such as the belief that they would never grow moldy and that two antagonists would be reconciled if they shared one. Good Friday hot cross buns were kept throughout the year for their curative properties; if someone "fell ill, a little of the bun was grated into water and given to the sick person to aid his recovery."[3] Some folks believed that eating them on Good Friday would protect your home from fire, while others wore them "as charms against disease, lightning, and shipwreck"![4]

Instead of moldy hot cross buns, try our Fava Bean Hummus with Bitter Herbs.

Fava Bean Hummus with Bitter Herbs
Serves: 4   **Cooking time: 15 minutes**

2 cups dried fava beans

2 Tbsps. tahini

1 clove garlic, minced

2 Tbsps. olive oil, plus more for the end of the cooking process

1 tsp. cumin

1 tsp. turmeric

½ tsp. salt

½ tsp. pepper

2 tsps. lemon juice

4 endives, separated

1 Tbsp. fresh parsley, finely minced

1 Tbsp. fresh mint leaves, roughly chopped

4 pita breads, toasted with a light drizzle of olive oil, salt, and pepper

1. Soak fava beans in 3 cups warm water for 20 minutes, until tender.
2. Drain the water and put the beans in a food processor or large pestle, and pulse or grind them until smooth.
3. Add the tahini, garlic, olive oil, cumin, turmeric, salt, pepper, and lemon juice and pulse or grind in the pestle until all the ingredients are fully incorporated.
4. Pour out the hummus onto a plate, drizzle with more olive oil (approximately 1 more Tbsp.), garnish with fresh parsley and mint, and serve with separated endives leaves and pita bread.

FOOD FOR THOUGHT

On Good Friday the faithful venerate the wood of the cross. Although this pious act may be interpreted cynically as worshiping an instrument of death, it is in fact a recognition of how Jesus took what was designed for death and reconfigured it into a sign of hope, no matter the pain or sorrow. Today, consider the crosses in your life, hold them gently in your hands, and pray that God will give you the strength to carry them and even see their value.

HOLY SATURDAY

holy Saturday is in some respects the ultimate Sabbath or day of rest. We Christians sometimes forget that the Hebrew Sabbath falls on a Saturday and that the Old Testament's rigorous rules against activity on the Sabbath—such as the command to sit in one's house and not move from one's seat (Exodus 16:29)—foreshadow Our Lord's stillness in the tomb the day after His burial.

But not all Christians could keep still this day. In some places, such as Poland, boys who were fed up with forty days of eating fish would take a dead herring and ritually execute it by hanging it from a tree and then burying it with glee in a mock funeral! In other places, such as Costa Rica, Holy Saturday is a time for *bromas*, or practical jokes, like stealing your neighbors' belongings and putting them in the town plaza. The association of Holy Saturday with practical jokes makes sense, since it was during the Paschal Mystery that the biggest joke of all was played on the Enemy, when Jesus Christ allowed the devil to stir up mankind against His innocent life without realizing that it was precisely Christ's death that would free mankind from the devil's bondage. Some Church Fathers even described Christ on the cross as the bait on a hook that Satan foolishly took.

In Naples, Italy, *casatiello* is a special donut-shaped bread filled with lots of pepper, pecorino cheese, and cured meats. It is easily recognizable by the whole eggs that are placed on top and secured by a cross of dough. Neapolitan *casatiello* is offered to family and friends only from noon on Holy Saturday until lunch on Easter Monday. In the old days (pre-1950s), the Easter Vigil service was held in the morning of Holy Saturday and ended around noon, and when that service ended so did the Lenten fast.

Tuscan *scarpaccia* does not have as close a tie to Easter as *casatiello*, but it was developed as a spring specialty by sailors making good use of their gardens. This crispy bread with integrated zucchini is delicious, and preparing it will not detract too much from your Easter preparations.

Scarpaccia

Serves: 4–6   **Cooking time: 45 minutes**

2–3 zucchini, cut into thin rounds

1–2 medium-sized onions, cut into thin slices

3 Tbsps. olive oil, divided, plus 2 tsps. more for the end of the cooking process

1 tsp. salt, divided

1 tsp. pepper, divided

1 cup all-purpose flour

⅓ cup of corn flour, plus 2 tsps.

2 Tbsps. fresh basil leaves, ripped

1. Preheat oven to 400°F.
2. Heat 1 Tbsp. of the olive oil in a sauté pan on medium-high heat and cook the zucchini and onions until the zucchini is slightly caramelized and onions are translucent.
3. Season with ½ tsp. of the salt and ½ tsp. of the pepper and set aside.
4. To a large bowl, add the all-purpose flour, ⅓ cup of the corn flour, 1 cup of water, 1 Tbsp. of the olive oil, the remaining ½ tsp. salt, and the remaining ½ tsp. pepper and mix together until a light batter is formed.
5. Add the sautéed onions and zucchini and mix all together.
6. Prepared a rimmed baking sheet by greasing it with the last Tbsp. of the olive oil.
7. Pour the entire zucchini mixture into the pan and spread it out evenly.
8. Sprinkle with a light coating of corn flour and drizzle 2 tsps. of olive oil over the mixture and ripped basil leaves over the entire dish.
9. Place in the oven for 35–40 minutes, until it's golden brown and crispy.
10. Garnish with more fresh basil leaves or any other herbs and serve.

LENT

FOOD FOR THOUGHT

This is a day that requires patience, for after a long Lent and a dolorous Good Friday, it is difficult to wait any longer for Easter Sunday morn or for the Holy Saturday night Vigil. What are you most impatient about in your life and why? As you meditate on the reasons, ask God to help you be patient with Him, others, and yourself.

CHAPTER 19

Eastertide

"Christ is risen! Indeed He is risen!"

Congratulations to you. By God's grace you have survived the meager days of Lent and are now ready for the fat days of Paschaltide. Our forebears in the faith found numerous ways of marking this holy season with rich breads and meats that help the soul rejoice and the body rebound quickly from the Great Fast. In this chapter we introduce you to some of these traditions and steer you toward the most feasible options for the modern table.

EASTER SUNDAY, THE RESURRECTION OF OUR LORD JESUS CHRIST

Easter shines, as Saint Gregory Nazianzen puts it, like the sun among the stars, for it celebrates in a glorious way the bodily resurrection of Jesus Christ from the dead, a belief that is the cornerstone of our faith (see 1 Corinthians 15:14).

Easter also once marked the end of a rigorous fast. As we have seen, eggs and all other dairy products were forbidden during Lent and still are among Eastern Orthodox and Eastern Rite Catholics. The only problem with this mortification is that nobody told the chickens. While folks fasted, the hens kept laying, and by Eastertide there were plenty of eggs in store. Easter eggs and Paschal breads rich with eggs (one Ukrainian recipe uses eighteen eggs for a single loaf!) were prepared with abandon. Pascha, Eternity Cakes, and Koulitch are just a few of these many delightfully decadent Easter breads.

Some Christian cultures have turned Easter dinner into an allegory of new life in the risen Christ. In Ukraine and other Slavic nations, a main course of ham symbolizes our liberation from the Mosaic law and its kosher restrictions (see December 25 for Baked Ham with Brown Sugar and Pineapple); linked sausages represent Christ breaking the chains of Hell; horseradish evokes the bitter herbs of the old Passover feast (and the bitterness of Christ's Passion, now sweetened by His resurrection); Easter bread, or Pascha, recalls Christ's rising from the dead; butter and cheese symbolize spiritual nourishment as from mother's milk; and salt signifies purification and preservation. And then there is the humble egg, in some respects the supreme symbol of the resurrection, for out of the "hard shell" of the tomb comes the miracle of new life.

All the ingredients are brought to church beforehand, either on Holy Saturday or Easter Sunday morning, and blessed by the priest. In some places, the priest travels from house to house blessing the foods. The feast begins when the father of the family takes a blessed egg, breaks it, and distributes it to all at table. It is a beautiful tradition.

Another age-old favorite, for obvious reasons, is lamb: through His Passion, death, and resurrection, Jesus Christ is the true Passover Lamb who takes away the sins of the world and averts the angel of death by His slain Blood. There is even a special blessing for Easter lamb in the old *Roman Ritual*:

> O God, who during the deliverance of Thy people from Egypt commanded through Thy servant Moses that a lamb be slain in the likeness of our Lord Jesus Christ, and instructed that afterwards the blood of the same lamb be put on the door-posts of the houses: do Thou deign to bless and sanctify this meat, which we Thy servants desire to receive for Thy praise, through the resurrection of the same Jesus Christ, our Lord, who liveth and reigneth unto endless ages. Amen.[1]

Our recipe for Parmesan Herb–Crusted Lamb Chops is a fusion blend, the diverse ingredients of which represent the universality of our faith and our obligation to use the fruits of the earth and the work of human hands in service to others. And the herbs are a nice tie-in to the bitter herbs of the Jewish Passover, the olive oil to the Garden of Gethsemane (as well as the oils used during our Baptism), and the bread crumbs to the risen Christ present in the Eucharist.

Parmesan Herb–Crusted Lamb Chops

Serves: 4   Prep time: 25 minutes   Cooking time: 30 minutes

THE MARINADE

2 Tbsps. garlic, minced

2 Tbsps. fresh ginger, grated

1 Tbsp. honey

3 Tbsps. lemon juice

2 Tbsps. olive oil

2 Tbsps. fresh mint leaves, minced

THE HERB CRUST

2 cups panko or other bread crumbs

½ cup parmesan, grated

1 bunch fresh parsley

1 bunch fresh thyme

1 sprig fresh rosemary

THE LAMB

2 frenched racks of lamb

4 Tbsps. olive oil

1 Tbsp. kosher salt

1 Tbsp. black pepper

1. Preheat oven to 400°F.
2. Combine the ingredients for the marinade and allow the rack of lamb to marinate on both sides.
3. Combine the ingredients for the herb crust and press the rack of lamb into the crusting on both sides.
4. Put rack of lamb on a baking sheet with a baking rack and cook for 20–25 minutes, or until the internal temperature reaches 125°F.
5. Use the rest of the marinade to make a sauce by heating it in a saucepan over medium heat until it lightly boils.
6. When lamb is cooked, pull the lamb out and tent with foil so that the lamb stays warm while resting, about 10 minutes before slicing.
7. Slice into chops and serve with the mint marinade sauce.

FOOD FOR THOUGHT

Make Easter a type of a "new year" by making an informed resolution to live joyfully, even in times of trial. And then tonight, before you go to bed, practice saying "Alleluia" with a sincere heart.

THE ASCENSION OF OUR LORD JESUS CHRIST

No mere "Welcome Home" or "Mission Accomplished" party, the feast of the Ascension of Our Lord Jesus Christ forty days after He rose from the dead is, in a certain sense, the *greatest* feast of the year. That, at least, is the opinion of Blessed Columba Marmion (1858–1923), who wrote that the "Ascension is the greatest [of the feasts of Our Lord] because it is the supreme glorification of Christ Jesus."[2] It was on this day that Jesus Christ, not with the blood of goats but with His own Blood, entered into the heavenly Holy of Holies and completed the final stage of our redemption before taking His seat at the right hand of the Father, where He continues to intercede for us.

Several superstitions grew up around the holiday, such as the belief that anyone who worked in the field or garden today would meet great misfortune, and that any clothing that has been touched by a needle on the Ascension will attract lightning and kill the wearer. Bizarre though they may be, these superstitions point to the importance of keeping the Ascension holy.

And keeping holy often involves throwing a feast. It was once a custom in Europe to eat fowl on the Ascension because this was the day that Our Lord "flew" to Heaven. Pheasants, partridges, pigeons, and even crows found their way to the dinner table. So what does it mean to eat crow on Ascension Thursday? Perhaps this is what the other apostles served Saint Thomas to tease him about his earlier doubts concerning the resurrection.

Bakers in western Germany chose a more delectable path by making pastries for the occasion in the shape of various birds. Finally, there is a firstfruits tradition for Ascension Thursday. In some parts of France, apple fritters (*beignets aux pommes*) are a popular choice.

Our Roasted Asian Quail honors the old tradition of feasting on a bird that can fly, and the Asian flavoring is an affirmation that Jesus Christ will come again from the East.

Roasted Asian Quail

5–6 quail

2 Tbsps. ketchup

2 Tbsps. brown sugar

1 tsp. salt

1 Tbsp. lemon juice

2 tsps. sesame seeds

1 Tbsp. sriracha

3 Tbsps. dark sesame seed oil

2 Tbsps. honey

3 cloves garlic, minced

1 Tbsp. fresh ginger, minced

¼ cup white wine

¼ cup soy sauce

2 Tbsps. vegetable oil

1. Wash the quail inside and out, dry with a paper towel, and bring them to room temperature.
2. Preheat the oven to 375°F.
3. In a nonreactive pan, mix all of the other ingredients together. Add the quail and rub the marinade all over the birds, inside and out.
4. Squinch together about 1 foot of aluminum foil into a small circle, on top of which a quail will sit. Make one for each of the quail you will cook.
5. Place the aluminum foil rounds on two baking sheets.
6. Shake off any excess marinade from the quail and place the birds on the aluminum foil ring molds, making sure there is room around each quail
7. Cook in the oven for 30–40 minutes, or until the quail is dark brown and the skin is crispy, being careful not to burn or overcook.
8. Pour the excess marinade into a small saucepan and cook over low heat until it reduces and thickens into a glaze.
9. Use the glaze as a dipping sauce for the roasted quail.

FOOD FOR THOUGHT

Jesus ascending into Heaven defies gravity, and the Spirit of God raises our spirits even when we are burdened and depressed. Today, think of the people who suffer from depression, and pray that God will lift them up. And don't forget to look to the Heavens as well. The old Collect for this feast sums up this outlook nicely, asking that just as we believe that our Redeemer ascended today into Heaven, we may ourselves dwell in mind amidst heavenly things.

EASTERTIDE

PENTECOST OR WHITSUNDAY

Our Lord fulfilled His promise to send the Holy Spirit on the Hebrew feast of Shavuot or Pentecost, the conclusion of a first-fruits festival held fifty days after the Passover (Exodus 23:16). Ten days after His Ascension, Jesus sent the Paraclete to His disciples in the form of a mighty wind and tongues of flame, with the result that they began to speak in different languages. The feast is also called White Sunday or Whitsunday in English, not because of the vestments (which are red) but because this day was once used for baptisms, and the newly baptized wore white robes for the occasion—a fitting custom, for Saint Peter baptized three thousand souls on the first Pentecost (Acts 2:41).

Food was an important part of the festivities. For obvious reasons, dove was the most popular dish. In England, gooseberry pudding was traditional. Why? Search us. Maybe it was an indirect tribute to the fruits of the Holy Spirit.

Dove is out of season in the spring, and gooseberry is not common in the United States, so instead try this poignant reminder of the gift of glossolalia (that's a fancy term for speaking in tongues—impress your friends!). Our Smoky Spiced Barbeque Beef Tongue Steaks capture both the flavors of the flame and the shape that it took as it descended upon the disciples.

Eating beef tongue may push some Americans outside their comfort zone, but isn't that what the Holy Spirit enabled the disciples to do—to stop cowering behind closed doors and to brave new frontiers? So take it all in good stride—or tongue in cheek.

Smoky Spiced Barbeque Beef Tongue Steaks
Serves: 4   **Cooking time: 2½ hours**

3–4 lbs. beef tongue

¼ cup of your favorite barbeque sauce

1 jalapeno pepper, minced

2 Tbsps. of honey (if your barbeque sauce isn't made with honey)

2 tsps. soy sauce

2 tsps. sesame seeds

4 cloves garlic, finely minced

2 Tbsps. olive oil

2 Tbsps. salt

2 Tbsps. pepper

2 Tbsps. oregano

2 bay leaves

2 lemon slices

1. Clean the tongue by washing and scrubbing it thoroughly with a clean scrubber.
2. Put the tongue in a large pot, filled with enough water to cover it by 1 inch.
3. Add the salt, pepper, oregano, bay leaves, and lemon slices to the water and simmer the tongue on medium heat for 1½ hours.
4. In the meantime, use a bowl to combine the barbeque sauce, jalapeno, honey, sesame seeds, soy sauce, and garlic.
5. When the tongue is boiled, discard the water and allow the tongue to cool to the touch.
6. Use a small knife to cut an incision into the outer whitish-gray skin that covers the tongue. Remove all of that tough outer membrane by hand and discard it.
7. Cut the tongue meat into 1-inch-square cubes and place in the barbeque marinade for 30 minutes.
8. Heat up your grill to medium-high heat.
9. Take the tongue out of the marinade and grill it for just 2–3 minutes per side.
10. Pour the remaining marinade into a small saucepan with 1 Tbsp. of water and boil until it thickens into a sauce.
11. Plate the tongue, cover it with the sauce, and serve with your favorite salad or starch.

FOOD FOR THOUGHT

The hymn "Veni Creator Spiritus" and its English equivalent, "Come Holy Ghost, Creator Blest," are perfect hymns to sing on this day, and there is even a plenary indulgence attached to doing so publicly. More great food for thought can be found in the Mass Sequence of the day, "Veni Sancte Spiritus," which we include here. It is a marvelous reflection on the work of the Holy Spirit in our lives.

Holy Spirit, Lord of light,
From Thy clear celestial height
Thy pure beaming radiance give.

Come, Thou Father of the poor,
Come with treasures which endure,
Come, Thou Light of all that live.

Thou, of all consolers best,
Thou, the soul's delightsome Guest,
Dost refreshing peace bestow.

Thou in toil art comfort sweet,
Pleasant coolness in the heat,
Solace in the midst of woe.

Light immortal, Light divine,
Visit Thou these hearts of Thine,
And our inmost being fill.

If Thou take Thy grace away,
Nothing pure in man will stay;
All his good is turned to ill.

Heal our wounds; our strength renew;
On our dryness pour Thy dew;
Wash the stains of guilt away.

Bend the stubborn heart and will;
Melt the frozen, warm the chill;
Guide the steps that go astray.

Thou, on those who evermore
Thee confess and Thee adore,
In Thy sevenfold gifts descend:

Give them comfort when they die,
Give them life with Thee on high;
Give them joys that never end.[3]

❧

Reference Guide to the Post-Vatican II Calendar

In organizing the year, *Dining with the Saints* primarily follows the traditional 1962 calendar, in use before the Second Vatican Council. The old calendar has a larger number of entries (over two hundred saints were removed from the calendar in 1970, as well as liturgical seasons like Pre-Lent); and more festivities means more feasting. That said, some of the saints canonized after 1962, such as Padre Pio, Father Damien of Molokai, and Pope John Paul II, have been duly added to our list, as well as numerous local saints who never made it to the universal calendar.

And not to worry: if you wish to follow the new calendar, you have two ways of doing so. First, the italicized date of an entry title is the date on which that feast appears in the 1970/2002 Novus Ordo calendar *if* that date is different from the 1962 calendar. If there is only one date, then either there is no difference between the two calendars regarding the holy day in question or the holy day is not on the new calendar. Second, consult this appendix. It lists all the feast days of the new calendar in chronological order. If a date on which you are feeling festive is empty, look it up in the main section of the book. There might be a local holy day on that date or a holy day from the 1962 Missal. Surely our merciful Father won't begrudge you consulting the vast traditions of the Church.

DATE ON THE NEW CALENDAR	HOLY DAY	DATE ON THE TRADITIONAL CALENDAR
JANUARY		
1	Octave of Christmas/ Solemnity of Mary	January 1
2	Basil the Great	June 14
6/2-8	Epiphany	January 6
8	Our Lady of Prompt Succor	January 8
17	Anthony, Hermit	January 17
20	Sebastian	January 20
21	Agnes	January 21
24	Francis de Sales	January 29
28	Thomas Aquinas	March 7
FEBRUARY		
1	Brigid	February 1
2	Candlemas/Presentation of the Lord	February 2
3	Blaise	February 3
5	Agatha	February 5
10	Scholastica	February 10
18	Simeon	February 18
MARCH		
3	Katharine Drexel	March 3
17	Patrick	March 17
19	Joseph	March 19
22	Catherine of Sweden	March 22
25	Annunciation	March 25

DATE ON THE NEW CALENDAR	HOLY DAY	DATE ON THE TRADITIONAL CALENDAR
MARCH		
varies	Lent	varies
	Laetare Sunday	
	Palm Sunday	
	Holy Thursday	
	Good Friday	
	Holy Saturday	
	Easter Sunday	
APRIL		
2	Francis of Paola	April 2
5	Isidore of Seville	April 4
20	Anicetus	April 17
21	Anselm	April 21
23	George	April 23
28	Louis de Montfort	April 28
29	Catherine of Siena	April 30
MAY		
1	Joseph the Worker	May 1
1	Peregrine	May 1
2	Athanasius	May 2
4	Florian	May 4
10	Damien de Veuster	April 15
16	Brendan	May 16
16	Honoratus	May 16
22	Rita	May 22
26	Philip Neri	May 26

DATE ON THE NEW CALENDAR	HOLY DAY	DATE ON THE TRADITIONAL CALENDAR
30	Joan of Arc	May 30
MAY		
varies	Ascension	varies
	Pentecost	
JUNE		
1	Justin	April 14
4	Caracciolo	June 4
6	Norbert	June 6
9	Ephrem	June 18
11	Barnabas	June 11
13	Anthony of Padua	June 13
24	John the Baptist	June 24
26	Josemaría Escrivá	
29	Peter and Paul	June 29
JULY		
1	Junípero Serra	July 1
3	Thomas the Apostle	December 21
4	Elizabeth of Portugal (universal)	July 8
5	Elizabeth of Portugal (U.S.)	July 8
6	Maria Goretti	July 6
11	Benedict	March 21
22	Mary Magdalene	July 22
24	Sharbel Makhluf	

DATE ON THE NEW CALENDAR	HOLY DAY	DATE ON THE TRADITIONAL CALENDAR
JULY		
25	James the Greater	July 25
26	Joachim and Anne	July 26
29	Martha	July 29
31	Ignatius of Loyola	July 31
AUGUST		
1	Lammas Day	August 1
2	Eusebius of Vercelli	December 16
4	John Mary Vianney	August 9
8	Dominic	August 4
10	Lawrence	August 10
11	Clare of Assisi	August 12
12	Jane Frances de Chantal	August 21
15	Assumption	August 15
16	Roch	August 16
16	Stephen of Hungary	September 2
17	Hyacinth	August 17
18	Helena	August 18
21	Pius X	September 3
23	Benizi	August 23
23	Rose of Lima	August 30
25	Louis	August 25
28	Augustine	August 28
SEPTEMBER		
3	Gregory the Great	March 12
5	Teresa of Calcutta	
12	Holy Name of B.V.M.	September 12

DATE ON THE NEW CALENDAR	HOLY DAY	DATE ON THE TRADITIONAL CALENDAR
SEPTEMBER		
13	John Chrysostom	January 27
17	Hildegard	September 17
19	Januarius	September 19
20	Eustace and Companions	September 20
23	(Padre) Pio of Pietrelcina	
26	Cosmas and Damien	September 27
27	Vincent de Paul	July 19
28	Lorenzo Ruiz	September 28
29	Michael, Gabriel, and Raphael	September 29
OCTOBER		
1	Thérèse of Lisieux	October 3
2	Guardian Angels	October 2
4	Francis of Assisi	October 4
6	Bruno	October 6
15	Teresa of Ávila	October 15
16	Margaret Mary Alacoque	October 17
17	Ignatius of Antioch	February 1
18	Luke	October 18
22	John Paul II	
25	Miniatus	October 25
31	All Hallows' Eve	October 31
NOVEMBER		
1	All Saints' Day	November 1
2	All Souls' Day	November 2

DATE ON THE NEW CALENDAR	HOLY DAY	DATE ON THE TRADITIONAL CALENDAR
NOVEMBER		
4	Charles Borromeo	November 4
11	Martin of Tours	November 11
15	Albert the Great	November 15
16	Gertrude the Great	November 16
16	Margaret of Scotland	June 10
17	Elizabeth of Hungary	November 19
23	Clement I	November 23
23	Miguel Pro	
25	Catherine of Alexandria	November 25
30	Andrew the Apostle	November 30
DECEMBER		
varies	Advent Sundays	varies
3	Francis Xavier	December 3
4	Barbara	December 4
6	Nicholas	December 6
7	Ambrose	December 7
8	Immaculate Conception of B.V.M.	December 8
12	Our Lady of Guadalupe	December 12
13	Lucy	December 13
14	John of the Cross	November 24
25	Nativity of the Lord	December 25
26	Stephen	December 26
28	Holy Innocents	December 28
31	Sylvester	December 31

WORKS CONSULTED

············ ❧ ············

Adler, Tamar. *An Everlasting Meal: Cooking with Economy and Grace.* New York: Scribner, 2011.

Anselm of Canterbury. "Praefatio." In *Liber de Fide Trinitatis et de Incarnatione Verbi contra Blasphemias Ruzelini sive Roscelini.*

Augustine. *Confessions.* 2nd ed. Translated by F. J. Sheed. Edited by Michael P. Foley. Indianapolis: Hackett, 2006.

———. Sermon 10 on the Saints.

d'Avila-Latourrette, Victor-Antoine. *Twelve Months of Monastery Soups.* Ligouri, Missouri: Ligouri, 1996.

Bacci, Pietro Giacomo. *The Life of St. Philip Neri.* Vol. 2. Translated by Frederick Ignatius Antrobus. London: Kegan Paul, Trench, Trübner & Co., 1902.

Benedict XVI. "Angelus Address." Randwick Racecourse, Sydney, Australia. July 20, 2008. https://www.vatican.va/content/benedict-xvi/en/angelus/2008/documents/hf_ben-xvi_ang_20080720_sydney.html.

———. "Letter of His Holiness Benedict XVI to Cardinal Giacoma Biffi Special Envoy to the Celebrations on the Occasion of the Ninth Centenary of the Death of Saint Anselm." April 15, 2009. https://www.vatican.va/content/benedict-xvi/en/letters/2009/documents/hf_ben-xvi_let_20090415_biffi-st-anselmo.html.

———. "Saint Gertrude the Great." October 6, 2010. https://www.vatican.va/content/benedict-xvi/en/audiences/2010/documents/hf_ben-xvi_aud_20101006.html.

Benedict of Nursia. *The Rule of Saint Benedict.*

Berger, Florence S. *Cooking for Christ: The Liturgical Year in the Kitchen*. Des Moines, Iowa: National Catholic Rural Life Conference, 1949.

Maronite Patriarch of Antioch. *The Book of Offering: According to the Rite of the Antiochene Syriac Maronite Church*. Bkerke, Lebanon: Maronite Patriarchate of Antioch, 2012.

Bouyer, Louis. *Newman: His Life and Spirituality*. San Francisco, California: Ignatius Press, 2011.

Bowler, Gerry. *The World Encyclopedia of Christmas*. Toronto: McClelland & Stewart Ltd., 2000.

Breviarum Romanum. 4 vols. Ratisbona, 1939.

Brown, Raphael. *The Little Flowers of St. Francis*. New York: Image Books, 1958.

Burton, Katherine and Helmut Ripperger. *Feast Day Cookbook*. Philadelphia: David McKay Company, Inc., 1951.

Butler, Alban. *The Lives of the Primitive Fathers, Martyrs, and Other Principal Saints*. Vol. 1. Edinburgh: J. Moir, 1798.

———. *Butler's Lives of the Fathers, Martyrs, and Other Saints*. 4 vols. Edited by Rev. F. C. Husenbeth. Great Falls, Montana: St. Bonaventure Publications, 1997.

Catholic Encyclopedia. 25 vols. New York: The Gilmary Society, 1907–1912. Available online at http://www.newadvent.org/cathen/.

Cather, Willa. *Death Comes for the Archbishop*. New York: Vintage Classics, 1990.

Chapman, Emily Stimpson. *The Catholic Table: Finding Joy Where Food and Faith Meet*. Steubenville, Ohio: Emmaus Road Publishing, 2016.

Chesterton, G. K. *Orthodoxy*. San Francisco: Ignatius Press, 1995.

———. *Saint Thomas Aquinas and Saint Francis of Assisi*. San Francisco: Ignatius Press, 2002.

Fisher, M. F. K. *The Art of Eating*. New York: Macmillan, 1990.

Foley, Michael P. *Drinking with Saint Nick: Christmas Cocktails for Sinners and Saints*. Washington, D.C.: Regnery History, 2018.

———. *Drinking with the Saints: The Sinner's Guide to a Holy Happy Hour*. Washington, D.C.: Regnery History, 2015.

———. *Drinking with Your Patron Saints: A Sinner's Guide to Honoring Namesakes and Protectors*. Washington, D.C.: Regnery History, 2020.

———. *Why Do Catholics Eat Fish on Friday? The Catholic Origin to Just About Everything*. New York: Palgrave Macmillan, 2005.

———. *Why We Kiss under the Mistletoe: Christmas Traditions Explained*. Washington, D.C.: Regnery History, 2022.

Fontes Vitae S. Thomae Aquinatis. Edited by D. Prümmer, O.P. Toronto: Privat & Revue Thomiste, 1912.

Francis de Sales. *Introduction to the Devout Life*. Point Roberts, Washington: Eremitical Press, 2009.

Greeley, Alexandra and Fernando Flores. *Cooking with the Saints*. Nashua, New Hampshire: Sophia Institute Press, 2019.

Guéranger, Dom Prosper, O.S.B. *The Liturgical Year*. 15 vols. Translated by Dom Laurence Shepherd, O.S.B. Great Falls, Montana: St. Bonaventure Publications, 2000.

Guidonis, Bernardus. "Vita Sancti Thomae Aquinatis." In *Fontes Vitae S. Thomae Aquinatis*. Edited by D. Prümmer, O.P. Toronto: Privat & Revue Thomiste, 1912.

Herrick, Robert. "A Ceremonie in Gloucester."

———. "Ceremony upon Candlemas Eve."

Holweck, Frederick. "Holy Innocents." *The Catholic Encyclopedia*. Vol. 7. New York: Robert Appleton Company, 1910. http://www.newadvent.org/cathen/07419a.htm.

The Holy Bible. Douay-Rheims Version. Baltimore: John Murphy Co., 1914.

Homans, George C. *English Villagers of the Thirteenth Century*. New York: W. W. Norton, 1975.

Ignatius of Antioch. *Epistle of Ignatius to the Romans*. Translated by Alexander Roberts and James Donaldson. From *Ante-Nicene Fathers*, Vol. 1. Edited by Alexander Roberts, James Donaldson, and A. Cleveland Coxe. Buffalo, New York: Christian Literature Publishing Co., 1885. Revised and edited for New Advent by Kevin Knight. http://www.newadvent.org/fathers/0107.htm.

John Chrysostom. "Homily 7 on the Acts of the Apostles." Translated by J. Walker, J. Sheppard, and H. Browne. Revised by George B. Stevens. In *Nicene and Post-Nicene Fathers*, *First Series*. Vol. 11. Edited by Philip Schaff. Buffalo, New York: Christian Literature Publishing Co., 1889. Revised and edited for New Advent by Kevin Knight. http://www.newadvent.org/fathers/210107.htm.

Kass, Leon R. *The Hungry Soul: Eating and the Perfecting of Our Nature*. Chicago: University of Chicago Press, 1999.

Kaufman, William I. *The Catholic Cookbook*. New York: Citadel Press, 1965.

Lefebvre, Dom Gaspar. *Saint Andrew Daily Missal*. St. Paul, Minnesota: E. M. Lohmann Co., 1952.

Marmion, Columba. *Christ in His Mysteries*. Translated by Alan Bancroft. Bethesda, Maryland: Zaccheus Press, 2008.

Mary of Agreda. *The Mystical City of God*. Translated by George J. Blatter. Chicago: W. B. Conkey, 1914.

Count de Montalembert. *The Life of Saint Elizabeth of Hungary, Duchess of Thuringia*. Translated by Mary Hackett. Dublin: James Duffy, 1848.

Oxford English Dictionary Online. 2nd ed. Available online at http://dictionary.oed.com/entrance.dtl.

Parlanti, Mary. *From the Kitchen of Mary Parlanti: With Love*. Lexington, Kentucky: Parlanti Foods, 2010.

Patalinghug, Leo. *Epic Food Fight: A Bite-Sized History of Salvation*. Servant, 2014.

———. *Grace Before Meals: Recipes and Inspiration for Family Meals and Family Life*. New York: Image, 2010.

———. *Saving the Family: The Transformative Power of Sharing Meals with People You Love*. Manchester, New Hampshire: Sophia Institute Press, 2019.

———. *Spicing Up Married Life: Satisfying Couples' Hunger for True Love*. Hunt Valley, Maryland: Leo McWatkins Films, Inc., 2012.

Patalinghug, Leo, and Stella Snyder. *Grace Before Meals*. 2nd ed. Hunt Valley, Maryland: Leo McWatkins Films, Inc., 2007.

Paul VI. "Béatification du Moine Maronite Charbel Makhlouf." December 5, 1965. https://www.vatican.va/content/paul-vi/fr/speeches/1965/documents/hf_p-vi_spe_19651205_charbel-makhlouf.html.

Peters, Jason. *The Culinary Plagiarist: (Mis)adventures of a Lusty, Thieving, God-Fearing Gourmand*. Eugene, Oregon: Front Porch Republic Books, 2020.

Pigozzi, Caroline. *Pope John Paul II: An Intimate Life: The Pope I Knew So Well*. Brentwood, Tennessee: FaithWords, 2008.

Pius XII. Apostolic Letter. April 13, 1942. In *Acta Apostolicae* Sedis, Annus XXXIV, Series II, Vol. IX (1942).

Rituale Romanum. Rome: Desclee, 1943.

Shaw, Teresa M. *The Burden of the Flesh: Fasting and Sexuality in Early Christianity.* Fortress Press, 1998.

Thomas Aquinas. *Summa Theologiae.*

De Tocco, Guillelmus. "Vita Sancti Thomae Aquinatis 32." In *Fontes Vitae S. Thomae Aquinatis.* Ed. D. Prümmer, O.P. Toronto: Privat & Revue Thomiste, 1912.

Trapp, Maria. *Around the Year with the Trapp Family* (New York: Pantheon, 1955).

Vázquez de Prada, Andrés. *The Founder of Opus Dei: The Life of Josemaría Escrivá.* Vol. 3, *The Divine Ways on Earth.* New York: Scepter Publishers, 2005.

Vitz, Evelyn Birge. *A Continual Feast: A Cookbook to Celebrate the Joys of Family and Faith throughout the Christian Year.* San Francisco: Ignatius Press, 1985.

Weiser, Francis X., *The Christmas Book.* New York: Harcourt, Brace and Company, 1954.

———. *The Easter Book.* New York: Harcourt, Brace and Company, 1954.

———. *The Holy Day Book.* New York: Harcourt, Brace and Company, 1956.

———. *The Handbook of Christian Feasts and Customs: The Year of the Lord in Liturgy and Folklore.* New York: Harcourt, Brace and World, 1958.

———. *Religious Customs in the Family: The Radiation of the Liturgy into Christian Homes.* Collegeville, Minnesota: Liturgical Press, 1956.

———. *The Year of the Lord in the Christian Home.* Collegeville, Minnesota: Liturgical Press, 1964.

NOTES

Introduction

1. Anne Fishel, "The Benefits of Family Dinner for Adults," The Family Dinner Project, May 11, 2021, https://thefamilydinnerproject.org/blog/benefits-family-dinner-adults/.
2. Alban Butler, *The Lives of the Primitive Fathers, Martyrs, and Other Principal Saints*, vol. 1 (Edinburgh: J. Moir, 1798), 173.

January Saints

1. John Chrysostom, "Homily 7 on the Acts of the Apostles," trans. J. Walker, J. Sheppard, and H. Browne, rev. George B. Stevens, in *Nicene and Post-Nicene Fathers, First Series*, vol. 11, ed. Philip Schaff (Buffalo, New York: Christian Literature Publishing Co., 1889), rev. and ed. for New Advent by Kevin Knight, http://www.newadvent.org/fathers/210107.htm.
2. Francis de Sales, *Introduction to the Devout Life* (Point Roberts, Washington: Eremitical Press, 2009), 149.
3. Ibid., 148.
4. Ibid., 149.

February Saints

1. Ignatius of Antioch, "Epistle of Ignatius to the Romans," trans. Alexander Roberts and James Donaldson, in *Ante-Nicene Fathers*, vol. 1, ed. Alexander Roberts, James Donaldson, and A. Cleveland Coxe (Buffalo, New York: Christian Literature Publishing Co., 1885), rev. and ed. for New Advent by Kevin Knight, http://www.newadvent.org/fathers/0107.htm.

March Saints

1. See Thomas Aquinas, *Summa Theologiae* II-II.147.8.
2. For a summary of twentieth-century dietary research, see Teresa M. Shaw, *The Burden of the Flesh* (Minneapolis, Minnesota: Augsburg Fortress Publishers, 1998), 126–27.

3. Bernardus Guidonis, *Vita Sancti Thomae Aquinatis* 28, in *Fontes Vitae S. Thomae Aquinatis*, ed. D. Prummer (Toronto: Privat & Revue Thomiste, 1912), 232–33. Translation by Michael Foley.
4. Guillelmus de Tocco, *Vita Sancti Thomae Aquinatis* 32, in *Fontes Vitae S. Thomae Aquinatis*, ed. D. Prummer (Toronto: Privat & Revue Thomiste, 1912), 154. Translation by Michael Foley.
5. Ibid., 56.
6. See Francis X. Weiser, *Handbook of Christian Feasts and Customs* (New York: Harcourt, 1958), 323–25.
7. Benedict of Nursia, *The Rule of Saint Benedict*, chapter 39.
8. Ibid., chapter 41.
9. Ibid., chapter 24.
10. See Saint Irenaeus of Lyons, *Against Heresies*, book 5, chapter 19, section 1.
11. Benedict XVI, "Angelus," Vatican website, July 20, 2008, https://www.vatican.va/content/benedict-xvi/en/angelus/2008/documents/hf_ben-xvi_ang_20080720_sydney.html.
12. *The Book of Offering according to the Rite of the Antiochene Syriac Maronite Church* (Bkerke, Lebanon: Maronite Patriarchate of Antioch, 2012), 28.
13. Weiser, *Handbook*, 304.

April Saints

1. Isidore of Seville, *Etymologies* 6.19.63–64. Translation by Michael Foley.
2. Ibid., 20.1.1.
3. Benedict XVI, "Letter of His Holiness Benedict XVI to Cardinal Giocoma Biffi Special Envoy to the Celebrations on the Occasion of the Ninth Centenary of the Death of St. Anselm," The Vatican, April 15, 2009, https://www.vatican.va/content/benedict-xvi/en/letters/2009/documents/hf_ben-xvi_let_20090415_biffi-st-anselmo.html.
4. Anselmus, "Praefatio," *Liber de fide trinitatis et de incarnatione verbi contra blasphemias Ruzelini sive Roscelini*, Patrologiae cursus completes, series Latina 32–47, ed. J.-P. Migne (Paris: J.-P. Migne, 1841–1857), col. 158.

May Saints

1. Katherine Burton and Helmut Ripperger offer a simple recipe for a Saint Joseph's Day Peasant's Breakfast in their *Feast Day Cookbook* (Philadelphia: David McKay Company, 1951), 71. Cut three strips of bacon in small pieces "and fry over a low flame until completely done. Cube the potato and brown with the bacon. Finally, break an egg over the whole (do not beat previously) and stir it slowly into the bacon and potato until set. Season and sprinkle with finely cut chives. This is for one portion and can be multiplied at will."
2. George J. Blatter, trans., *Mystical City of God* (Hammond, Indiana: W. B. Conkey, 1914), chapter 72, paragraph 765.
3. Prosper Guéranger, O.S.B., *The Liturgical Year*, vol. 8, trans. Laurence Shepherd, O.S.B. (Great Falls, Montana: St. Bonaventure Publications, 2000), 403.
4. John Henry Newman to John Dobree Dalgairns, in Louis Bouyer, *Newman: His Life and Spirituality* (San Francisco, California: Ignatius Press, 2011), 269.

5. Pietro Giacomo Bacci, *The Life of Saint Philip Neri*, vol. 2, trans. Frederick Ignatius Antrobus (London: Kegan Paul, Trench, Trübner & Co., 1902), 47.
6. Ibid., book 2, chapter 7, 196.

July Saints
1. Willa Cather, *Death Comes for the Archbishop* (New York: Vintage Classics, 1990), 38.
2. Pope Paul VI, "Beatification of the Maronite Monk Charbel Makhlouf," December 5, 1965, translation from the original French by Mike Foley, https://www.vatican.va/content/paul-vi/fr/speeches/1965/documents/hf_p-vi_spe_19651205_charbel-makhlouf.html.
3. Florence S. Berger, *Cooking for Christ: The Liturgical Year in the Kitchen* (Des Moines, Iowa: National Catholic Rural Life Conference, 1949), front matter.

August Saints
1. Quoted by Saint Francis de Sales in his *Introduction to the Devout Life* (Point Roberts, Washington: Eremitical Press, 2009), 158.
2. Augustine, *Confessions*, 2nd ed., trans. F. J. Sheed (Indianapolis: Hackett, 2006), 10.31.44.
3. Ibid., 10.6.8.

October Saints
1. Raphael Brown, ed., *The Little Flowers of Saint Francis* (New York: Image Books, 1958), 73.
2. Ibid., 88–91.
3. Ibid., 328.

November Saints
1. Katherine Burton and Helmut Ripperger, *Feast Day Cookbook* (Philadelphia, Pennsylvania: David McKay Company Inc., 1951), 140.
2. Pius XII, Apostolic Letter, April 13, 1942, *Acta Apostolicae Sedis* XXXIV, 90. Translation by Michael Foley.
3. Benedict XVI, "General Audience," Vatican, March 24, 2010, https://www.vatican.va/content/benedict-xvi/en/audiences/2010/documents/hf_ben-xvi_aud_20100324.html.
4. Benedict XVI, "General Audience," Vatican, October 6, 2010, https://www.vatican.va/content/benedict-xvi/en/audiences/2010/documents/hf_ben-xvi_aud_20101006.html.
5. Count de Montalembert, *The Life of Saint Elizabeth of Hungary, Duchess of Thuringia*, trans. Mary Hackett (Dublin: James Duffy, 1848), 177.
6. "Kattern, n.," *Oxford English Dictionary*, 2nd ed. (1989), available online at http://dictionary.oed.com/entrance.dtl. The "Clemen" is Saint Clement, whose feast day falls on November 23.
7. "Cattern Cakes (St. Catherine's Day)," Kingsdown, Lynsted and Norton Newsletter Recipe Column, http://www.lynsted.com/Recipes/Cookbook/Cattern_Cakes.html.
8. For a recipe, see Evelyn Birge Vitz, *A Continual Feast* (San Francisco, California: Ignatius Press, 1985), 283.

Advent

1. For the meals of Italy, Mexico, and Provence, see Evelyn Birge Vitz, *A Continual Feast: A Cookbook to Celebrate the Joys of Family and Faith throughout the Christian Year* (San Francisco: Ignatius Press, 1985), 125–32.

The Twelve Days of Christmas

1. See Augustine, Sermon 10 on the Saints; Frederick Holweck, "Holy Innocents," *The Catholic Encyclopedia*, vol. 7 (New York: Robert Appleton Company, 1910), http://www.newadvent.org/cathen/07419a.htm.

Epiphany and the Time Thereafter

1. The custom was also tied to charity. In France a piece of cake was put aside "for Our Lord" and given to a poor person. Another French tradition required each person to pay for his piece of cake. The money collected, called "the gold of the Magi," would be given to the poor or to help pay for the education of a promising but disadvantaged youth.
2. Gerry Bowler, *The World Encyclopedia of Christmas* (Toronto: McClelland & Stewart Ltd., 2000), 128.
3. Robert Herrick, "Ceremony upon Candlemas Eve."
4. See Exodus 13:2, 12–13; Numbers 18:15–16.

Mardi Gras or Carnival

1. "Shrove, v." *Oxford English Dictionary*, 2nd ed. (1989), available online at http://dictionary.oed.com/entrance.dtl.

Lent and Holy Week

1. Cited in Francis X. Weiser, S.J., *Handbook of Christian Feasts and Customs: The Year of the Lord in Liturgy and Folklore* (New York: Harcourt, Brace and World, 1958), 177–78.
2. Robert Herrick, "A Ceremonie in Gloucester."
3. Katherine Burton and Helmut Ripperger, *Feast Day Cookbook: The Traditional Catholic Feast Day Dishes of Many Lands* (Montreal, QC: Catholic Authors, 2005), 52.
4. Francis X. Weiser, S.J., *Handbook of Christian Feasts and Customs: The Year of the Lord in Liturgy and Folklore* (New York: Harcourt, Brace, and Company, 1958), 201.

Eastertide

1. "Deus, qui per famulum tuum Moysen, in liberatione populi tui de Aegypto, agnum occidi jussisti in similitudinem Domini nostri Jesu Christi, et utrosque postes domorum de sanguine ejusdem agni perungi praecepisti: tu benedicere et sanctificare digneris hanc creaturam carnis, quam nos famuli tui ad laudem tuam sumere desideramus, per resurrectionem ejusdem Domini nostri Jesu Christi, qui tecum vivit et regnat in saecula saeculorum. Amen." *Rituale Romanum* (Rome: Desclée, 1943), 239. Translation by Michael Foley.
2. Columba Marmion, *Christ in His Mysteries*, trans. Alan Bancroft (Bethesda, Maryland: Zaccheus Press, 2008), 347.
3. Edward Caswall, trans., "Holy Spirit, Lord of Light," Hymnary, https://hymnary.org/hymn/HAGA1895/283.

Index of Recipes

Index of Holy Days, Seasons, and Saints

About the Authors

FATHER LEO PATALINGHUG is an award-winning chef and author, a widely acclaimed speaker, the founder of the international food and faith movement Plating Grace, and the host of *Savoring Our Faith* on EWTN. A priest of the Voluntas Dei community, he lives in Baltimore.

MICHAEL P. FOLEY, the author of *Drinking with the Saints*, *Why Do Catholics Eat Fish on Fridays?*, and a dozen other books, teaches in the Great Texts program at Baylor University in Waco, Texas.